VOICES
OF THE
VOICELESS

Women, Justice,
and Human Rights
in Guatemala

MICHELLE TOOLEY
Foreword by Walter Wink

HERALD PRESS
Scottdale, Pennsylvania
Waterloo, Ontario

Library of Congress Cataloging-in-Publication Data
Tooley, Michelle, 1953-
    Voices of the voiceless : women, justice, and human rights in
Guatemala / Michelle Tooley.
        p. cm.
    Includes bibliographical references (p. -) and index.
    ISBN 0-8361-9057-2 (alk. paper)
    1. Women's rights—Guatemala. 2. Women—Guatemala—Social
conditions. 3. Human rights—Guatemala. 4. Political persecution—
Guatemala. 5. Social justice—Guatemala. I. Title.
    HQ1236.5.G9T66 1997
    323.3'4'097281—dc21   96-53278

The paper used in this publication is recycled and meets the minimum
requirements of American National Standard for Information Sciences
—Permanence of Paper for Printed Library Materials, ANSI Z39.48-
1984.

*Our sacred dream is to say
our people are weavers — a people
who have woven history
with our hunger, sacrifice, and blood.*

Rigoberta Menchú

To the women of Guatemala
who have increased justice
in their country
and who give hope to all
who yearn for peace and justice
in our world.

Contents

List of Figures 11
Foreword by Walter Wink 12
Author's Preface 14

1 Introduction 19
    Women and Social Change in Latin America 21
    Organization 25

2 Injustice in Guatemala 29
    Decade of Democracy: 1944-1954 36
    Guatemala: National Security State, 1954-1985 40
    The State of the Union with Civilian Presidents:
        1985-1996 44
        Alvaro Arzu's Presidency 50
        Human Rights Policy 54
        Human Rights Violations 56
        Amnesty Laws 59
        Forced Military Recruitment and Civil Patrols 59
        Mayan Indians and the Struggle for Survival 60
        Economic and Social Situation 61
        Poverty 62
        The Feminization of Poverty 63
        Maquiladoras 65
        Refugee Resettlement 66
    Conclusion 69

3 Voices of the Voiceless: The Response of Women
in Guatemalan Human Rights Groups 70
   Rigoberta Menchú 72
   Committee for Peasant Unity 76
      Government Repression 78
   Grupo de Apoyo Mutuo 79
      Government Repression 82
   CONAVIGUA 83
      Government Repression 87
   Women and the Means of Social Change 88

4 Injustice Through Powers and Authorities 96
   Powers and Authorities: Power Structures
      and Inner Spirits 100
      Response 101
   Powers and Authorities: Confronting Evil 103
      Response 104
   Powers and Authorities: Inner and Outer Nature 105
      Response 107
         Inner Personal Demonic Possession 108
         Outer Personal Demonic Possession 109
         Collective Possession 110
   Domination System: Violence 113
      An Alternative Vision: The Reign of God 114
      Nonviolence 115
      Response 117
   Domination System: Inequality 122
      Economic Inequality 123
      Gender Inequality 128
      Response: Economic Equality 131
      Response: Gender Equality 133
   Domination System: Despair 135
      Response: Confrontation and Conversion 136

5 **Toward a Theory of Social Justice** 138

    The Nature of Injustice 144

    In the Beginning: Injustice 146

    Justice as Participation 147

        Economic Justice 152

        Political Justice 155

        Gender Justice 157

        Cultural Justice 160

    Justice as Radically Historical Narrative 165

    Justice as Praxis 171

    Justice as Solidarity 175

6 **Conclusion** 178

    Guatemalan Women and the Struggle for Justice 178

        Perception of Threat 179

            Genocide Through Poverty and Militarism 179

            Climate of Fear 181

            The Scandal of Silence 182

    Means of Social Change 184

    Guatemala: A World with Justice 187

        Justice as Participation 187

        A New Image of Power 189

        The Dangerous Memory of Suffering 190

    North American Women: Partners in Justice 190

        Barriers to Justice-Actions 191

        A Cloud of Witnesses 192

    Conclusion 194

Notes 197

A Select Bibliography 211

Index 228

The Author 232

List of Figures

Figure

1. Massacres in Guatemala: 1982-1991 49
2. Extrajudicial Executions in Guatemala: 1981-1991 49
3. Disappearances in Guatemala: 1981-1991 51
4. Disappearances: 1978-1985 51
5. Personal, Social, and Instrumental Rights:
    An Interpretation of *Pacem in Terris* 150

Foreword

MICHELLE Tooley's passionate recounting of the tragedy that is Guatemala is more than simply a cry of the heart for a suffering people. It is a systematic theory of social justice that seeks to hone the Christian message to alleviate the oppression that has for five centuries held Guatemala's indigenous peoples in virtual slavery.

A staggering 89 percent of Guatemalans live in poverty, 76 percent of children under five are malnourished, and 100,000 people have been assassinated since 1960 with no one charged. Yet the dominant religion of the country is Christianity. How is it possible that Christian principles and beliefs have not yielded a more compassionate and equitable society? More compassionate—what am I saying? The church has itself been up to its ears in complicity with the exploiting powers. Without the church's imprimatur on the injustices visited on Guatemala's poor, the wealthy landholders would never have been able to seize the land, much less retain it.

Tooley chronicles the sad history of this colorful land. She brings the story up to the present in a way that unmasks United States involvement in perpetuating Guatemala's rich elites and extraction industries. The U.S. government deposed a democratically elected president, installed a handpicked despot, and armed him and his successors with virtually irresistible might. Yet the people have resisted, against overwhelming odds.

The bloody, interminable war is now over and democratic government is in power, but the world waits to see if increased political democracy will lead to economic democracy. This appears unlikely as the free market, liberated from communist constraints, sweeps through the world, destroying middle classes, welfare states, and social nets that could rescue the weakest, sickest, and poorest. The greed of the superrich is rising and the despair of the unemployed, the downsized, and the homeless is escalating. Today no one, in any class, is safe from the invisible hand and its invisible truncheon.

Most Guatemalans have so far been trying simply to survive. However, the cessation of hostilities may only mean looking up from a small clearing in the jungle to the "junglefication" of the entire world economy. Just when Guatemalans are emerging again into the light, they may find lights for the poor being extinguished the world over. One billion adults worldwide were either unemployed or underemployed in 1995, up from about 820 million just the year before.

In light of such facts, solidarity takes on new meaning. We are in this together. We North Americans who once looked down on our neighbors to the south now find ourselves facing our own economic stresses. We will find a way out of this collective madness or go down together. That is why it is so valuable that Tooley has done more than simply recite Guatemala's torment. She has used that people's travail as the foundation for a social ethic that can serve the churches in the global struggle for justice.

This eminently readable book is both inspirational and informative. I only hope enough Christians respond to it with the fiery commitment that can bring change to a system of domination that seems hell-bent on pulling the columns of the world down on its own head and the heads of us all.

—*Walter Wink, Professor of Biblical Interpretation*
Auburn Theological Seminary, New York

Author's Preface

THE idea for this book grew from two events. First, ten years ago, I taught children of undocumented aliens at a small Spanish Presbyterian church in Fort Worth, Texas. At that time, Fort Worth schools did not allow undocumented children in public schools. Volunteers staffed six alternative schools which met from four to five nights each week.

Throughout the year, I heard bits and pieces of stories from children who had come to the United States as economic or political refugees. One night I arrived at "school," Iglesia Presbyteriana Gethsemane, to find no children. The director reported that the Immigration and Naturalization Service had raided one of the other schools, located in a Catholic church, and had searched the priest's desk for children's names. The directors called off our school and others in the city for the night to protect the children and their parents from deportation.

That night I heard from the director stories of our children's families; stories from Honduras, Guatemala, El Salvador, and Nicaragua; stories of wars that left victims in their wake. As the year progressed, I heard more stories from parents. They told of injustice and oppression in their countries and of their visions of a new life in the United States.

Then five years ago a friend and I visited Santa Apolonia, a small town in the mountains of Guatemala. OXFAM, Diakonia (a Swedish nongovernment organization), and Louisville United Against Hunger sponsored a widows' project in a neighboring village. The nuns who managed the project, the School Sisters of St. Francis, lived in Santa Apolonia.

My friend and I had been in Guatemala for two weeks, traveling through the beautiful countryside, seeing the deceptively peaceful face of Guatemala without looking beneath the surface. We were innocents abroad, although neither of us should have been. Our introduction to the real Guatemala occurred in Santa Apolonia, a village of women and children. The military had killed most of the men, believing that they were guerrillas or sympathetic to guerrillas. The nuns came to Santa Apolonia to help the survivors begin a new life. They began an orphanage for abandoned children, helped the women form a weavers' co-operative, and trained women in agricultural skills. The sisters and the women together worked to rebuild the village.

But in spite of the hope generated through the orphanage and cooperative, the shadow of tragedy remained. Victims were children, like Angelina, abandoned by her alcoholic mother at birth, unable to speak or walk as a result of inadequate nutrition; young boys who remembered the sight of their fathers and uncles being tortured and shot; and women, living in fear when soldiers drove through the small village.

Trips to Guatemala have been invaluable experiences. With the help of Witness for Peace, I talked with poor people, mainly women, who work to improve human rights. I went to learn from those who are practitioners. They told me the stories of their lives, often litanies of tragedies. Men and women shared their ideas about the sources of injustice as well as their hopes and dreams for a just Guatemala.

To the people involved in the struggle for human rights in Guatemala, I owe a great debt of gratitude. I am especially grateful to Witness for Peace; to Fr. Jim Flynn of Kentucky Interreligious Task Force On Central America; and to Gail Phares of Carolina Interreligious Task Force On Central America. Fueled by their great love for Guatemala and wise analyses of the political and economic situation, they helped me to hear and understand the struggles of Guatemalans.

But this book does not stop with the borders of Guatemala. If my reading of Guatemalan women's story is correct, their story has great relevance for women in the United States today. With the current backlash to feminism and the women's movement, women are targets of active and passive oppression. Women, especially women of faith, must be actively involved in the struggle to end injustice wherever found. As Christian women with a social responsibility to protect the vulnerable and liberate the oppressed, we must listen to the cries of exploited women and act in solidarity with them.

Although a book is a solitary endeavor, it is also the product of a community that nurtured and encouraged me. Melanie and David Wilkinson, and their children, Micah and Meredith, have been good friends; they have listened to my struggles and helped me at every stage of my journey. I am grateful for the friendship of Perry Hildreth. During turbulent years at Southern Baptist Theological Seminary, he has been sympathetic and has offered wise counsel.

My church congregation, Jefferson Street Baptist Community at Liberty, and our peacemaker group have encouraged me in every possible way—through prayers, letters, and gifts of bread. The Sisters of Loretta offered me a peaceful and hospitable place to write and think. The graduate women's group, especially Jane Kendrick-Lites, Joyce Oliver, Jana Mayfield, Lilian Lim, and Chris Henson, has been a rich source of understanding and support. In a time in my denomination when women have been silenced, these women and others have courageously refused to be silenced, offering instead prophetic words and compassionate actions.

I am deeply grateful for the contributions of Glen Stassen; he has encouraged this work since its inception and has helped nurture it to maturity. He has been prophet, professor, mentor, and friend; from him I have learned better how to be a peacemaker.

—*Michelle Tooley*
  Lufkin, Texas

VOICES OF THE VOICELESS

1

Introduction

THE national symbol of Guatemala, the quetzal, is a bird with brilliant red, green, and blue feathers, and a long tail feather. Although brilliantly colored, the quetzal makes no sounds, sings no songs. Mayan legends record that the quetzal refused to sing or lost its voice when the Spaniard Pedro de Alvarado and his 300 men arrived and slaughtered 30,000 Mayans.

Throughout the history of Guatemala, except for a ten-year period, the poor, like the quetzal, have been voiceless.[1] The poor are indigenous people—women, farm workers, factory workers, refugees, and those who live in garbage dumps. The poor have been challengers with little social or political influence. They have been physically present but socially and politically invisible.

Guatemala is a country devastated by oppression and injustice. The people of Guatemala suffer from war, poverty, and violence. They have endured 500 years of oppression, first by external colonial powers, now by an internal economic and military elite. Through social, economic, and political control, the powerful have kept the poor captive, drastically limiting their freedoms and human rights. Violence has taken a heavy toll on the Guatemalan people. Bread for the World has targeted Guatemala as one example of a country where militarization is a major cause of hunger and poverty. UNICEF estimates that 109 out of 1,000 children die before the age of five.[2] A startling 89 percent of Guatemalans live in poverty and 67 percent in extreme poverty.[3] The Institute for Food and Development Policy has determined that 76 percent of Guatemalan children under five are malnourished.[4] Only 2.2 percent of landowners hold two-thirds of the arable land.[5]

Although economic and social indicators testify to millions of people living in dehumanizing poverty, the scandal of Guatemala is the flagrant abuse of other human rights as well. Since 1960, 100,000 people have been assassinated with no one charged for the murders. The violence continues to escalate. Every day's newspaper brings reports of assassinations, attacks on civilians, and increased intimidation and repression. Most sources attribute the deaths and other acts of violence to the military or right-wing death squads loosely affiliated with the military. A minority of the persons killed have been combatants. Forty thousand people have been "disappeared." In the 1980s one million people became internal refugees and 150,000 fled the country to avoid being tortured or killed. Refugees, an estimated 140,000, hover on the Mexican border of Guatemala. After ten years in exile, they are ready to return to their homes but few have land to which to return. The military admits to destroying 440 indigenous villages during the 1980s. Today, 70,000 mainly indigenous people who survived the massacres live in "model villages" supervised by the military.

Many people hoped that the disappearances and assassinations would end with the transition to a civilian government in 1985 but a 1990 article reports that political violence is on the rise.[6] Because of the disappearances, assassinations, and constant repression, Guatemala has been called a land of prisoners, a land of eternal tyranny.

During the thirty years of violence, human rights groups have emerged and died due to systematic repression by the police, army, and paramilitary death squads. But in the past decade, a popular movement has erupted in Guatemala. Human rights groups, both secular and Christian, have emerged and grown, even amid repression. Before this decade, participants in human rights groups were middle-class *ladinos.*[7] Today groups represent most segments of Guatemalan society, with heavy representation by indigenous men and women.

In Guatemala women have created a community of active participation through involvement in human rights groups. In spite of their lack of power in the public sphere, women are working for justice in a country devastated by violence and poverty. Their actions are self-empowering. They are increasing the justice in Guatemala. Through a variety of means, women recognize and confront violence in Guatemalan society—political, economic, and social violence.

By hearing the story of Guatemalan women, women in the United States can draw hope from their story and recognize and confront the violence and injustice in our own society. Recognition of the structures of racism, sexism, militarism, and economic injustice should lead to conscientization—raising the consciousness of ourselves and others to situations of injustice. Women in the United States need to act together with self-empowering initiatives to end crippling oppression and injustice in our own neighborhoods, country, and world.

Women and Social Change in Latin America

In several Latin American countries with repressive military regimes and appalling socioeconomic conditions, women have been first to protest imprisonments, disappearances, assassinations and other human-rights violations. In the midst of societies where women have little social, economic, or political power, they have acted collectively with extraordinary courage.

In some Latin American countries, women's efforts for social change occurred in the context of a women's movement. In Brazil, the women's movement began as women's clubs in Christian base communities during the 1960s and 1970s. Women who lived in *favelas* and poor working-class neighborhoods experienced firsthand the social and economic policies of the military dictatorship. These women used the mothers' clubs to fight for basic survival needs—affordable food, a decent wage, adequate schools, daycare centers, and access to safe water. These community-based mothers' clubs became the organizational base for the feminist movement in Brazil.

In 1979, middle-class feminists joined with poor and working-class women in the struggle for daycare in São Paulo. The movement, Movimiento de Luta por Creches (MLC) or Movement of Struggle for Day Care, called for daycare centers close to women's work, financed by the state or private industry. The MLC formed coalitions with other groups who supported daycare, wrote articles for newspapers, and planned meetings to educate their constituents and members of government, both local and state. Soon, several political parties—even the ruling Democratic Social Party—demonstrated their support for women's concerns by creating women's divisions within their parties. By 1982 there were 141 daycare centers in São Paulo, all financed by the municipal government.

In Bolivia women entered the struggle for social justice when their husbands and companions were jailed for protesting poor working conditions in the mines. Sixty women staged a hunger fast in protest and after ten days won concessions from the mining company. Their husbands were released from jail and the government improved working conditions. Following their initial action, the women organized themselves into the Housewives Committee of Siglo XX, a group that became the model for Housewives Committees in every Bolivian mining camp.

The Housewives Committee had a dual focus: to improve working conditions for the miners and living conditions for their families. Besides conditions at the mine, the women demanded improved housing and schools, access to safe water, and affordable food. Members of the Housewives Committee directed their actions—hunger strikes, marches, and demonstrations— toward both the government and the mining company. The women sent petitions to the government and mining company; they wrote letters protesting schools, health care, and working conditions at the mines.

Although most of their tactics were nonviolent, the women occasionally resorted to violence. Since men could not threaten strikebreakers, for fear of imprisonment, women in the Housewives Committee would throw stones at strikebreakers and drag them away. Tensions at the mine frequently resulted in violence initiated by both the miners and the mining company. The women also offered emergency medical care for miners hurt during skirmishes with the authorities.

The Madres de Plaza de Mayo in Argentina and the Co-Madres in El Salvador have championed the cause of human rights in their countries. They have created a new breed of human rights groups in Latin America, "motherist" groups.

> These protagonists are not the traditional political actors from parties or unions, [but] in the majority of cases, are simple mothers of families who are not militants and do not belong to any part of the opposition. [They are] women who, by their condition as mothers, wives, sisters, or daughters of the victims, have been intensely, culturally mobilized by the repression, [in a manner] without precedent in Latin American history.[8]

Mothers, like the Madres de la Plaza de Mayo and the Co-Madres, test the limits of political action by publicly demanding justice from their government. Social and political circumstances, rather than ideology, propel them into action. They begin as women who, under normal circumstances, would not be politically active. But with the death or disappearance of relatives, they join a group and are transformed into political actors. With their actions of civil disobedience, these women provide historical models for women in oppression.

The Madres de la Plaza de Mayo began in the center of Buenos Aires, Argentina, in 1977 as fourteen women wearing white head scarves gathered to protest the disappearance of their children. Their weekly protests at the Plaza de Mayo occurred in the context of a brutal military regime where all forms of public dissent were forbidden. Initially dismissed by government officials as Las Locas, the crazy women, the movement grew in three years to protests with over 2,000 women. By 1982 more than 2,500 women marched to the Plaza each Thursday.

Besides weekly marches and demonstrations, the women presented petitions, one with 24,000 signatures, calling for investigations into the abductions, assassinations, and acts of torture. The Madres delivered hundreds of writs of habeas corpus to the courts and gave press releases to the media. In spite of the kidnapping of nine Madres, harassment by government security forces, and fears for personal safety, the Madres refused to accept the finality of the disappearances. One Madre commented, "Our desire to find our sons was stronger than our fright."[9] In addition to growth of their movement within Argentina, the Madres made valuable contacts with human rights groups internationally, contacts that led to the Madres testifying before the Inter-American Human Rights Commission in 1979.[10]

In Chile, following the 1973 coup, forty relatives of the disappeared gathered to form Agrupación, the Group of Relatives of the Detained-Disappeared. Agrupación differs from the Madres and other motherist groups in one way: although they, like other motherist groups, have no previous political experience, many of the women in Agrupación had children in a leftist group that advocated violent change in Chile. Still, this group of mothers practiced nonviolent methods and advocated nonviolent change through political reform.

Like the women in Las Madres de Plaza de Mayo, members of Agrupación pressed the government to investigate the disappearance of their children. They staged protests, carrying placards and photos of missing relatives. They spoke to the United Nations, the Organization of American States, the International Court of Justice, and to the media, hoping to "break the silence" surrounding their missing relatives. When the Chilean National

Congress passed an amnesty law for all offenses committed between 1973 and 1978, the Agrupación staged a hunger strike until the government began an investigation of over six hundred cases of disappeared persons. They presented letters and petitions to different government officials. After clandestine cemeteries were discovered at Lonquen and Yumbel in 1979, the Agrupación led marches to the graves and held public masses.

Throughout their protests, the women of Agrupación and Las Madres de Plaza de Mayo, as well as the women of Bolivia and Brazil, emphasized that they were women and mothers. Although their actions were revolutionary in a society where public forms of expression were either limited or forbidden, they have continued to act, convinced that life can be better for their sons and daughters. The news of their actions have spread throughout Latin America and the world, bringing a glimmer of hope to oppressed people in countries with almost no hope.

Within the past twelve years women in Guatemala have added their voices to the movement for social change in Latin America. Poor and middle-class indigenous and *ladina* women are finding their voices through the vehicle of church groups and human rights groups. Women, especially wives and mothers, have been active in the struggle for social and political change. The participation of women and their strong role in leadership has been particularly significant in the movement for social and political change in Guatemala.

Organization

To understand the situation in Guatemala and its relevance for women and other victims of injustice throughout the world, I examine the conceptions of justice held by women in human rights groups. To achieve this, I provide a framework to interpret their views of justice by examining the conceptions of justice held by two ethicists, David Hollenbach and Karen Lebacqz; a theologian, Gustavo Gutiérrez; and a political theorist, Michael

Walzer. Since people concerned with justice must be aware of the sources and manifestations of injustice, I include Walter Wink's studies on the powers and authorities.

In addition to the categories for understanding social structures from Wink and the descriptions of justice from Gutiérrez, Walzer, Lebacqz, and Hollenbach, I focus on the stories of women in Guatemala. Human rights groups and church groups are empowering people through their actions and activities. These groups enlarge the political opening and create hope. Women involved in groups discover skills and abilities; they find that can be effective in forms of action and ministry outside the home.

Chapter two examines injustice in Guatemala, with emphasis on Guatemala's history and the economic, political, and social situation. I describe the current situation and recent history of Guatemala, taking care to name and describe evil structures and systems.

Many women have responded to the injustice in Guatemala through involvement in human rights groups and church groups. In chapter three, women in human rights groups tell their stories and the stories of their organizations. Granted, we must know statistics, read history, and understand the political dynamics. These, however, must be supplemented by personal narratives if we are to understand more fully how political, economic, and social realities shape society and influence the marginalized majority of Guatemala. From their experiences and their analyses, we recognize the sources of injustice and see the shapes of justice. Through their activities and priorities, we see their social change strategies, their entry points, and how they confront injustice.

The actions of Guatemalan women have implications for North American women trapped in a pattern of rampant individualism that prevents them from engaging in compassionate actions to ease suffering and injustice in their own neighborhoods or in the larger global community. North American women paralyzed by injustice, oppression, and discrimination can learn from the experience of Guatemalan women.

Believing that justice cannot be understood adequately without attending to issues of domination, I include Walter Wink's
trilogy on the principalities and powers in my framework. Chapter four contains a theological analysis of injustice which uses
Wink's work as a foundation. Wink addresses the problem of injustice from the viewpoint of the powers and authorities in the
New Testament. His analysis offers categories for understanding
injustice in contemporary society. The powers and authorities
are institutions of authority, created by God, but fallen and sinful. If created by God as a good creation, even though the powers are fallen, the powers are redeemable—not permanently fall-
en or without possibility of change.

The message of powers and authorities concerns the material
and spiritual nature of institutions. According to Wink, many
people lack categories for understanding social realities. We
blame evil individuals and miss the larger structure of institutions. We ignore sinful structures and systems. With no category
for understanding social realities, we are left with a vacuum
Glen Stassen says can be filled with secular stowaways like
laissez-faire ideology or simple avoidance. Injustice is the result.

In chapter five I examine justice as conceived by Gutiérrez,
Lebacqz, Walzer, and Hollenbach. Instead of surveying their
writings on justice, I examine central themes that resound with
Guatemalan women's ideas and practices of justice and the need
for justice actions in the United States. Although Gutiérrez,
Lebacqz, Walzer, and Hollenbach represent different religious
traditions and disciplines, all demonstrate concern for justice.

Justice is a recurring theme in Gutiérrez's books and articles
but one Gutiérrez does not clearly define. His picture of justice
must be "caught" by readers; justice is absolutely unquestion-
able in Gutiérrez. Certainly Gutiérrez begins with the experience of injustice, rather than a theory of justice. Lebacqz, echoing liberation themes, suggests that studies of justice begin appropriately with an exploration of the context of injustice.

Lebacqz says a glance at the world reveals "the rupture of justice and the reign of injustice."[11]

Walzer, political theorist formerly at Harvard University and now at the Princeton Institute for Advanced Studies, envisions a plurality of justice systems based on a social understanding of distributive justice and opposition to the injustice of domination. For Walzer, concentrations of economic power and political power are threats to justice. Hollenbach, a Catholic human rights theorist and professor of Christian ethics, stresses participation and mutuality in justice.

The last chapter compares the theological analysis of injustice in chapter four and the concepts of justice in chapter five with the historical reality of injustice in Guatemala and the United States and the response of women and other advocates of justice. A result of the comparison is a new, more comprehensive definition of justice shaped by the experience of women in Guatemala. This chapter identifies what compels women to move from the private sphere to the public sphere and how women's actions change their lives and the social and political situation. The responses of Rigoberta Menchú and the women in CONA-VIGUA (National Coordinator of Guatemalan Widows) and GAM (Grupo de Apoyo Mutuo) testify to their beliefs about groundings for human rights. This chapter also examines injustice in Guatemala in light of Wink's analyses of the powers and principalities in the New Testament and contemporary society.

Furthermore, the chapter proposes an understanding of justice that will be helpful for Guatemalan women throughout the world and women in the United States. First, a new understanding of justice that gives voice to the experience of victims of political oppression and economic exploitation will help clarify and strengthen their claims for justice. Similarly, a recovered emphasis on justice will help women in the United States to hear the stories of the oppressed. A renewed commitment to justice will empower women to engage in justice actions that help Guatemalan women and other oppressed persons.

2

Injustice in Guatemala

THE silencing of poor and indigenous people began with the invasion of Latin America by Christopher Columbus and other explorers 500 years ago. Mexico's *conquistador*, Hernán Cortés, commanded Pedro de Alvarado to verify reports of rich lands and new and different races. When the Spaniards arrived in Guatemala they found lush vegetation, fertile coastlands, tropical jungles, and an indigenous population in existence since 2000 B.C.E.

Alvarado left Mexico on December 6, 1523, with 120 cavalry, 300 infantry, and several hundred Mexican auxiliaries. He describes Guatemala as "well populated with strong towns."[1] Alvarado met little opposition until an initial battle with thirty thousand Quiché warriors. Even though the Quiché warriors outnumbered the Spaniards, they were no match for the military prowess, guns, steel, and horses of the Spaniards. Quiché sources report, "There were so many Indians that they killed that they made a river of blood."[2] Following the defeat of the Quiché, the Spaniards carried out a long and hard campaign against the Tzutuhil, Mam, Pocomán, Cakchiquel, Ixil, Uspantec, Kekchí, and other indigenous peoples in Guatemala.

Bartolemé de las Casas reports that five million Indian lives were lost in Guatemala due to the cruelty of Alvarado. While the number may be exaggerated, historians agree that Alvarado's regime was characterized by excessive cruelty and injustice. The

Spaniards maintained social control through terror and force. Guatemala historian Severo Martinez Paláez adds, "What we must recognize is that the cruel treatment of the Indians was not a sporadic phenomenon, but . . . inherent in the social structure of the colony." The Spaniards believed that because of the Indians' numerical superiority, such cruelty was "absolutely necessary to maintain. . . ."[3]

Although Alvarado initially came to Guatemala in search of gold, silver, and other riches, he soon discovered that the true wealth of Guatemala was land and control of labor to work the land. Alvarado rewarded followers with the free use of Indians. Despite Spanish laws designed to curb abuse of the indigenous population, he continued to enslave the indigenous peoples, so much so that Mexicans complained the low price of Guatemalan Indian slaves hurt Mexican slave trade.

In Guatemala, the Spaniards tried to create a utopia based on the Spanish principles of religion, government, and culture. In writing about the conquest of Mexico and Guatemala, Bernal Diaz del Castillo wrote, "We came here to serve God and the king and also to get rich."[4] Initially the conquistadores, followed by the oligarchy, created a society to serve the church, state, and the ambition of individuals.

To fuel the new society, the Spaniards used three methods of social control for creating wealth. First, the *encomienda*, a trusteeship with the right to labor and tribute, was given to Spanish conquistadores and colonists as a reward for service to the Crown. The king of Spain and later the governor rewarded loyal subjects, often soldiers or colonists, with tribute and labor from one village or a group of villages. The Indians worked in mines, built roads, and provided house and farm labor, all with little or no pay. By the early eighteenth century, the encomienda lost power in Guatemala.

Second, the *repartimiento* was essential to the colonial economic system. It allowed the state to take away up to 25 percent of the population of Indian villages to provide labor for landowners. The employers were required to pay the laborers one *real* (one-eighth peso) per day. The workers were expected to travel to the work site at their own expense and often were kept captive in substandard housing until the work was completed. The Indian population endured the effects of the repartimiento during the three centuries of colonization, from the sixteenth until the nineteenth centuries.

Third, the *reducción* or *congregación* was the Catholic Church's policy to create larger, more centralized towns. Representatives of the church persuaded or forced Indian communities of a few families to move to larger towns, supposedly to facilitate the instruction of the gospel by missionaries. The Dominicans claimed that the reducción also helped curb illegal oppression of Indians. Ironically, many of the larger towns were located near large *haciendas* or *fincas*; the Indians served as a ready source of forced labor for the hacienda or finca owners.[5]

In addition to the forced labor imposed by Alvarado and the Spaniards, Amerindians suffered from the introduction of European diseases by the Spaniards. In 1490 Latin America contained 20 percent of the world's population. Less than a century later, the region represented 3 percent of the world.[6] The effect on Guatemala was so great that it is almost impossible to overestimate the extent of the damage. Europeans brought smallpox, influenza, mumps, measles, typhus, and other contagious diseases to people with no immunity to European diseases.

Combined with the brutality of the conquest and forced labor, the epidemics reduced the population of the Guatemalan highlands from 70 to 90 percent in the first century after the conquest. In one pandemic of smallpox, influenza, and bubonic plague, one-third of the population of the highlands died. From 1520 until 1680, the highland Cuchumatán Indians declined by more than 90 percent, from 260,000 to 16,000.[7]

Independence from Spain in 1821 did little to improve living conditions for the majority of Guatemalans. In the nineteenth century one million people lived in Guatemala, two-third indigenous, one-third ladino, and forty thousand whites. The whites dominated the classist and racist society. Within the white population, Spanish-born landowners, government officials, and merchants were the wealthiest and most powerful. The oligarchy still maintained the practice of forced Indian labor. Many peasants continued subsistence farming on small plots of land. The plots were inadequate to provide for the basic needs of their families, which forced peasants into seasonal migration to work in coffee fields or on banana plantations.

From the time of the conquest, interbreeding between the Spaniard men and indigenous women created a new class of people, ladinos. Although they eventually evolved into a privileged ethnic minority, in the first few centuries after the conquest, ladinos were persecuted and shunned by both the white elite and Indians. Prohibited by law from holding office or from owning land in Indian villages, ladinos were often sharecroppers, tenant farmers, wage workers, or urban artisans.

Nineteenth-century politics revolved around liberals and conservatives. Conservatives, in power for much of the century, were estate owners and merchants who supported the Catholic Church and profited from government monopolies. In opposition to conservative ideology, liberals supported free trade, anticlericalism, and modernization of the economy.

Following independence, Governor Galvez implemented a liberal agenda based on an Enlightenment-influenced understanding of justice and equality. He abolished slavery, modernized the economy, and reduced the power of the Catholic Church. A nationalist, Galvez believed separate Indian cultures threatened the development of national identity. His tax reforms —on crops, slaughtered meat, and community funds—threatened the life of the village. Understanding that land was the major source of wealth in Guatemala, he proposed land reform that involved the seizure of "empty lands"—not from wealthy landowners but from peasants who had used lands for centuries but could not prove title. The empty lands included many communal lands held by Indian villages. Although Galvez and the liberal agenda claimed liberty and justice for all, the liberals exploited indigenous peoples and increased the inequality between rich and poor.

Into the Guatemalan political scene came an unlikely figure, Rafael Carrera. Carrera, a ladino born in a Guatemala City slum, kept swine in the small village of Malasquescuintla. With the support of the Galvez government, a wealthy landowner claimed the communal land surrounding Malasquescuintla. The village responded with numerous revolts, culminating in an attack by soldiers who raped Carrera's Indian wife and burned down his buildings. Described as "quiet with a dominating personality, a will and a talent for power," Carrera soon won the allegiance of his neighbors and other insurgent leaders in the highlands.[8] Following their victory over the Guatemalan army, Carrera and his followers insisted on a government that protected village lands and recognized the church.

In 1844, Carrera became president and remained president until his death in 1865 as a wealthy man. His wealth distanced him from peasant concerns, but he maintained his commitment to village communities and their lands.

Carrera was followed by a breed of liberals serving the gods of progress and order. Influenced by Compte, dictators Justo Rufino Barrios and Manuel Estrada Cabrera ushered Guatemala into the modern era. The dictators of this era were *caudillos*, charismatic, authoritarian leaders. After thirty years of conservative rule, the liberals again took control of Guatemala through a military coup led by Barrios. Concerned about the military strength of Guatemala, Barrios began the Escuela Politécnica, the national military academy, and professionalized the army.

Barrios diversified the economy, an economy based first on the export of indigo, then on the dye, cochineal. He expanded the cultivation and exportation of coffee. From 1870 until 1900 the coffee exportation and cultivation grew twenty times, resulting in economic growth for the oligarchy. The extremely rapid economic growth attracted foreign investors. Barrios welcomed foreign investors, funding their projects with loans from the Guatemalan government.

To provide cheap labor for the growing coffee industry, Barrios reinstituted forced labor and encouraged debt bondage.[9] His government expropriated village communal land—23,427 lots in the first year of his regime. The lack of sufficient land made peasants likely candidates for forced-labor projects. In the forced-labor program, up to one-fourth of village residents were given to landowners for up to one month annually. Debt bondage and forced-labor programs resembled slavery, with scarce attention by the authorities to abuse of the peasants. The repressive nature of forced labor, debt bondage, and other programs directed toward peasants led the British Consul to call the Barrios administration "one of the most cruel despotisms the world has ever seen."[10]

The decade of democracy, also called "the ten years of spring," began with the overthrow of General Jorge Ubico, dictator for thirteen years. Although the Guatemala Constitution forbids reelection, Ubico was· reelected twice. During his early years, he improved roads, instituted programs for agricultural diversity, and strengthened Guatemala's foreign trade. In spite of minor reforms and economic growth, from the beginning of his dictatorship Ubico turned toward violent and repressive solutions. Disturbed by the power and freedom of the press, he registered printing presses to control articles written by the opposition. He trusted no one in his own government. Early in his dictatorship, he forced all the members of the Supreme Court to resign, and then replaced them with allies. Ubico was fascinated by the military and used the military, death squads, and spies as tools of repression. An admirer of Hitler and Mussolini, he believed he was a reincarnation of Napoleon. After directing a massacre of students, workers, and prominent citizens in 1934, he told *Time* that "I am like Hitler, I execute first and give trial afterward."[11]

Throughout Ubico's years, he cultivated relationships with U.S. businesses in Guatemala, particularly the powerful triumvirate of the United Fruit Company, International Railways of Central America, and the United Fruit Steamship Company. To please both the United States and the United Fruit Company, during World War II Ubico expelled German coffee growers and expropriated their lands. The interests of the three companies became synonymous with the interests of the United States. By the 1930s the three companies controlled 40 percent of the Guatemalan economy.

By 1934, the United Fruit Company possessed 550,000 acres of Guatemalan land with only 115,000 acres in cultivation. United Fruit Company had a monopoly on rail transportation throughout the country and on shipping from the Pacific coast. The company paid minimal taxes and was exempt from regulations or inspections on the railways and shipping lines. Although United Fruit Company workers were paid well in comparison with other Guatemalans, employees were not allowed to bargain collectively or form unions. Any labor dispute or strike was crushed with force by the police and military.

Conditions of life in Guatemala deteriorated rapidly under Ubico. Two percent of the population owned 72 percent of the available farmland and the rural per capita income was $89.15. By 1944, even Ubico's allies were distancing themselves. Finally a people's movement arose that led to his resignation. First, in May 1944, forty-five lawyers called for the resignation of a judge who tried political opponents of the Ubico government. Then 200 teachers petitioned Ubico for a wage increase. When he refused, they boycotted a parade in his honor. In response, he fired the teachers and charged the teachers who had written the petition with conspiracy against the government.

Students at the University of San Carlos protested his actions against the teachers and called for a student strike. On June 23 teachers called a strike supported by students and other professionals. Ubico called the actions of the students and professionals "Nazi-fascist" and announced a state of emergency.[12]

Early in his administration Ubico had said that if 300 respected Guatemalans asked him to resign, he would. On June 24, 311 prominent Guatemalans signed the *Memorial de los 311* and delivered it to Ubico. People gathered at a meeting in Guatemala City that night to demand Ubico's resignation. In spite of the peaceful nature of the demonstrations and actions, the police retaliated with harassment, questioning, and beating hundreds of people.

The next day women dressed in mourning gathered at the Church of San Francisco, on the main plaza across from the National Palace, to pray for an end to the bloodshed. As the women processed from the church, the army fired on the group and killed a teacher, Maria Chincilla Recinos. In response Guatemala City closed down. Businesses and schools ceased operating. The opposition stopped talks with the government. The city was deserted. The opposition brought Ubico a letter stating the unanimous desire of the people of Guatemala for his resignation. The letter asked for an end to the attacks on citizens, restoration of the freedom of press and association, and the suspension of martial law. Ubico saw his control over the people and government of Guatemala rapidly disintegrate. Finally on July 1, 1944, he resigned in favor of a triumvirate.

Decade of Democracy: 1944-1954

Guatemala's history, especially the years following the 1954 *coup d'etat*, is punctuated with violence, repression, and subversive intervention by the United States.[13] The first decade after World War II is unique in Guatemala's history because it was the first and only period of significant socioeconomic reform. Two democratically elected presidents, José Arévalo Bermejo and Jacobo Arbenz Guzmán, introduced agrarian reform, improved education and health care, and abolished forced unpaid labor. In response to the land reform by Arbenz, an invading army headed by Colonel Carlos Castillo Armas, aided by the CIA, over-threw Arbenz.

Latin America took Franklin Roosevelt's New Deal to heart. Roosevelt's Four Freedoms speech became the foundation for a new Guatemala. The freedoms—of speech, of religion, from want, and from fear—sounded like the rebirth of a new world to most Guatemalans who had never known these freedoms. The freedoms in Roosevelt's speech represented a threat to Guatemala's small group who ruled the country with little thought for justice and equality.

In the twentieth century Guatemala was a semifeudal economy controlled by the oligarchy and the military. The new constitution of 1945 mandated an apolitical military whose function was to support the constitution. Arbenz and Arévalo proposed an economic democracy and an electoral democracy. The democracy would be truly participatory for the first time in Guatemala's history, including indigenous and ladino people in addition to the oligarchy and middle class. Under Arbenz, 60 percent of the economically active population, 300,000 to 400,000 people, were active in unions.[14] The electoral democracy gave voice to right, center, and left-of-center parties, including the Communist party.

The Arévalo government was responsible for the new 1945 constitution that outlawed racial discrimination and guaranteed equal access to health services. As a result of health clinics, access to clean water, and higher income, the infant mortality rate fell an average of 2.5 percent per year during the ten years of the Arévalo and Arbenz administrations.[15] The Arévalo administration enacted the first social security law and repealed the Vagrancy law.[16] The government began literacy campaigns and increased educational expenditures by 155 percent over four years. In 1947 the Arévalo government passed a labor code that restricted child labor, set daily hours and minimum wages, and legalized the right to strike and collective bargaining.

Although Arbenz passed the momentous agrarian-reform

law, President Arévalo made beginning steps toward land reform. He distributed land confiscated from German and Nazi
sympathizers. Arévalo drafted legislation that addressed concerns of small farmers. Under the Law of Forced Rental, farmers
with less than three acres could petition to rent unused land
from neighboring plantation owners. He formed the National
Production Institute to give advice, credit, and supplies to small
farmers.

Inequitable land distribution was a major barrier to economic growth and justice. A Minnesota professor concluded that
large landowners fear land reform because they might lose their
source of cheap labor if Indians own land.[17] A 1949 Library of
Congress study revealed that "raising the standard of living
through diversification and mechanization is greatly dependent
on changes in the distribution of the profits and the land."[18]

Jacobo Arbenz continued the reforms of the Arévalo administration and passed the agrarian-reform law, Decree 900. The
decree was based on a World Bank study that concluded that the
poverty of the highland peasants hindered Guatemala's economic growth. Access to land for more Guatemalans would
stimulate the stagnant economy. The legislation called for the
expropriation of land not cultivated for three years. The government would reimburse owners for the value of the land, based
on the owners' declarations of tax value. Under the legislation,
Arbenz lost a family farm. But the major target of the decree was
the United Fruit Company. Under the terms of the legislation
the government expropriated 381,000 acres from the United
Fruit Company, at a tax value of three dollars per acre. The United Fruit Company responded by demanding sixteen million
dollars for the true value of the land.[19]

Ubico and other opponents of the "ten years of spring"
quickly labeled both Arbenz and Arévalo communists, a charge
used to arouse popular prejudices. At the height of the Cold War
any advocate of economic and social reform was labeled communist. Both Arbenz and Arévalo wanted to transform Guate-

mala into a modern capitalist state, a true participatory democracy. Arévalo called his program of economic and social reforms "spiritual socialism" but rejected material socialism and said that communism was contrary to human nature. Political scientist José Aybar de Soto said that Ubico's use of the word *communism* to label anyone opposed to the government created a new socially accepted definition of communism.[20] Communist was used for anyone who was anti-Ubico, anti-repression, and pro-democracy.

In response to the changes during the Arévalo and Arbenz administrations, particularly the 1952 land-reform legislation that threatened the United Fruit Company, the United States took action. With the cooperation of the "Liberation Army" of Castillo Armas, the U.S. overthrew the government of Guatemala.

The "ten years of spring" threatened powerful economic, social, and political interests in Guatemala. The Catholic Church, the oligarchy, and the military in Guatemala watched as "their" country became a participatory democracy, with involvement by student associations, unions, cooperatives, and church groups. But not only Guatemalans were threatened by the social and economic revolution led by Arbenz and Arévalo. Guatemala's revolution represented a threat to the economic and political interests of the United Fruit Company. Guatemala could evolve into an authentically Latin American democracy, with a shape different from the form of democracy practiced in the United States.

Journalists Stephen Kinzer and Stephen Schlesinger call the June 1954 coup and the events leading up to the coup the most blatant North American intervention in the history of Latin America. The coup, called "Operation Success" and approved by President Eisenhower, was implemented by the CIA in cooperation with the United Fruit Company and a few dissidents from Guatemala. In the ten years prior to the invasion, Guatemala felt the increasing strength of U.S. threats against their social and economic reforms. In the months before the invasion, Guatemala asked both the United Nations and the Organization of American States to investigate threats from the United States, but U.S. influence prevented the approval of an investigation.[21]

Two of the most powerful men in the United States, John Foster Dulles, Secretary of State, and Allen Dulles, director of the CIA, had ties with the United Fruit Company.[22] The Dulles brothers spearheaded Operation Success. The dictator of Nicaragua, Anastacio Somoza García, provided a base for training the mercenary army and a landing strip for CIA-owned planes.

The invasion, more an invasion of disinformation than a real military threat, began with reports from a clandestine radio station, claiming to broadcast from "deep inside Guatemala." The radio broadcasts were taped by CIA operatives in Florida and sent from Nicaragua and the U.S. base on Swan Island. The broadcasts announced fictitious military victories and bombings all over Guatemala. In fact, CIA planes dropped a few bombs on Guatemala City and the mercenary army fought one battle at Zacapa, a small border town. Within days, President Arbenz resigned and the U.S. Ambassador, John Peurifoy, brought in Colonel Armas to be president.

Guatemala: National Security State, 1954-1985

The years following 1954 were characterized by erratic and increasingly corrupt military rule. Fraudulent elections, coups, and assassinations were the means for leadership transitions. Guatemala became famous as the birthplace of "the disappeared" and a country with no official political prisoners. Enemies of the government were either buried in clandestine cemeteries or left on the side of the road as a reminder to the general populace.

In spite of escalating violence and active repression, a popular movement erupted throughout the country in the 1970s. Cooperatives formed among farmers and artisans. Unions grew in membership. Catholic Action groups throughout Guatemala flourished.[23] Human rights groups formed to investigate and protest human rights violations.

The reforms achieved during the "ten years of spring" quickly disappeared. Eager to keep Guatemala free from "communism," the United States and its allies provided military training and supplies. After the CIA-sponsored coup, Castillo Armas returned much of the land expropriated by Decree 900. Four years after the coup, less than .5 percent of people who had received land under Decree 900 still held their land. In addition to returning land, Armas canceled 533 labor union registrations and erased labor legislation. Both the coffee oligarchy and the United Fruit Company recovered their lost land and again operated with a privileged position in Guatemalan society.

Ironically, a civilian president, Julio César Méndez Montenegro, provided the impetus for the present military. Throughout his presidency, Méndez, a reformer identified with the Arévalo and Arbenz revolution, battled with the army for control of Guatemala. The occasional acts of two small guerrilla groups provided the excuse for the head of the army, Colonel Carlos Arana Osorio, to institute death squads such as the Ojo por Ojo and Mano Blanca.[24] Méndez, powerless to handle the growing military, watched as the defense minister called a state of seige and gave control of Guatemala to the top military leaders. During Méndez's administration, the army crushed the small guerrilla movement, killing thousands of civilians in the campaign. After eliminating the guerrillas, the army targeted the popular movement—church groups, unions, cooperatives, and professional associations.

In 1970, Colonel Arana, head of the army and also known as the Jackal of Zacapa, won the presidency by vote of 4 percent of the population, 43 percent of those voting.[25] Guatemala watched as Arana and the death squads rained terror on the countryside in the name of anticommunism, counterinsurgency, and national security. Prepared by Ojo por Ojo, death lists of reformist politicians and union leaders appeared regularly. From November to March over 700 political killings occurred. Arana promised to eliminate all guerrillas "even if it is necessary to turn Guatemala into a cemetery."[26]

In 1978 General Romeo Lucas García won the presidency in an election the *Washington Post* called "a fraud so transparent that nobody could expect to get away with it." Lucas García was the candidate of the army and right wing political parties. Residents of Guatemala City experienced massive, selective repression. The Lucas government targeted unions, the University of San Carlos, and moderate-centrist political parties. In 1980 alone, 1,000 union members were assassinated. At the University of San Carlos deaths and disappearances were a daily occurrence. At one point, the army opened fire on a busload of engineering and medical students arriving for classes. The Christian Democrat party reported that 238 of its leaders were assassinated between 1980 and 1981. Christian Democrat and 1985 president Vinicio Cerezo remarked, "My government would have you believe that communism is the enemy of democracy in Guatemala when in reality it itself is freedom's foe."[27] Even Lucas García's vice-president admitted, "Death or exile is the fate of those who fight for justice in Guatemala."[28]

In the rural highlands, where five million Guatemalans lived, the killing was more widespread. Lucas García implemented a tactic used by the United States in Vietnam—a scorched-earth policy of burning entire villages and fields. In response to the massacres, the guerrilla movement experienced unprecedented growth, in spite of massive repression by the military. Although at no time did the guerrilla movement number more than 3,500, participation represented a response to the climate of fear created by the military and death squads. An Oxfam America study revealed that

> Indians began joining the guerrilla organizations not because of a deep ideological understanding of or commitment to their cause

but rather as a means of individual and community defense
against the selective killings and acts of terror by the army and
death squads.[29]

Prior to Lucas García's rule the bourgeoisie and the military
worked cohesively as a ruling coalition. During Lucas García's
presidency the coalition broke down, resulting in divisions
among the military and a lack of bourgeois confidence in the
military.

Efrain Ríos Montt, a centrist military officer, overthrew Lucas
in March 1982. Although he came to power in a coup, Ríos
Montt promised reform—elections, less corruption in the government and military, a safer Guatemala. During the 1982 coup
Ríos Montt promised to bring back democracy. With the support
of the urban middle class and a group of younger military officers Ríos Montt promised a responsible, moral government that
stopped death squads and ended government corruption. His
support by the junior army officers alienated other factions of
the military. His counterinsurgency program of *frijoles y fusiles*,
beans and bullets, combined a social program of food distribution with brutal repression in rural areas particularly targeted
against the Mayan Indians. The army continued the scorched-
earth policy, burning crops and forests, bombing and destroying
villages, and killing over 4,000 people during the first 63 days of
the regime. Ríos Montt instituted secret tribunals to try people
accused of political crimes. On television he explained that he
had declared "a state of siege so we could kill legally."[30]

A leader of the evangelical fundamentalist church *El Verbo*,
Ríos Montt received political and financial support from the religious right in the United States to fund a war against communism and a religious war.[31] Protestant conservatives joined Catholic conservatives in their support of the government social-
military program in the highlands. Anyone opposing the government program was accused of opposing the will of God.

During the eighteen months of the Ríos Montt administration, the rural-urban cleavage grew. The bloodbath, concentrated in the rural highlands, resulted in 30,000 deaths, 200,000 refugees on the border of Mexico, and one million internally displaced Guatemalans.

In response to the atrocities committed during the Ríos Montt regime, the four guerrilla organizations—the Organization of the People in Arms (ORPA), the Guerrilla Army of the Poor (EGP), Rebel Armed Forces (FAR), and some of the Guatemalan Workers Party (PGT)—formed a joint coalition, Guatemalan National Revolutionary Unity (URNG). They declared, "Since 1954, when the anti-Communist right wing and U.S. imperialism overthrew the democratic government of Arbenz, 83,500 people have been assassinated in Guatemala."[32] URNG announced its platform for a revolutionary government: full equality for indigenous peoples and an end to their cultural oppression, an end to domination by the rich, basic rights for all citizens, land reform, a representative government, equality for women, a new popular revolutionary army, and a nonaligned foreign policy.

A coup led by Oscar Mejía Victores and senior officers of the military ousted Ríos Montt in 1983. These officers, known as the most violent and as anticommunists, represented the interests of the rural elite. Death squads and the military continued to operate openly in rural areas, but massacres occurred less frequently. Assassinations escalated in urban areas as the Mejía Victores administration targeted union leaders, students, teachers, church and human rights workers.

The State of the Union with Civilian Presidents: 1985-1996

Since 1985 the people of Guatemala have elected three civilian presidents. Some have seen the change from a military president to a civilian president as indicative of Guatemala's transition to a democracy. These same people assume that political violence will subside and greater freedoms will occur. Power in Guatemala, however, remains in the hands of the military and the economic elite. Archbishop Oscar Romero's friend, Monsignor Ricardo Urioste said, "Elections are simply one note in the symphony of democracy." More steps must be taken before Guatemala qualifies as a democracy. The criteria for a democracy are—

> legal freedom to formulate and advocate political alternatives with the concomitant rights to free association, free speech, and other basic freedoms of person; free and nonviolent competition among leaders with periodic validation of their claim to rule . . . and provision for the participation of all members of the political community, whatever their political preferences.[33]

With elections and political openings Guatemala may be making a transition toward democracy but there are too many abuses of human rights and there is too little freedom to label Guatemala a democracy today. Political scientist Susanne Jonas argues that Guatemala cannot be considered even a limited political democracy while such extreme social inequalities exist—with no attempts for structural reform.[34]

The situation in Guatemala is reminiscent of a quotation from Lillian Hellman's *Pentimento*.

> Old paint on canvas, as it ages, sometimes becomes transparent. When that happens it is possible in some pictures to see the original lines: a tree will show through a woman's dress, a child makes way for a dog, a large boat is no longer on the open sea. That is called pentimento because the painter "repented," changed his mind. Perhaps it would be as well to say that the old conception, replaced by a later choice, is a way of seeing and then seeing again.[35]

Guatemala as a National Security state with the dominant power of the military is much stronger than a weak democratically elected president and fledgling human rights and church groups painted over it.

Guatemala has not always been governed by a military president or dictator but the power, at least since 1954, has come from a military that governs largely through fear and intimidation. Ximena Bunster-Burotto believes that the military state "depends on the oppression and exploitation of the poverty-stricken masses."[36]

In spite of thirty years of fear imposed by a military state, the 1985 constitutional process and presidential election gave Guatemalans hope for increased freedom and human rights. Restored, at least on paper, were a civilian government, the rule of law, and limited political pluralism. The platforms of the five candidates in the 1985 election differed little, but Vinicio Cerezo, a Christian Democrat, was the most progressive candidate. None of the candidates advocated more than modest reforms; none suggested restrictions on the power of the military. Cerezo offered the most possibility for change. During his campaign he promised to respect the rights of all citizens and to bring an accounting for the disappeared. He won the election by 70 percent of those who voted. For the first time in many years the election was nonfraudulent, but still over half of Guatemala's registered voters did not participate, an indication of their lack of faith in the electoral process.

Although many people praise the 1985 election as a step toward democracy and a move away from military domination, Jonas insisted that the Cerezo regime was a civilian continuation of the counterinsurgency state.[37] She based her conclusion on the military's own 1982 document, "National Plan for Security and Development," in which elections were a necessary stage in counterinsurgency strategy after the most intensive military phase was completed. It is common knowledge that the army allowed the election, unlike Chile, where a people's referendum paved the way for the removal of General Pinochet and the election of President Aylwin. Jonas suggests that the army and the ruling coalition needed the election—

1. to overcome the international isolation that Guatemala had incurred during its many years as the region's worst human rights violator—for political reasons, but above all, to attract international aid to alleviate the economic crisis;
2. to regain private-sector confidence and reactivate the economy; and
3. to establish internal stability and legitimacy, which had been seriously challenged by revolutionary and popular movements during the late 1970s and early 1980s.[38]

The government of Guatemala had been isolated in some international circles because of its reputation as a violator of human rights. Like other countries in Latin America, Guatemala felt the strength of the global recession and needed increases in foreign aid to expedite economic recovery. Many members of the military felt that a civilian government, still under the control of the military, would not be too great a cost for internal stability and economic recovery.

Cerezo's public affirmation of human rights at the United Nations and in Washington, D.C., bolstered Guatemala's international image. With the return to a civilian government and a supposed end to military rule, the United Nations reduced human rights monitoring. Mayor Andrew Young and the city of Atlanta, Georgia, promised training for Guatemala's police force. Taiwan, France, and West Germany also promised training for Guatemalan police. In addition, the United States, West Germany, Israel, Italy, Spain, Mexico, and Venezuela gave aid to Guatemalan security forces.

Cerezo's administration was a disappointment for Guatemalans interested in human rights and less militarism. Granted, modest reforms occurred. Cerezo set up a government human rights office, although the office rarely investigated claims. Cerezo even responded to the peasant *pro-tierra* movement by distributing land from six southern coast farms to 6,200 families.[39] Neither dissent nor involvement in popular movements was as dangerous as it had been in the previous sixteen years of military rule (see figures 1-4).[40] Nevertheless, Cerezo's administration tolerated increased levels of human rights abuses. Like the Guatemala of military dictatorships, bodies were found on the side of the road with marks of torture; mothers still cried because their sons and daughters had been abducted.

After his election, Cerezo identified increasingly with the military. In an interview he stressed the "absolute unity" between the government's agenda and the army's agenda.[41] On one occasion, Cerezo visited the war zone dressed in a military uniform; on another occasion he thanked the army for bringing democracy to Guatemala. It is difficult to ascertain whether Cerezo's identification with the military was political pragmatism or ideological affinity.

Even the modest reforms implemented by Cerezo troubled the civilian and military right wing. During 1988 and 1989 factions of the military attempted coups that proved destabilizing for the Cerezo government. Although Cerezo made no public statement after the 1988 and 1989 coups and rumors of coups, he became even more sensitive to demands from the right wing. Defense Minister Gramajo and his followers believed that a civilian government was necessary for stability and increased foreign aid. The right wing coalition believed that a civilian government would allow the popular movement and the guerrillas more freedom to grow in strength and number. The civilian and military right wing viewed Christian Democrats, a moderately progressive party, as a "watermelon" or green on the outside and red on the inside. Even though Christian Democrats were aligned with the army, the right wing coalition feared that Cerezo and the Christian Democrats would bring a form of democratic socialism to Guatemala.

On January 6, 1991, Jorge Serrano Elías became president of Guatemala and the first Protestant elected president in Latin America. Serrano, a right wing businessman who campaigned on a law and order platform, had served as president of the

Figure 1
Massacres in Guatemala from 1982-1991

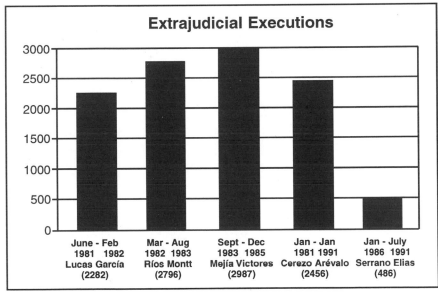

Figure 2
Extrajudicial Executions in Guatemala 1981-1991

Council of State during the dictatorship of Ríos Montt. The 1990 campaign differed little from the 1985 campaign, except the general populace found less reason to hope for change. During the 1990 campaign more than twelve leading politicians were murdered. Again, in spite of penalties for nonvoters, the turnout was abysmal—only 30 percent of the electorate voted.

As was true of Cerezo, Serrano talked much about peace and human rights. In spite of Serrano's public comments, the violence continued and even increased. In August 1992 a Witness for Peace worker commented that violence resembled early 1980s levels. He observed,

> The past several months in Guatemala have grown continually more tense. Continuing repression, much of it traced to governmental security forces, shakes the society. The Serrano administration, half-way through its second year in power, has proven incapable of responding to the needs of the people. . . . Political violence continues without pause.[42]

Human rights activists and other members of the popular sector remain targets for threat, intimidation, and torture at the hands of government security forces. In August 1991, Vice-President Gustavo Espina admitted that the military continues as the dominant institution.[43]

Alvaro Arzú's Presidency

On May 25, 1993, President Serrano suspended the Constitution, dissolved the Congress, Supreme Court, and the Constitutional Court, and announced a coup. His actions effectively suspended the freedom of speech, assembly, the press, and made political gatherings illegal. Although news stories reported Serrano's action as the arbitrary action of one individual, the coup and counter-coup were carried out with full knowledge and support of the military hierarchy. They were military coups behind a civilian facade.

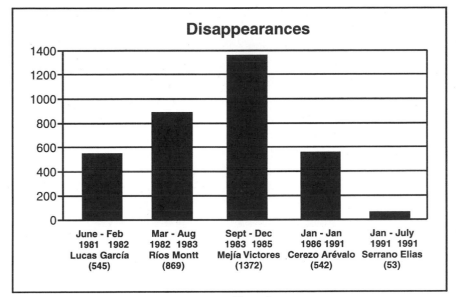

Figure 3
Disappearances in Guatemala 1981-1991

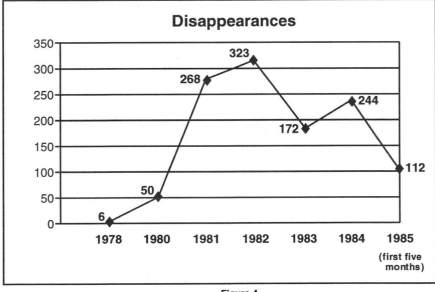

Figure 4
Disappearances 1978-1985

Following the coup, on May 27, 1,000 workers gathered outside the National Court to protest the suspension of the Constitution. Later that day over 2,000 people gathered in the National Cathedral for a protest mass. On May 31, 500 journalists protested the censorship of the press. The Clinton administration froze all aid to Guatemala, including joint military exercises and military training. In addition, the U.S. threatened suspension of preferential tariff treatment for the $200 million worth of Guatemalan imports. The European Economic Community cut all aid and proposed an economic blockade.

On June 1 the military ousted Serrano. Guatemala was for two days in turmoil and confusion as political leaders, conservative union representatives, and business leaders made plans for Guatemala's future. On June 2, the vice-president, Gustavo Espina, one of Rios Montt's closest advisers during the bloody years of the early 1980's, was declared president. Four days later, he resigned and fled for El Salvador. On June 7 the Guatemalan Congress elected Ramiro do León Carpio, the former Procurator of Human Rights, as the new president, in spite of objections from the military.

As Human Rights Procurator, de León supported the peace process and fiercely criticized the Serrano government, the military, and the civil patrols. As president, he reiterated his support for peace talks and flew to Brazil to build international support for his peace plan at the Iberoamerican Summit. His first action as president was to fire Defense Minister García Samayoa and replace him with General Roberto Perussina Rivera, former chief of staff of the Defense Ministry and leader of the hardliners in the army. In spite of his previous harsh criticism, as president de León affirmed the important role of the Army and the civil patrols. Clearly, the source of power still remained in the hands of the military and business elite.

In January 1996, Guatemala elected Alvaro Arzú Irigoyen of the National Advancement Party (PAN) as president. Representing an alliance of conservative business interests, President

Arzú and PAN hold as their priority modernization of the state. To modernize the state, Arzú wants to professionalize the army and create a more friendly environment for foreign investment and free trade. The platform of Arzú and PAN supports participatory democracy, sustainability, equity, and growth with stability. In January, Arzú promised to curtail the power of the military and end killings of civilians, echoing the three presidents' promises of respect for human rights.

Arzú's first action was to restructure the Army and remove 118 National Police officers. He removed one-third of the Army's twenty-three generals and promoted officers in favor of a negotiated settlement with the Guatemalan National Revolutionary Unity (URNG). In the midst of these changes, right wing groups in the military and death squads accelerated the violence. In the first five months of 1996, the Human Rights Procurator's Office received more than 7,000 reports of human rights violations. Common crime and kidnappings grew exponentially. Even high-ranking military officers' names, especially those who support a negotiated peace agreement, appeared on death lists.

In the same election, poor and indigenous Guatemalans were represented by a political party, the New Guatemala Democratic Front (FDNG). This party, the first left-of-center political party since Guatemala's "decade of democracy" in the 1950s, proposed candidates from the popular movement. In spite of violence and harassment directed at NGDF candidates and activists, Guatemalans elected six NGDF candidates to the Congress, including Amílcar Méndez from CERJ (Runujel Junam "Everyone Is Equal" Ethnic Communities), Rosalina Tuyuc from CONAVIGUA (National Coordinating Committee of Guatemalan Widows), and Nineth de Montenegro from GAM (Mutual Support Group).

In the aftermath of the January 1996 election, representatives of the New Guatemala Democratic Front, labor and human rights activists, religious workers, and journalists continued to be the targets of harassment and violence. In January, two

NGDF activists, Miguel Mejía of CERJ and his wife Lucía Tiu Tum of CONAVIGUA, were brutally assassinated. Also in January, Congressman Méndez' nephew was murdered. On April 11, 1996, masked men entered the home of Méndez and sexually abused his adopted daughter. He and other members of NGDF have received death threats by mail and telephone.

Since 1987 the Guatemalan government and the URNG have been involved in negotiations to end the thirty-six-year-old civil war. Between January 1992 and May 1996 five accords were signed: the Marco Accord providing for the peace process and the expansion of civil society, the Global Human Rights Accord, establishing the U.N. Mission to Guatemala, the Accord on the Clarification Commission forming the Truth Commission to investigate human rights violations following the signing of all accords, the Accord on the Identity and Rights of Indigenous People, addressing the issues of indigenous persons in Guatemalan society, and the Accord on Socio-Economic and Agrarian Issues, addressing social development, education, health, rights of women and workers, and land ownership. The last accord will address the role of the army in a democratic society and the reintegration of the URNG into Guatemalan political life and civil society.

Human Rights Policy

Human rights groups and church groups concerned with human rights struggle to change human rights policy. There are two levels of human rights. One level refers to negative rights, such as the right not to be killed. The other level refers to positive rights for food, health care, education, human dignity. Also there are two levels of human rights policy: normative policy, or what the government proclaims, and *de facto* policy, or the enacted policy. Human rights groups in Guatemala are concerned with negative and positive rights, normative and *de facto* policy. Members of human rights groups insist there are ample guarantees for human rights within the 1985 constitution and through international agreements like the Universal Declaration of Human Rights signed by the Guatemalan government. The problem remains of how to enact the normative policy and improve the *de facto* policy.

The 1985 Constitution contains guarantees of human rights and civil rights. Article two promises life, liberty, justice, security, and peace. Article thirty-four prohibits slavery and insists that no one can be forced to serve in civil defense groups. Within the Constitution are guarantees of freedom of association and freedom of assembly. In spite of a history of injustice to indigenous peoples, even ethnic groups are protected in the Constitution. The Constitution is so progressive that semiliterate peasants, members of the human rights group CERJ, use it to protect peasants' human rights.

However, the 1985 Constitution also protects powers of the military state. In addition to guarantees of human and civil rights, the Constitution sanctions the institutions of the counterinsurgency state implemented in the early 1980s. These include civilian self-defense patrols, model villages concentrated in "development poles," and Inter-Institutional Coordinating Councils —a military structure that administers development projects at every level of government.

Besides guarantees in the Constitution of 1985, the government of Guatemala has signed and ratified other international human rights instruments. Through the United Nations, Guatemala has signed three general pacts: the Universal Declaration of Human Rights in 1948; the 1966 International Pact of Economic, Social, and Cultural Rights; and the International Pact of Civil and Political Rights. Genocide is prohibited in the 1948 Convention for the Prevention and Punishment for the Crime of Genocide. Children's rights have been protected through the United Nations Convention for the Rights of Children. In international pacts and conventions the Guatemalan government officially has opposed discrimination, slavery, torture, and the mistreatment of refugees and workers. Several conventions address the rights of women. These include the 1952 Convention of the Political Rights of Women, the 1957 Convention over the Nationality of the Married Woman, and the 1979 Convention on the Elimination of all Forms of Discrimination against Women.

Human Rights Violations

Human rights violations occur often in Guatemala. In fact, Guatemala has the worst record of human rights abuse in the Western Hemisphere. The gathering of data on violations of human rights is complicated by the danger to human rights monitors. In 1990 and 1991 the United Nations reported more human rights monitors killed in Guatemala than any other country in the world.

Two types of violence exist in the Guatemalan society. First, most Guatemalans experience generalized violence as daily terror. Generalized violence includes attacks on churches during mass, burning of villages, harassment during demonstrations —any situation where random acts of violence occur. Second, systematic violence occurs when security forces gather specific names, addresses, and other information on victims. Frequently in Guatemala these have been religious workers, human rights workers, judges, journalists, members of unions, and students. The army or death squads methodically track down the victims and intimidate, torture, or kill them.

Women are not exempted from violence. Latin American human rights activist Dr. Orlando García writes,

> Latin American men have traditionally been the victims of war; now it is women who, because of their political activism or because of their sexual vulnerability, are increasingly the targets of sadistic military and police officials. These are not crimes of passion, but the crimes of politics gone mad. And women are the easiest targets—our mothers, our wives, our sisters.[44]

Women who are jailed often suffer gender-related violence, which may take the form of rape, strip searches, verbal harassment, or other types of physical and psychological abuse.

Female members of the Mutual Support Group, GAM, and the National Coordinating Committee of Guatemalan Widows, CONAVIGUA, as well as other women working for social change in Guatemala, report constant harassment by members of the military, police, and intelligence personnel. In their efforts to document disappearances women frequently visit army bases and police stations. On their visits women are harassed verbally and sexually. Their experiences of violence have opened their eyes to the violence suffered by women in daily life. In spite of rape, torture, and threats, women have continued to be an active force for human rights.

Gender-related violence happens in the home and in work situations. Women endure abysmal working conditions in factories. Not only are many jobs not open to females and salaries less than their male co-workers are offered if they do find employment, but often women are subjected to sexual advances from supervisors. In the home as well, women are victims of domestic violence. Out of every ten women murdered in Guatemala, four are killed by their husbands.[45]

After the election of a civilian president in 1986, again in 1990 and 1996, many people hoped for an end to the violence. Not only does the violence continue, but the main perpetrator of the violence is still the military. Even the U.S. State Department Human Rights Report on Guatemala concludes, "Reliable evidence indicates that security forces and civil patrols committed, with almost total impunity, the majority of human rights abuses during 1990."[46] In spite of clear evidence of the army's involvement from the State Department, Amnesty International, Americas Watch, and other monitors of human rights, still no high-ranking military officer has been prosecuted for a crime. From 1988 through 1992 violence by military death squads increased dramatically. *The Defense Monitor* reports that disappearances and political killings occurred at a rate of two per day in 1990 and three per day during the first eight months of 1991.[47]

The Working Group on Forced and Involuntary Detentions of the United Nations Commission on Human Rights ranked Guatemala third in the world for detentions and "disappearances" in 1992. The Guatemala Human Rights Commission documented 1,389 human rights abuses during 1992. The Commission discovered 465 murders, 27 illegal detentions, 191 death threats, 102 cases of torture, 356 attempted murders, and 83 bombings of civilian areas.

In addition to the human rights violations linked to government security forces, repression takes other forms in Guatemala. In most cases Guatemalan workers are denied the right to free political, popular, and union organization. The Pro Justice and Peace Committee of Guatemala believes that the right of free organization is not possible in Guatemala. Leaders of student associations, labor organizations, and professional organizations are often threatened, kidnapped, and assassinated. Although some unions exist, the unions function in the midst of a violent and repressive society.

The great majority of workers in Guatemala do not belong to unions. The government refuses to defend the rights of the workers. Both the government and the private sector have used repressive means to stop unions. Workers who try to organize are threatened, intimidated, or fired. Members of government security forces frequently crush demonstrations by shooting into the crowd or forcibly stopping the demonstration.[48] Only within the past few years have two factories in the massive clothing industry been allowed to form unions.

Human rights violations in Guatemala also include violations of economic and social rights. In February 1988 Archbishop Prospero Penados del Barrio declared,

> The economic and social situation afflicting the country is desperate. There is a clear outcry against burdensome taxes. . . . We know there is terrible insecurity and that economic and social deterioration have reached record levels.[49]

A majority of Guatemalans are denied the right to participate fully in their society. Many Guatemalans are denied the right to food, clothing, and health care because of the pervasive poverty and the great inequality between the rich and poor.

Amnesty Laws

In 1986 the Rios Montt government granted amnesty to all persons implicated in political crimes and related common crimes committed from March 1982 to January 1986. Before the inauguration of civilian president Cerezo, the military extended the amnesty for all prior human rights abuses. President Cerezo interpreted the laws as a mandate for prohibiting investigation of past human rights abuses. Amnesty International fears that the amnesty laws lead the police and military to believe they can act extrajudicially without punishment. As many as 150,000 people have been politically assassinated since 1954. Military personnel have been prosecuted in only one case and many people doubt that the officers will serve their entire sentences.

Forced Military Recruitment and Civil Patrols

Although military service is required in Guatemala, the law is not applied except to poor young males. Guatemala has no draft or formal procedure to encourage military service. Instead the army enters a place where large crowds gather—soccer games, church services, the weekly market, festivals, bus terminals—and forcibly gathers young men, taking them to a military base far from their village for training.

Beginning in 1982 the military initiated mandatory paramilitary civilian self-defense patrols, *patrullas de auto-defensa civil* or PACs, ostensibly designed to eliminate the guerrilla movement and to arm civilians against subversive incursions. Actually civil patrols serve as a method of social control over villages, another way of repressing peasants. Members of the civil patrol range between the ages of fifteen and sixty, although boys as young as ten have been seen in some civil patrols. Men of villages and hamlets are required to serve, without pay, to defend their towns. In spite of the 1985 Constitution affirming only voluntary civil defense service, more than one million men, one-fourth of Guatemala's adult population, have been forced to participate in civil patrols. Even President Cerezo admitted that less than one-third of the civil patrollers serve voluntarily.[50]

The army forces men in civil patrols to hunt for guerrillas and to intimidate anyone with sympathy for guerrillas, to guard entrances to their village, to kill fellow villagers suspected of subversive activities, to participate in massacres, stoning civilians, and using machetes on neighbors and friends. Civil patrols act as the army's eyes and ears in a village, making reports to local army representatives when a villager is suspected of subversive activities. As recently as 1989 civil patrols assisted the army in the forced relocation of a village near Nebaj. Two hundred civil patrollers and fifty soldiers burned down the buildings in town and marched the villagers to Nebaj.

Mayan Indians and the Struggle for Survival

The 22 groups of Mayan Indians do not speak with one voice; they do not act together politically or socially. But they do share a common heritage, a heritage of violence and oppression, a heritage of poverty and discrimination. They are not the only victims of discrimination in Guatemala, but they represent a significant majority of the more than 80 percent of Guatemalans who are poor.

As a moderate-centrist Christian Democrat, Vinicio Cerezo voiced his concern about Guatemala's indigenous ethnic groups. In his inaugural address on January 14, 1986, he affirmed the rights of all citizens, including the Indians, to participate equally in Guatemala's democracy and to be guaranteed human rights. Unfortunately, Cerezo's words did not correspond to his actions. His administration made modest reforms—changing rural development programs from military to civilian control and dismantling surveillance operations by interinstitutional coordinators. Nevertheless, while Cerezo condemned political violence against indigenous groups in public statements, massacres in Indian villages were not investigated because of amnesty laws, model villages and civil patrols remained in place, and the military continued rural counterinsurgency programs.

Throughout the years from 1524 to the present time, indigenous peoples have maintained their identity and worldview. In spite of the brutality of conquest, disease, and forced labor, Indian villages defended rights and customs, resisted Spanish religious reform, and practiced their religion. Often when communal lands were expropriated, using legal advisors Indians argued land cases before the colonial courts. Historian Jim Handy writes that throughout the 450 years of Guatemalan history,

> with amazing consistency, protest has always first taken nonviolent, legal form. Only with repeated demonstration of the inability or unwillingness of government to respond effectively to these protests have peasants turned violent.[51]

Granted, the indigenous peoples of Guatemala have not been passive—they have been angry and active. In spite of myths perpetrated about the docile Indians grateful to serve their Spanish conquerors, indigenous peoples have protested their exploitation and domination. From 1524 until 1944 more than thirty-six Indian rebellions occurred—typically only after nonviolent action and legal alternatives failed.[52]

Economic and Social Situation

Gernot Kohler writes of "global apartheid," an international system of social, economic, and political control which works to separate the largest portion of the population of the world— those who are poor, people of color, and women, especially within the developing world—from the smallest portion of the population who are wealthy.[53]

Most Guatemalans, men and women, indigenous and poor, are victims of apartheid as Kohler defines it. Although they did not use the word apartheid, both the Guatemalan Bishops Conference and the Inter-American Commission on Human Rights affirmed that severe *de facto* racial and cultural discrimination exists in Guatemala.[54] Two percent of the population controls 70 percent of the wealth. Indigenous people, from 50 to 60 percent of the population, have been the target of the government's counterinsurgency plan. By the government's own admission at least 440 indigenous villages were destroyed by the military in the early 1980s. Survivors who are not internal or external refugees have been relocated in model villages which resemble concentration camps.

Poverty

More than nine million people live in Guatemala. According to the United Nations Human Development Index, Guatemala has the lowest development index in Central America.[55] Over 86 percent of Guatemalans live in poverty.[56] Out of the 61 percent of Guatemalans who live in rural areas, 75 percent have no access to health care and 82 percent have no access to clean water.

About 50 percent of the population of Guatemala is indigenous. Twenty-three groups of Mayan Indians live in Guatemala with different languages, cultures, and customs. A majority of indigenous peoples are concentrated in the highland region, although twenty years of armed conflict and government relocation progams have forced many indigenous people to move to Guatemala City or other regions of the country. Social indicators demonstrate the lack of services for the indigenous population. The illiteracy rate for indigenous people is 77 percent; the life expectancy is 44 years.

In 1980 more than 400,000 families lacked sufficient land for subsistence. An 1982 Agency for International Development study reports that land distribution in Guatemala is the most unequal in Latin America.[57] Between 1964 and 1979 land distribution deteriorated in 16 of 22 departments. Two percent of the landowners own 65 percent of farmland. In Guatemala City at least 325,000 live in marginalized areas, some on the sides of mountains, others in cardboard or wooden shacks, some in garbage dumps.

In spite of pockets of wealth Guatemala appears almost paralyzed by pervasive poverty. Since 1980 real wages and purchasing power have steadily declined, and prices have increased exponentially.[58] Unemployment is 12 percent and underemployment is 35 percent of the economically active population. Since 1980 open unemployment has increased more than 600 percent. Real wages and purchasing power declined 46 percent from 1983 through 1986, with more than one-third of the decline occurring during the first year of Cerezo's presidency.

Cerezo's economic plan focused on holding down wages and stabilizing the currency. No efforts were made to reduce unemployment or control price increases. Low prices on the international market for cotton, coffee, and sugar caused more unemployment. Often landowners switched to nontraditional export crops that are less labor intensive or are harvested mechanically, resulting in the loss of jobs for seasonal laborers.

The Feminization of Poverty

The years of violence and repression have resulted in increased poverty among women. Economic and social indicators are much worse for women than men in Guatemala. Women's groups estimate that over half the labor force is female, yet most women are employed in the informal sector as domestic help, artisans, farm workers, and factory workers. Females represent only 19 percent of the formal labor force. Because of the war waged throughout Guatemala in the 1970s and 1980s, 38 percent of urban women are widows and 56 percent of rural women are widows.[59]

These women and other women whose husbands have been "disappeared" become wage earners. Some women work in the informal sector in their village; others move to Guatemala City or other urban areas to find employment. An estimated one-half of the heads of household in El Mesquitel slum in Guatemala City are women.[60] The health and education indicators also reveal the difficulty of life for Guatemalan women. Among all Guatemalan women the illiteracy rate is 55 percent; among rural women it increases to 85 percent. The maternal morbidity rate is the highest in Latin America, as is the life expectancy for women.

Latin American political culture reinforces the traditional roles of wife and mother for women. In Guatemala, as in other countries in Latin America, machismo results in special privileges for males in society. Women are responsible for socialization of children; they are the guardian of moral values within the context of the home. Internalizing their prescribed social role, they are often passive and subservient, not because they are less capable or intelligent but because they lack experience outside the home. A majority of women in Guatemala have little or no formal education. Many indigenous women do not speak Spanish, only their indigenous language.

During the 1980s third world debt, global inflation, and a national economy sympathetic to foreign business greatly increased the problems of the poor and pushed the small middle class closer to poverty. Debt repayment led to structural adjustment policies that cut social services and capped wage and price indexes—all policies that drastically affect the poor. Latin American scholars identify women as particularly vulnerable to the effect of increased inflation and third world debt.

Governments believe that women will survive this "superexploitation" without special attention.[61] Governments save money on programs and services that would benefit women and families on grounds that women will cope, regardless of circumstances. UNICEF calls this process "the invisible adjustment." UNICEF says that the "present crisis of social disinvestment is being financed principally from the resources of a social fund provided by the superhuman effort by poor women to support themselves and their children."[62]

Maquiladoras

Although forced labor was abolished in 1944, poor economic conditions experienced by the majority of Guatemalans have led to a type of labor forced by economic desperation, *maquila* factories.[63] The maquila industry has experienced exponential growth because of the abundant source of cheap labor, expanding in the past five years from five factories to over 250 factories that employ 45,000 workers, 80 percent of whom are women. Workers are paid substandard wages averaging $1 to $2 per day in a society where from $5 to $6 is required for basic needs. Working conditions are abysmal.

The maquilas are warehouselike buildings with poor lighting and little ventilation. Workers rarely receive health benefits and are often fired if they miss work due to illness. Kurt Petersen, a researcher for Yale University's Center for International Rights, discovered that most seamstresses work at least fifty hours and often sixty or seventy hours each week.[64] It is not uncommon for workers to be locked in a building overnight or throughout a weekend.

Women are victimized by the maquila system. Not only are they the recipients of inadequate salaries and poor working conditions at the factories, they are often the targets of physical and sexual abuse. Desperate for jobs to feed their families, they often tolerate abuse. In many factories managers coerce women to give sexual favors in offices and storage rooms. In a Korean-owned factory every fifteen days women are lined up and beaten in the stomach to make sure they are not pregnant. Pregnant women are fired.

An additional injustice has been the refusal of companies and the government to allow workers in the maquila industry to unionize. Phillips-Van Heusen, a United States clothing company, recently allowed workers to form a union, after an initial protest of the company's salaries and working conditions by six employees and a two-year boycott sponsored by the U.S./ Guatemala Labor Education Project. The six employees who first complained to Guatemala's Labor Inspector were fired from the company two days after making their complaints. The mistreatment of the six employees spurred one hundred workers to form a union.

Unions in Guatemala must be officially recognized by the government. Both the Guatemalan government and Phillips-Van Heusen initially opposed the organization of workers and refused to recognize the union. In addition to firing six employees, the management of the two Phillips-Van Heusen factories offered payments to workers to resign from the union, shifted union supporters to more difficult positions, warned workers that they would lose jobs, and threatened to close the factories.[65]

Workers persisted in the struggle in spite of opposition, strengthened by the pressure of international labor and human rights solidarity groups. After almost two years of pressure, in the fall of 1992 the Phillips-Van Heusen management and the government of Guatemala officially recognized the union. The union is the first in Guatemala's maquila sector.

Refugee Resettlement

During the early 1980s an estimated one million people fled their villages, some because of the government's scorched earth policy, some because of attacks and intimidation by government security forces, some because of poverty. An Indian woman who is a religious educator writes,

> This week in the villages where I work, the army, mixed in with civil patrols, massacred an entire village which is called Agua Fría, near Los Pajales on the limit of Baja Verapaz and Uspantán. They didn't leave one survivor. They were all covered with gasoline and burned alive, children, women, and men.[66]

In response to the massacres of friends and relatives many peasants became internal refugees, escaping to the mountains, to relatives in other towns, or to the growing slums of Guatemala City. Many peasants in the highlands escaped to the mountains, often suffering cold, hunger, malnutrition, and illness. In addition to the lack of medical attention, harsh weather and no sources for food, the mountain settlements were frequently ambushed or bombed by the army. Those who escaped to the mountains were considered guerrilla accomplices by the army.

More than 70,000 peasants were forced into the 24 model villages, referred to by the U.S. State Department as "rural settlements" or "halfway houses." The Guatemalan government advertised the villages as "modern communities for displaced peasants." In fact, the model villages, located in areas of conflict, are forced resettlement camps under military control. In the model villages the government provides housing, food, and work. The Inter-American Commission reported that the model village program "was separating the Indians from their native lands and making them more dependent on the government for food and work."[67] Peruvian Nobel laureate Adolfo Perez Esquivel calls the model villages "concentration camps."[68]

Many refugees fled to Mexico or the United States. Refugees to the United States rarely are granted political asylum. Since 1980 approximately 99 percent of applications for political asylum from Guatemalan refugees have been denied. Since the United States supports the government of Guatemala, approval of applications for political asylum is an admission that the United States supports a government denying civil or human rights to its citizens.

At least 100,000 Guatemalans crossed the border into southern Mexico. For ten years 46,000 Guatemalans have lived in exile in United Nations refugee camps in Chiapas, Mexico. In 1987 the refugees formed the Permanent Commission of Representatives of the Guatemalan Refugees in Mexico to negotiate repatriation with the Guatemalan government. After five years of negotiations and peace talks, on October 8, 1992, the government signed an accord to allow the refugees to return home in a collective and organized fashion, to own land in their home regions, and to live without discrimination or persecution.

Less than one month after the accord, the army began a campaign against communities in the Ixcan and Quiché region designated for refugee return. A military patrol of 450 men attacked the communities of Cuarto Pueblo and Los Angeles, killing sixty peasants, burning houses, robbing valuable objects, and killing domestic animals. During the attack the army slaughtered over 200 domestic animals; destroyed 130 hundred-pound bags of rice, corn, and beans; and burned chapels, schools, clinics, community centers, and houses.

After the attacks an army spokesperson, Captain Julio Alberto Yon Rivera, announced that the army dismantled five guerrilla camps where army personnel discovered marijuana. In response, representatives from the destroyed communities reiterated that the army destroyed civilian communities and burned crops—not guerrilla camps with marijuana.

In spite of violence in the highlands, on January 20, 1993, the first refugees crossed from Mexico into Guatemala. After a celebratory mass in Guatemala City, the refugees left for resettlement areas in the highlands departments of Huehuetenango and El Quiché. Although the refugees have reentered Guatemala with hopes for the future, they remember the terror that drove them from home. They will be living in areas targeted as areas of conflict by the army because of small guerrilla forces in the region.

Since the 1980s the government has claimed that the refugees are either guerrillas or are sympathetic to the guerrillas. In 1987 the Minister of Defense, Alejandro Gramajo, said, "Guerrillas have infiltrated the refugees' ranks, preparing them with Marxist doctrines."[69] The refugees face resentment not only from the military, but also from people who remained in their native villages and suffered repression. In spite of problems with the military, lack of land, and resentment from other peasants, the repatriation process continues and offers a glimmer of hope to displaced Guatemalans.

Conclusion

The examination of Guatemalan political, social, and economic reality reveals 500 years of repression, first by Spanish invaders, then by the military and economic ruling coalition. The history of Guatemala reads like a litany of sorrows. Historian Jim Handy says the current situation in Guatemala is

> the result of an economic and social system that has marginalized peasants, deprived them of their land, forced from them their labor with little or no compensation, and refused them protection from economic and physical attack.[70]

The peasant population—indigenous people and poor ladinos—struggled against tyrants, unjust legislation, and a socioeconomic order that protects those in power with money and guns.

Many of us believe that with increased education and life experience human beings progress toward justice and peace. The Berlin Wall comes down, military force is used for humanitarian ends in Somalia, domestic programs like Head Start and Job Corps are funded by Congress. Guatemala is a strong and painful reminder that frequently life, unlike fairy tales, does not have happy endings, that history is not always about progress, that the sin in structures and systems, in persons and groups, is all-pervasive and all-encompassing, seemingly irredeemable. Given the situation in Guatemala, where is the hope? Where is the justice?

Anthropologist Margaret Mead once said, "It has been women's task throughout history to go on believing in life when there was almost no hope." The experience of women in human rights groups and church groups in Guatemala bears witness to the truth of Mead's quote. Especially in the past ten years women have determined to create more peace and justice by eliminating hopelessness. They have enlarged the political opening and participated fully in the popular movement. To their narratives, the stories of women who are the voices for the voiceless, we now turn.

3

Voices of the Voiceless: The Response of Women in Guatemalan Human Rights Groups

THE sound of women's voices rise from a dusty Mexican hillside close to the Guatemalan border. A community of 200 Jacalteco people from a small village in Guatemala live in this village, a United Nations refugee camp. The seemingly sleepy community, one hour by burro from the nearest road or water source, is the scene of activity today. Women from several neighboring refugee camps have gathered to discuss their activities for the coming month and to reflect on the past year.

They recall that shortly after they and their families fled to Mexico from war-torn Guatemala, they formed a women's group named after an elderly activist named Mama Maquín. Adelina Cal Maquin had led a peaceful demonstration to reclaim land in her village, Panzós, Guatemala, where she and 100 fellow Kekchí Indians were massacred. In choosing Mama Maquín's name for the group, the women were facing their fears and asserting their determination.

The women of Mama Maquín want to educate and empower all Guatemalan women in refugee camps in preparation for the day they return to Guatemala. In Guatemala, these women were afraid to organize because they feared reprisals from the military, but in refugee camps they are free to organize. They organize to educate each other about their rights as women and to work for better education and health care. They organize to preserve their culture and history. The women in Mama Maquín tell stories of life in Guatemala in the past; they encourage the community to plan for the day when they will return home. The women support youth when they decide never to carry a gun or torture another human being.

At La Sombra Refugee Camp, the group decided that the community needed a corn grinder and community stoves. In spite of a membership almost totally illiterate, the group put together a proposal and negotiated with the United Nations High Commissioner on Refugees. The UNHCR delivered two stoves and a corn grinder to the community and a cylinder of gas to every family. The women also stress self-improvement, encouraging literacy classes, building the confidence of women as they learn about leadership through experience. At the end of their meetings, they sing a song that summarizes their struggle.

> We are women struggling for justice and equality;
> We women of Mama Maquín won't take abuse.
> We'll struggle until the new dawn
> For the dignity and equality of women.
> When women struggle,
> The world begins to change.

For the first time in the history of Guatemala, women have been prominent in human rights organizations. Previously they have been separated from men and the dominant culture by dress, language, education, and social and economic patterns.[1] The violence of the early 1980s, after more than thirty years of military rule, served as a catalyst for women's involvement in collective action, both in women's groups and in groups with male and female leadership. In the popular movement women have provided a strong voice for social change, for peace and development.

The battle has not been won. Women are still the objects of exploitation and discrimination, because of their ethnic group, their gender, and their class struggle. In spite of almost overwhelming cultural, psychological, economic, and political oppression, however, women have participated in the popular movement. Their actions have empowered women and men throughout Guatemala to become involved in the struggle for justice.

This chapter chronicles three of the strong voices for peace and justice in Guatemala—one woman, Rigoberta Menchú and the organization that she works with, and two women's groups, GAM and CONAVIGUA. Like Mama Maquín in the refugee camps in southern Mexico, women in Guatemala have modeled new ways of being human as they continue traditional roles and discover new dimensions of their identity as Guatemalan women.

Rigoberta Menchú

Rigoberta Menchú, a Quiché Mayan Indian in her thirties as of this writing, grew up in an environment of poverty and oppression in Guatemala. In *I, Rigoberta* she describes her life and the life of her people as they endured terrorism and repression by the military. She also tells of her growing involvement in the movement for nonviolent social change. Nominated by Nobel Peace Prize recipients Desmond Tutu and Adolfo Perez Esquivel, Menchú received the 1992 Nobel Peace prize for promoting the human rights of Guatemalan indigenous peoples and indigenous peoples throughout the world.

Menchú was born in the village of Chimel, in the Quiché region of Guatemala, the region hardest hit by the military repression of the 1970s and 1980s. She was the sixth of nine children. Her family owned a small patch of land in their village in the mountains, but because the land did not produce enough food, they migrated to fincas on the southern coast for eight months each year. On the fincas, adults and children picked coffee beans, weeded coffee plants, and picked cotton. Her two eldest brothers died while the family worked on the large plantations, one from malnutrition, the other from pesticide poisoning.

When Menchú was ten years old, a wealthy landowner seized their land and their neighbors' lands. Representatives of the landowner threw the families out of their homes, destroyed their possessions, and took possession of the land. Vicente Menchú, Rigoberta's father, asked unions in FASGUA, the Guatemalan Federation of Independent Unions, to help the villagers in the struggle for their land. After Menchú's conversations with FASGUA, he began organizing villagers to participate in protests through farmworkers' unions.

Government officials imprisoned Vicente Menchú for protesting against landowners. Although his family complained to the government, they realized the futility of their complaints. The government authorities served the same interests as the wealthy landowners. After eighteen months in prison, Menchú was released and traveled home to El Quiché. Within weeks he resumed his work with unions, traveling from town to town, gathering support from farmworkers for the labor organizations. On several occasions, he was beaten and tortured. In spite of repeated death threats, Menchú continued his work with unions, moving from town to town at night for safety.

The Menchú family understood that the root of peasants' problems was ownership of the land. Menchú said, "The rich have become rich because they took what our ancestors had away from them, and now they grow fat on the sweat of our labor."[2] Poor Guatemalans are exploited through unjust labor practices, hunger, poverty, and malnutrition. In response to the injustice, several members of the Menchú family became involved in community organizing. Vicente Menchú helped found Comité Unidad Campesina (CUC) in 1977 and worked tirelessly on peasant issues until his death. Rigoberta's mother worked with CUC and talked with women about the struggle for social change. Rigoberta's younger brother served as the secretary of his community, helping to organize villagers.

Rigoberta learned about organizing through her work as a catechist for children, which she began when she was ten years old. Six years later, she joined a clandestine group of peasants in Huehuetenango who traveled from finca to finca educating and organizing farmworkers. In 1979 Menchú joined CUC, first working on any job available, later as an organizer and leader.

Because of their involvement in the struggle for social change, the Menchú family was labeled subversive and communist by the government and landowners. In September 1979 the military kidnapped Rigoberta's sixteen-year-old brother, Petrocinio. In weeks army officials in Chajul sent word announcing punishment for imprisoned guerrillas and subversives. Several family members traveled to the army base and found their son and brother. He was barely recognizable because of days of torture. They watched as army officers burned the boy and his companions to death.

The burning of the young men at Chajul was one of many incidents of repression in the El Quiché region. It inflamed the CUC. They organized a march of students, workers, orphaned children, Christians, and union members in Guatemala City on January 31, 1980. Peasants took over radio stations to broadcast their concerns. They first occupied the Swiss Embassy, then the Spanish Embassy, in order to seek international exposure. In spite of the Spanish ambassador's pleas for no military action, soldiers set fire to the Spanish Embassy building, killing Vicente Menchú and 37 other Quiché Indians.

While struggling with grief for Vicente and Petrocinio, Rigoberta and her mother continued their work in the villages of the highlands with all the more determination. Her mother traveled throughout neighboring villages, voicing her concerns about hunger and poverty. She shared her experiences of loss with other mothers and continually motivated women to action. Her actions did not escape the attention of the military. In April 1980 Menchú's mother was kidnapped, raped, and tortured until she died.

Within months of her mother's death, death threats prompted Rigoberta to flee from Guatemala. Since her exile in 1981, Menchú has lived in Mexico. She has continued to be a leader and spokesperson for CUC. In 1982 Menchú and other exiled Guatemalans founded the Unified Representation of the Guatemalan Opposition (RUOG) to keep the interests of the Guatemalan people before the international community. Through CUC and RUOG, Menchú has lobbied the United Nations for UN-sponsored peace talks and condemnation of Guatemala's human rights violations.

Throughout the past ten years Menchú voiced concerns about human rights abuse in Guatemala and about the oppression of indigenous peoples throughout the world. In addition to serving as an official observer of the UN General Assembly and the UN Commission on Human Rights, in 1986 Menchú joined the Board of the International Indian Treaty Council, a UN nongovernmental organization. As a spokesperson for minorities and women, she served on the UN Subcommission on the Prevention of Discrimination of Minorities and helped form the United Nations Working Group on Indigenous People.

Menchú has been an advocate for the rights of indigenous peoples. Adolfo Perez Esquivel said that she "is the voice for all indigenous, which has been silenced for five centuries."[3] At the Third Continental Encounter of 500 Years of Indigenous, Black, and Grassroots Resistance in Managua, Nicaragua, in October 1992, she challenged the crowd "to make the Americas again blossom with life, flower with respect, and flourish with peace."[4]

In addition to receiving the 1992 Nobel Peace Prize, Menchú has received other international recognition for her work in human rights. Both she and Nelson Mandela were named honorary members of the Committee for Non-Governmental Organizations of Belgium. In 1990 the Latin American Association for Human Rights in Uruguay gave her the Monsignor Proaño Human Rights Award. UNESCO selected her as the recipient of the 1990 Educational Peace Award.

Committee for Peasant Unity

CUC formed in 1977, with Vicente Menchú as one of its founders. It began not as a formal centralized organization but as small grassroots groups of peasants in the highlands and in fincas along the southern coast dedicated to defending peasants' rights. Government authorities refused to recognize CUC as a legal union. As CUC grew in number and strength, the army began repression of leadership, especially in El Quiché. Because of the kidnappings and deaths of leaders, CUC operated clandestinely until May 1978.

On May 29, 1978, the army opened fire on an unarmed crowd of 700 Kekchí Indians in Panzós, wounding 300 and killing over 100. The crowd had gathered in a peaceful demonstration to protest the expropriation of their land by army generals and developers.[5] The bodies of the 100 Indians were dumped into two mass graves dug by bulldozers the day before the massacre. In response to the massacre, CUC announced its existence publicly with a condemnation of government action at Panzós and organized a demonstration in Guatemala City with more than 80,000 people protesting the massacre—the largest demonstration in over 25 years. One year after the Panzós massacre, an anniversary demonstration drew 100,000 supporters.

With this act CUC was officially recognized, under the name of Comité Unidad Campesina, as an organization defending all peasants rights, both Indians and ladinos. CUC works on such issues as conscription into the army, jobs and wages on plantations and sugar mills, land struggles, and government repression. The 1980 Declaration of Iximché expressed CUC's goals.

For a society based on equality and respect; so that our Indian peoples can develop our culture, fractured by the criminal invaders; for a just economy in which no one exploits others; so that the land may be communally held, as it was in the time of our ancestors; for a people without discrimination; in order to end all repression, torture, kidnapping, assassination, and massacres . . . so that we gain equal rights as workers; so that we don't continue to be used as objects of tourism; for a just distribution and use of our wealth, as in the times when the life and culture of our ancestors flourished.[6]

CUC grew dramatically following the massacre at Panzós and the burning of the Spanish Embassy. Most of CUC membership came from the highlands, the area most impoverished and with the highest percentage of indigenous peoples. But in spite of a membership that was primarily indigenous, CUC did not project an antiladino perspective. Certainly their objectives focused on oppression of indigenous peoples and respect for indigenous culture but CUC also recognized the domination of poor ladinos by the minority elite. CUC was the first organization to bring together indigenous and migrant farmers with poor ladino farmworkers. Contacts with ladinos in CUC and other social change groups helped Menchú and other indigenous peasants to understand that poverty unites the Indian and the ladino.

In February 1980 CUC organized a strike of cotton and sugar workers on the southern coast, beginning on one plantation with 750 workers. During the strike, Rigoberta Menchú and other members of CUC posted signs and painted banners criticizing the landowners. They distributed leaflets inviting people to join CUC. Within days 70,000 to 80,000 workers joined the strike. This paralyzed agricultural operations for fifteen days and compelled the government to meet CUC's demands to increase the minimum wage.

Because of government repression, CUC could not operate openly nor could they communicate through government-controlled media. To spread their message, members of CUC first spray-painted slogans on cattle. When they discovered that

landowners slaughtered the cattle with their slogans, they painted their slogans on stray dogs. They called boycotts and regularly informed the news media of their actions. On the first of May,
Labor Day, peasants walked or rode buses to Guatemala City to
participate in CUC's strikes and demonstrations where CUC
members set up barricades, held lightning meetings, and threw
propaganda bombs.

In January 1981 CUC joined a coalition of six human rights
groups to form the 31 January Popular Front, commemorating
the massacre at the Spanish Embassy. They realized that one
scandal of the government counterinsurgency program is the
conspiracy of silence. To break the silence Rigoberta Menchú
and other coalition representatives traveled throughout the
world telling the story of Guatemala to church and human rights
groups. In January 1989 CUC again led a massive strike on the
southern coast at the height of sugarcane season, with 50,000 to
70,000 seasonal workers and permanent workers demanding
salary increases to keep up with the 400 percent increase in the
cost of living in the past ten years. The strike ended after a week,
due to heavy militarization of the sugar factories and the presence of soldiers surrounding the strike area.

Government Repression

Both CUC and Menchú have been the target of government
repression. In May 1988 Menchú and other members of RUOG
returned to Guatemala to discuss ways to resolve the conflict.
During the visit she was arrested by the Guatemalan military
and held until international solidarity groups demanded her release. During a 1989 visit, death threats prompted her to leave
Guatemala.

As soon as Menchú's candidacy for the Nobel Peace Prize
was made public, Guatemalan president Jorge Serrano Elias
nominated Elisa Molina de Stahl, a wealthy ladina woman who
works with blind and deaf people. After Menchú won the Nobel
Peace Prize, Foreign Minister Gonzalo Menendez Park insisted

she was linked to "groups that have damaged Guatemala's image outside the country."[7] He added that the award was no blow to Guatemala's human rights image because no unpunished abuses occur in Guatemala. Chief military spokesperson Julio Yon Rivera declared, "She has only defamed the fatherland. To give her the prize would be a political victory for the guerrillas."[8]

When Menchú returned to Guatemala following the announcement of the award, two teenage women who helped prepare meals for Menchú were abducted, beaten, and stripped. They were accused of being guerrillas and threatened with death before their release.

Likewise since CUC emerged as a peasant organization it has been the target of government repression—selective at first, then widespread. During the 1980 Labor Day demonstration, the army killed industrial workers and peasants. Following the 1980 strike, plantation owners fired employees and ignored the new minimum wage. The army harassed and killed both leaders and participants. The repression following the massacres at Panzós and the Spanish Embassy and the 1980 strike prompted many members of CUC to make the transition from CUC to participation in the guerrilla movement.

Grupo de Apoyo Mutuo

During the past decade, women—especially wives and mothers—have been active in the struggle for social and political change. In response to the thirty years of violence, human rights groups have occasionally emerged only to be systematically repressed by the police, army, and paramilitary death squads. An exception is GAM, which has the longest history of survival as a human rights organization in Guatemala.

Twenty-five wives and mothers of the disappeared on June 5, 1984, met at the home of Archbishop Prospero Penados de Barrio to listen to the story of the Co-Madres, a human rights group in El Salvador. At the meeting the women formed the Mutual Support Group for the Reappearance with Life of Our Family Members, commonly referred to by its Spanish acronym, GAM, to find their disappeared family and friends. By November 1984, two hundred and fifty were members of GAM, and six hundred and seventy belonged to GAM in 1985. Americas Watch's 1988 report estimates a membership of 1000. In a recent interview Nineth de Garcia reported that GAM currently has 2,500 members.[9] As the organization grew, the members of GAM expanded the original goal to include demanding the immediate release of all disappeared Guatemalans and bringing an end to extrajudicial assassinations and disappearances.

GAM has consistently championed the cause of human rights in Guatemala. Although GAM has male members, 90 percent of its constituency is female and 80 percent is indigenous. GAM has been called "the moral conscience of Guatemala and the thorn in the flesh of the military and the right-wing government ruling Guatemala."[10]

GAM's president, Nineth de Garcia, is a schoolteacher and former law student whose husband was abducted in 1984. She says that the movement began at the morgues when three wives and two mothers gathered to identify corpses, in hopes of finding their disappeared sons and spouses. The first rule for GAM members is to be united in all their activities, whether they are speaking to the president of Guatemala, making public announcements, or holding a mass. Garcia insists that it is important to use all talents and abilities to publicize what has happened in Guatemala.

Thus far GAM's actions to bring about social change in Guatemala have been nonviolent. Most of GAM's actions are included in Gene Sharp's categories of nonviolent protest and persuasion and nonviolent intervention: public speeches, letters of opposition, public statements, declarations of indictment, and group petitions. They have written or supplied information for newspaper articles and have used banners and posters. They have sponsored vigils, marches, parades, funeral processions, and protest meetings. GAM has implemented sit-ins, nonviolent harassment, nonviolent occupation, and has created an alternative institution to investigate human rights abuses.[11]

Prior to the formation of GAM, families looked for their relatives only through official channels—inquiries to the government and police, visits to army bases, morgues, and hospitals. In the first few months of the group's existence, the members were eager not to blame the government, so they restricted their activities to petitions and newspaper advertisements of children asking, "Daddy, Where Are You?" Their initial activities drew no response from the Guatemalan government nor from the international press.

In October 1984 GAM expanded their strategy to include more socially disruptive practices. GAM members continued to document disappearances of family members and friends. A crowd of 150 GAM members and 800 sympathetic priests, students, and union members joined in the eighteen-mile March for Peace into Guatemala City. They ended the march at the National Palace, where they threw carnations on the palace steps. In late 1984, GAM publicly denounced the army and intelligence units as perpetrators of the violence. An estimated 250 GAM members occupied the National Congress building to protest congressional apathy to human rights abuse.

In 1985 GAM members began a weekly pots-and-pans protest in front of Public Ministry offices. They petitioned Congress for a law giving rights to political prisoners. By this time their protests and marches were growing and drawing international media attention. Following the murder of two GAM leaders, a protest march was transformed into a symbolic funeral dirge for the two leaders. One thousand marchers participated. GAM supporters marched outside the U.S. Embassy, in hopes of meeting with Presidential Envoy Harry Schlandeman, but he refused to meet with them. In August 1985, GAM members submitted 900 habeas corpus petitions to the Supreme Court. Before the December presidential election, 150 members of GAM occupied the Metropolitan Cathedral for five days.

Following the election of President Cerezo, GAM leaders requested a meeting with the president and presented the government with a petition, signed by 15,000 Guatemalans, requesting that Cerezo establish an investigatory commission. GAM members, carrying posters of the disappeared and pictures of soldiers torturing peasants, marched behind the army at the Independence Day parade. They also marched behind soldiers during the Army Day parade.

By 1987 the investigatory commission promised by Cerezo had not materialized. In protest, GAM members again occupied the Guatemalan Congress. Through their investigations GAM members compiled information about their relatives' disappearances. They marched to the Human Rights Attorney's office to present information on the disappearances. Later they published two lists of army, police, and military intelligence personnel who participated in the abductions and killings.

At a press conference, Nineth de Garcia and other GAM leaders charged that President Cerezo, the former UN Ambassador, the former Education Minister, and officials in the U.S. Embassy knew information about disappeared individuals. At other press conferences, Nineth de Garcia presented complaints about the existence of hidden cemeteries, secret prisons at army bases, and crimes that were direct violations of the 1985 Constitution. On June 21, 1988, GAM, with student groups and unions, sponsored the Day Against Forced Disappearances. The group marched to the National Palace and protested all the disappearances, especially the June 21, 1980, abduction of 27 union leaders.

Government Repression

Sharp correctly asserts that a serious challenge to authority brings repression.[12] Since GAM changed its strategy in 1984 from quiet nonconfrontative protest and individual action to collective actions that organized and mobilized relatives and friends of the disappeared, Sharp's prediction has proven correct. The military government of General Mejia repeatedly tried to intimidate and discredit GAM. Members of GAM received threatening phone calls and death threats in the mail. In a Chimaltenango village, the Civil Patrol threatened local members of GAM. The army told peasants coming into Guatemala City from the countryside that GAM was "subversive" and "against the government."[13]

In 1985 General Mejia referred to GAM as a pressure group directed by subversives and making trouble for peaceful Guatemalans. A government spokesperson added that GAM's actions would not be tolerated. Within two weeks two of GAM's leaders, Hector Gomez and Rosario Godoy, were dead. Gomez was abducted on a busy street in the middle of the afternoon; his mutilated body was discovered the next day. Rosario Godoy delivered the eulogy at his funeral. In three days Godoy, her two-year-old son, and 21-year-old brother were found dead in a ditch outside Guatemala City. The government called the deaths an accident. After the killings three GAM leaders and fifteen members of the Gomez family went into exile.

Before Mejia left office he passed an amnesty law that protects members of the military and police from prosecution for human rights abuses. During Cerezo's administration, GAM has not been directly threatened by the government, but Cerezo has called GAM "masochistic," urging them to "forget the past."[14] The Cerezo government has tried to divide GAM by claiming that the ladino leadership of GAM did not reflect indigenous interests. Also the government allocated funds as financial reparation for anyone who lost a family member and would not protest; less than twelve GAM members accepted Cerezo's offer.

CONAVIGUA

In the 1980s throughout Guatemala small groups of women banded together for support in the middle of violence and re-

pression. Women united initially because of their common loss-
es. During the violence of the early 1980s, many women, especially indigenous women, became widows as their husbands
were killed by the military forces of the government of Guatemala. In addition to the deaths of husbands, sons and fathers disappeared or were forced into military service, never to be seen
again. Daughters and mothers were violated by soldiers and
members of the civil patrol. Rosalina Tuyuc describes the terror
of 1980-1983.

> Women watched powerlessly as soldiers entered their villages,
> burned houses and fields, kidnapped husbands and children.
> They watched as soldiers threw babies into fires or boiling water.
> They watched as half-dead husbands were buried alive. In front of
> children members of the military raped mothers and daughters.[15]

Before organizing, women thought that only men could participate in social change movements. They believed women acted only in the home as they cared for the children, cooked, and
cleaned. Few women had the advantage of a public school education and many were fluent only in their indigenous language.
Women felt powerless to act outside the home, in the public
sphere, for change. Women also were paralyzed by fear for
themselves and for their children. Initially the groups of women
shared their experiences of pain and grief. Through the course
of their conversations, pain and suffering served as a catalyst for
action. They decided that organizing against the repressive government and army was not only possible but necessary for social
change.

On September 11 and 12, 1988, the local groups gathered for
a national assembly of widows to discuss the repression in Guatemala as it affected women, especially widows, and the poor. At
the conclusion of the assembly, they formed one national organization, CONAVIGUA, the National Coordinator of Guatemalan Widows. Their introductory statement concludes with these
words:

In our villages only our great sacrifices have kept us alive together with our sons and daughters. Without men at home and without any help from the government, we have to take care of everything —work in the corn field, clean our house, go down to the coast for seasonal work. These and other things we have done in order that we and our children might live. So for this we have organized, to meet our needs, to defend ourselves from the abuses that we suffer, and so that we can forever live in peace.[16]

CONAVIGUA is led by a democratically elected National Council with local and regional groups scattered throughout the country. Today more than 11,000 women participate in CONAVIGUA. Although CONAVIGUA began as a group of widows and other women who had lost family members to repression, the organization has broadened its base to include all women interested in the struggle for human rights. Most women in CONAVIGUA are indigenous, although ladina women also participate. Country and city women, widows, married women, and single women participate.

The women of CONAVIGUA take seriously their objectives. These include: commitment to work for basic human needs (food, medicine, and housing), to struggle against forced service in the military and civil patrols, to protect widows and other women from rape and other abuse, to recover the bodies of relatives and to give them a Christian burial, to respect human rights, to achieve governmental provision of education, and to get women's voices heard in the political, social, and economic life of Guatemala.[17]

From its beginning as a national organization, CONAVIGUA participated in parades and demonstrations. On March 8, 1989, thousands of women celebrated the International Day of Women with parades in Guatemala City and the departments of Chimaltenango, Sololá, El Quiché, Quetzaltenango, and Totonicapan. On Father's Day, June 17, 1989, the children of CONAVIGUA women marched to the National Palace with banners asking, "What happened to my father? Where is my father buried? Why have you killed my father?"

Women of CONAVIGUA recognize that injustice occurs in Guatemala because of the conspiracy of silence. To break the conspiracy of silence, women tell their personal and collective stories of pain and suffering to anyone who will listen. Since September 1988 they have used radio, television, and newspapers to denounce acts of violence. They write press releases, interview with international press representatives, and cultivate contacts with media. When they present reports or statements to any person or agency in the government, they release the same information to the press. Members of the National Coordinating Council take turns living at the office in Guatemala City, serving as resource persons for international church and human rights groups that visit Guatemala.

In addition to actions in opposition to violence and the lack of human rights, CONAVIGUA leads classes, workshops, and courses for women. In three departments CONAVIGUA teaches adult literacy, legal rights, and human rights. They sponsor artisan groups and agricultural cooperatives where women learn valuable skills and strengthen their economic power by entering the market as a group instead of individuals.

CONAVIGUA realizes that popular movements must struggle together for the recognition of human rights. Frequently they form coalitions with other groups for parades, demonstrations, and other collective actions. They are part of Union and Popular Action Unity (UASP), a coalition of unions and human rights groups. The partners of UASP have participated in protests for higher salaries for farm workers, teachers, state employees, and factory workers. On July 18 and 19, 1991, CONAVIGUA, GAM, CERJ, CONDEG, and the Communities of Population in Resistance (CPR) of the Ixcán and El Sierra sponsored a national conference to discuss the repression and impunity practiced by the government.

CONAVIGUA supports the collective return of refugees. On January 24, 1993, the women of CONAVIGUA joined the returned refugees and other popular organizations in a march from the Civic Plaza in Guatemala City to the Central Plaza outside the National Cathedral. Over 25,000 people gathered for a mass and speeches for the 2500 returned refugees. Rosalina Tuyuc, member of the coordinating council of CONAVIGUA told the crowd,

> Some say this return is dangerous but we the people, the oppressed, we say this return brings us strength to struggle for peace. All that you have learned in refuge you will offer to this struggle. This is your land; we are your people.[18]

Government Repression

Since its beginning, CONAVIGUA has been the object of death threats and harassment from the military and right wing groups loosely associated with the military. The army has accused CONAVIGUA members in villages, regional groups, and in Guatemala City of being collaborators with the URNG or of being disloyal to their country. The National Police and civil patrols threaten women, warning them not to meet or organize, harassing them as they travel from town to town for meetings or demonstrations.

Military forces often harass CONAVIGUA because of their nonviolent actions. Since CONAVIGUA is strongly opposed to forced military recruitment and participation in civil patrols, the widows often support men or boys who refuse to serve or offer resistance to service. In October 1991 the military accused the local council of San José Poaquil in Chimaltenango of being terrorists because the women stopped the forced military recruitment of thirty local youth.

In May 1991 the Military Commissioners of Perantén in the Department of Huehuetenango accused several poor widows of belonging to the guerrillas because they received school supplies and fertilizer from CONAVIGUA. During the following month, another widow and member of the local group of CONAVIGUA, Juana Ajualip, was accused of being a guerrilla and threatened with death by assassination by the Military Commissioner of Choraxaj, Joyabaj in the department of El Quiché.

In 1991 the National Police invaded the Guatemala City office of CONAVIGUA at 12:05 a.m. CONAVIGUA staff and members from rural areas who live in rooms above the offices were awakened when the police broke down the door, entering without a search warrant. Policemen looked through desks and papers and interrogated women and children. Following the attack on the national office of CONAVIGUA, various regional offices received threats.

In 1991 a group called Anticommunist Unity distributed a bulletin naming the leaders of CONAVIGUA and other popular organizations:

> Amilcar Mendez, Byron Morales,
> Armando Sanchez, Rosalina Tuyuc,
> Nineth de García, Juan Mendoza.
> The last popular communist leaders
> Who will die massacred
> Because we will not be happy until they die.[19]

In addition to threats and harassment, members of CONAVIGUA have been tortured and killed for their human rights activities. In 1990 a civil patrol in El Quiché killed María Mejía, a member of CONAVIGUA, after she stated that she did not want her son to participate in the civil patrol. The National Police assassinated the peasant María Teresa Anavisca on March 13, 1991, when she tried to reclaim her land on the Olga María plantation.

Women and the Means of Social Change

What propels people without political power, people whose lives have been shaped by tragedy, to act against a powerful and repressive government? Martin Luther King's analysis of the Civil Rights struggle gives us a clue.

There comes a time when the cup of endurance runs over, and men are no longer willing to be plunged into the abyss of despair. . . . Oppressed people cannot be oppressed forever. The yearning for freedom eventually manifests itself. . . . Something within him has reminded him of his birthright of freedom, and something has reminded him that it can be gained.[20]

The freedom that the people of Guatemala seek is freedom from an oppressive government and military institution that deny citizens civil and human rights. Piven and Cloward insist that the yearning for freedom is not sufficient to mobilize a group to act.

The emergence of a protest movement entails a transformation both of consciousness and behavior. The change in consciousness has at least three distinct aspects. First, "the system"—or those aspects of the system that people experience and perceive—loses legitimacy. Large numbers of men and women who ordinarily accept the authority of their rulers and the legitimacy of institutional arrangements come to believe in some measure that these rulers and these arrangements are unjust and wrong. Second, people who are ordinarily fatalistic, who believe that existing arrangements are inevitable, begin to assert "rights" that imply demands for change. Third, there is a new sense of efficacy; people who ordinarily consider themselves helpless come to believe that they have some capacity to alter their lot.[21]

Piven and Cloward's explanation of a protest movement touches elements of relative deprivation. Relative deprivation theory explains that deprivation or misery leads the poor to revolt. With human rights abuses in Guatemala, the misery level was high, but CONAVIGUA's and GAM's philosophy and methodology need a more meaningful explanation than relative deprivation offers.

The actions and methodology of CUC, CONAVIGUA, and GAM fit best into the political process model of the resource mobilization school. Political process theorists stress that collective action is as much a function of the political realities confronting members and challengers as it is of peasant grievances, group organization, availability of resources, or socioeconomic change.[22] A key concept in political process literature is the structure of political opportunities, a term used to explain the outcomes of protest movements, such as the Civil Rights Movement, Welfare Rights Movement, and the Unemployed Worker Movement. Charles Brockett defines the structure of political opportunities as "the configuration of forces in a group's political environment that influences that group's assertion of its political claims."[23]

Important variables in the structure of political opportunities in the political process model are peasant grievances, the presence of allies and support groups, access to the political system, and capacity and the inclination of state repression. When the structure of political opportunities changes to the advantage of challengers, the power discrepancy between challengers and the elite diminishes, increasing the challengers' political power and legitimacy, and improving the possibility of their success.[24]

In the political process model, a social movement is defined as "rational attempts by excluded groups to mobilize sufficient political leverage to advance collective interests through noninstitutionalized means."[25] Members of CUC, CONAVIGUA, and GAM are poor, indigenous people who have been politically and socially excluded from mainstream Guatemalan life. During the thirty years of military rule, they were the main targets of repression. All three groups also include poor and middle-class ladinos, who have not been granted civil or human rights. Their priority on collective action has given members more political leverage to improve human rights.

The political process model acknowledges the unequal distribution of power and resources, preventing people and groups from pursuing interests through legitimate means. For political protest theorists, collective action is the independent variable. Initially family members and friends of the disappeared acted individually. Through GAM and CONAVIGUA women have discovered the power of collective action as they search for their missing family members and act in solidarity with other victims of repression. Some actions are spontaneous, such as the mourning and demonstration for the two GAM leaders in 1985, but most actions have been planned to build loyalty among group members and to mobilize a larger constituency.

The political process model recognizes that political opportunity structures may further the cause of the excluded group. In GAM's case, the membership almost doubled in the first year of Cerezo's administration. Although Cerezo did not champion the causes of human rights, the fact that his administration was civilian instead of military created a greater climate of political openness. Not only did GAM's membership grow but citizens joined unions and participated in strikes and protests. The 1985 constitution guarantees greater civil and human rights; groups such as CONAVIGUA, GAM, and CERJ have used the constitution to protect peasants' basic human rights.

The political process model correctly targets the importance of allies and support groups to the mobilization of groups without political power. Through coalitions with other groups, CUC, GAM, and CONAVIGUA have strengthened solidarity among peasants and weakened the domination of the military and private sector.

In addition to allies and support groups within Guatemala, outside agents—religious workers, human rights groups, union organizers, and development workers—have been crucial to the development of grassroots leadership. Catholic Action and foreign missionaries, especially Maryknolls, were responsible for the development and radicalization of indigenous leaders. The Menchú family, and thousands of highlands Indians, received political, social, and religious training through Catholic Action groups. Through the influence of religious workers, peasants' attitudes were transformed from fatalistic to activistic. Peasants not only learned how to be leaders, they actually took the lead in asserting their rights, in spite of the threat of repression. Religious workers also supported the development of indigenous organizations, such as the one Rigoberta Menchú worked with before her involvement in CUC.

Contacts with international nongovernment organizations have proved invaluable to Guatemalan social change groups. International groups have provided alternative sources of economic assistance and protection to vulnerable groups and individuals. Rigoberta Menchú has created more awareness of Guatemala's political situation through her involvement in the United Nations and RUOG. International Peace Brigades accompany leaders in GAM and CONAVIGUA, both for international visibility and personal safety. Through education and advocacy, groups like Witness for Peace and the Mennonite Central Committee act in solidarity with fledgling human rights groups as well as strong groups like GAM, CONAVIGUA, and CUC.

Other allies for social change groups have been the news media, both within Guatemala and international, both mainstream and alternative. Media attention contributed significantly to expanded political opportunities. All three groups found news sources through alternative media, mainly through international human rights groups and church groups. GAM, more than CUC, CONAVIGUA, or any other social change group, nurtured mainstream media contacts and created news opportunities. Through organization and mobilization, GAM "converted a favorable structure of political opportunities into an organized campaign of social protest."[26]

Repression is a serious factor for peasant mobilization in Guatemala. Obviously, many countries possess the capacity for repression but choose coercion instead of force. Guatemala, on the other hand, chooses violent repression as the primary method of social and political control. Ted Gurr argues that "historical traditions of state terror . . . probably encourage elites to use terror."[27] Because of the tradition of repression throughout the past thirty years, elites of Guatemala readily use repression to keep existing class structures in place. Certainly the memory of past repression is part of the risk involved in collective action. When CUC formed in 1978, however, the memory of past repression did not successfully discourage involvement. In 1980 alone a series of strikes involved 70,000 sugarcane workers, 40,000 cotton pickers, and 10,000 coffee harvesters. CUC's strength and its threat to elites resulted in indiscriminate state violence that resulted in the assassination of 110 union leaders and over 300 peasant leaders in 1980.[28]

Aldon Morris and Cedric Herring point out that in spite of the strength of collective action, extensive repression by the government or dominant group may lead to the death of a movement.[29] Violent repression does not always have a negative impact on mobilization, however. In the case of Guatemala, the extreme violence of the early 1980s antagonized many people and motivated them to enter popular resistance movements.

Repression by the military has shaped but not weakened GAM. During 1984-1985, several GAM leaders went into exile. The leader who remained, Nineth de Garcia, is now accompanied by members of International Peace Brigades. During periods of heavy repression, attendance at weekly meetings decreased, but membership continued to grow. But GAM was born during a period of heavy repression and membership grew steadily during the 1980s. On the day of the demonstration mourning for the two GAM leaders, 35 people joined GAM. In 1985 the membership grew from 350 to 670. Rigoberta Menchú's family and community were propelled into action initially to defend their community and later to work with unions and CUC. CONAVIGUA and GAM both were a direct result of the violence of the early 1980s, when husbands and fathers of women were assassinated or disappeared.

Social movements are more than protests planned and implemented by the members of social change groups. A social movement is a dynamic process also influenced by the actions of crowds and public opinion. Pamela Oliver contends that the value of crowds has been neglected in social movement theory.[30]

Crowds attract media attention and give the movement more credibility in the eyes of the nation and world. Crowds have given energy to CUC, CONAVIGUA, and GAM's protests by participating in marches and demonstrations. The January 1993 return of 2,500 refugees to Guatemala gave energy and credibility to the popular movement, as did the awarding of the Nobel Peace Prize to Rigoberta Menchú a month earlier. The return resulted in crowds of 25,000 at celebrations in Guatemala City, as well as crowds of people lining roads throughout Guatemala as buses with refugees journeyed to the capital and later to their homes in Polígono Catorce.

In 1984 when there were 250 members of GAM, 1000 people participated in the March for Peace. In a 1987 demonstration 700 GAM members and 3000 people from popular organizations gathered to support GAM's request for a commission to investigate human rights abuses. Likewise CUC attracted large crowds and a growth in membership through marches, demonstrations, and strikes. CUC's strikes on the southern coast in 1980 and 1989 paralyzed hundreds of sugar and cotton plantations. In 1980 an estimated 70,000 to 80,000 farmworkers participated.

The fusion of ethnic diversity is particularly frightening to the Guatemalan government and private sector. CUC's strike brought together poor ladino and indigenous workers and full-time workers with seasonal laborers.

A social movement is shaped by its constituency. More than 90 percent of GAM's membership is female, mainly poor indigenous women. CONAVIGUA's membership is 100 percent female and like GAM is made up of mainly indigenous women.

Guatemala has a culture characterized by machismo and patriarchal dominance. Latin American culture is organized around the patriarchal family. A woman's subordination is tied to her role in the family unit. Gender roles tend to be static; the woman is responsible for the private sphere—reproduction, the house, and the family; men are responsible for the public sphere. Both CONAVIGUA and GAM realize that the rights of women are overlooked in Guatemala. Because of the patriarchal nature of society, women have not been allowed to develop economically or intellectually. Women have been busy caring for children and animals. Women have been a cheap source of labor in plantations, farms, and factories. Women have suffered when children were kidnapped, husbands were assassinated, or their daughters were tortured or raped. Women have seen and experienced violence firsthand. Women's involvement in human rights groups and other sections of civil society begins to shatter the passive image of women.

Rigoberta Menchú and the women of GAM and CONAVIGUA tell a story—a story of exclusion from economic participation, domination by powers and authorities, exploitation by the dominant culture, and violence from repressive regimes. But as they tell their story, they resist reacting with bitterness, cynicism, and hopelessness. Instead, they act as agents of transformation, turning the conspiracy of silence and the intimacy of pain into social protest. Mothers and wives and daughters, they enter the political arena as novices, novices who defiantly and openly question the state. No longer are they silently weeping women who privately bear their pain. Through collective action they are transformed into political actors helping to gain recognition for the 60 percent indigenous, for the 87 percent majority living in poverty, for widows and orphans, and all people who lack access to the political system.

4

Injustice Through Powers and Authorities

WHEN Myrna Mack Chang turned fifteen her parents, wealthy Guatemalans, sent her to an elite Catholic high school. Maryknoll Sisters, radicalized by Vatican II and the Second Conference of Latin American Bishops in Medellín, Colombia, taught Mack and other daughters of Guatemala's elite. Mack grew up in a world of power and privilege that comes with economic and social status; her world was insulated from political violence and economic oppression.

During Mack's high school years, Maryknoll Sisters exposed her to the writings of Paulo Freire, Dorothy Day, Gustavo Gutiérrez, Dom Helder Cámara, Martin Luther King Jr., and others. Her education extended beyond the classroom to the slums of Guatemala City, to meetings of farmworkers and factory workers, and work with and for the poor of Guatemala. Mack's high school years and her involvement with the poor sensitized her to the rampant domination of poor and indigenous people by the minority elite.

After obtaining her Ph.D. in anthropology and gaining international acceptance as a social anthropologist, Mack began a study of displaced indigenous communities in the Guatemalan highlands. During the study, she voiced concerns about the conditions that led to the formation of the Communities of Population in Resistance (CPR). After many death threats, she was abducted and brutally murdered by government security forces on September 11, 1990.

By the time Rigoberta Menchú turned fifteen, she had already experienced ethnic and economic oppression. Although Menchú and Mack were citizens of the same country, they did not experience the same privileges and opportunities—Myrna was wealthy and ladina; Rigoberta was poor and indigenous.

Before her fifteenth birthday two of Menchú's brothers had died, one of malnutrition, the other due to pesticide poisoning. Because her family lacked enough land for subsistence farming, they worked in the fields of coffee and cotton plantations eight months of each year. From their home in the highlands, the Menchú family and other laborers were crowded onto trucks and transported to the fincas. At the fincas, overseers treated indigenous labor like slaves. They received abysmal housing, little food, verbal abuse, and poor salary and working conditions.

When she was fifteen Menchú worked for eight months as a maid in a Guatemala City ladino household. Her employers forced Menchú to use her first two months' salary to buy additional clothes. While the maids ate cold hard tortillas, the family dog consumed the same meat and rice the family ate. Besides their rude remarks about her indigenous ancestry, the family treated Menchú with contempt because of her inability to speak Spanish. On several occasions the three sons threw dishes at Menchú. After eight months' work, her employer paid her sixty *quetzales* ($12). As in Menchú's case, rarely do employers pay the legally required minimum wage to domestic help, factory workers, or farm laborers. No government agency effectively regulates the amount or frequency of wages.

Myrna Mack experienced injustice because of her choice to identify with poor and indigenous people in Guatemala—particularly the internally displaced political refugees in the CPR. Because of her identification with internally displaced refugees, members of the elite and military regarded her as a traitor to her class. Rigoberta Menchú, on the other hand, inherited injustice because of her identity as an indigenous person in a region where Mayan Indians have been oppressed for 500 years. As an indigenous person, she experienced political, economic, and social injustice.

Myrna Mack and Rigoberta Menchú offer poignant examples of injustice in Guatemala. Such injustice wears many faces: poverty, poor nutrition, unemployment, underemployment, unequal land distribution, militarism, racism, classism, and sexism.

Despite being pervaded by injustice, Guatemala is far from alone in its struggle with injustice. Injustice knows no national boundaries. The earth groans with cries of injustice. Relief workers in the Sudan comfort children who have endured weeks without food. A mother in Sarajevo gives birth to a baby with the sounds of bombs ringing in her ears. Former coal workers in eastern Kentucky move into an abandoned school bus. The residents of a small village, forced off land by a large agribusiness corporation, relocate to fragile rain forest land. A single parent in Philadelphia continues in her job as secretary despite sexual harassment by her supervisor. A Detroit steel worker is laid off five years before retirement from the only job he has ever held. Men and women work in the blistering heat for long hours and little pay picking oranges and tomatoes along the Texas-Mexico border. Species after species of plants become extinct because of land cleared in an Ecuadoran rain forest for cattle to supply hamburger meat to fast-food chains. A ten year old in Burma cries out in the night, frightened by the sound of gunfire, fearing the footsteps of soldiers. Korean shop owners in Chicago barricade themselves in small stores each night, waiting for the gangs that have threatened to burn them out.

Given the reality of injustice, compassionate Christians and disciples from all religious traditions support a move from injustice to justice. In spite of definitions of justice and well-meaning people, the problem remains—how to move from the lived reality of injustice to justice.

The situation in Guatemala, eastern Kentucky, Zaire, and throughout the world cries out for a response from churches and Christians. Instead of responding with care and compassion, we have been so consumed by individualistic and materialistic understandings of evil, injustice, and oppression that we no longer see situations of injustice as the mission of the church. The church too often sees the Bible as referring only to personal or satanic rather than structural evil.

During a four-month sabbatical in Latin America, Walter Wink became overwhelmed by despair as he confronted evil and injustice. With the goal of writing a book about peacemaking in Latin America, Wink and his wife visited churches and human rights groups who struggle daily with oppression and injustice. They interviewed torture victims, families of the "disappeared," and church workers. Instead of finding hope, Wink grew despondent. He writes, "The evils we encountered were so monolithic, so massively supported by our own government, in some cases so anchored in a long history of tyranny, that it scarcely seemed that anything could make a difference."[1]

Wink found help in the biblical concepts of the powers and authorities. In fact, *Naming the Powers*, the first volume of the *Powers* trilogy, grew out of the despair he experienced in Latin America. In his *Powers* trilogy, Wink examines the language of power throughout the Bible. He believes we have ignored institutionalized evil and the domination of fallen powers in the structures and systems of society. This has led to injustice and domination and our own sense of inadequacy and incomprehension. Wink suggests that the demonic in today's world "has a peculiar proclivity for institutional structures."[2] Have we been naive in our understanding of the powers and authorities, spiritualizing them or ignoring their presence and power? How can Wink's analysis of the powers and authorities further the understanding of injustice and act as a catalyst for justice?

Wink believes justice cannot be understood adequately without attending to issues of domination. Wink's trilogy offers categories for understanding domination and oppression in contemporary society. The powers and authorities are institutions of authority created by God—but fallen and sinful.

The message of the powers and authorities is a message about both the material and the spiritual nature of institutions. According to Wink, many people lack categories for understanding social realities. We blame evil individuals and miss the larger authority structures and systems. With no category for understanding social realities, we are left with a vacuum that Glen Stassen says can be filled with secular stowaways like laissez-faire ideology or simple avoidance. The result is debilitating injustice. People concerned with justice must be aware of the sources and manifestations of injustice.

Powers and Authorities: Power Structures and Inner Spirits

To clarify the meaning of the powers and authorities, Wink examines the language of power throughout the New Testament. He asserts that the powers are relevant to contemporary experience but must first be studied in their original context. Wink offers meticulous word studies of New Testament power language and impressive examinations of troublesome texts regarding the principalities and powers.

Wink begins by identifying his biases; he does not assume the myth of objectivity. Wink collects data concerning the language of power from the New Testament, the Septuagint, the pseudepigrapha, rabbinic literature, and the writings of early Christian theologians.

Wink uses seven hypotheses as the interpretive grid for his study of the language of power in the New Testament. 1. The language of power pervades the whole New Testament. 2. The language of power in the New Testament is extremely imprecise, liquid, interchangeable, and unsystematic. 3. Despite all this imprecision and interchangeability, certain clear patterns of us-

age emerge. 4. Because these terms are to a degree interchangeable, one or a pair or a series can be made to represent them all.
5. These powers are both heavenly and earthly, divine and human, spiritual and political, visible and invisible. 6. These powers are both good and evil. 7. Unless the context further specifies, we are to take the terms for power in their most comprehensive sense.[3] Wink emphasizes that the powers are created by
God. If created by God as a good creation, the powers are redeemable—they are not permanently fallen or without possibility of change.

Response

Wink's insistence that we recognize both the power structure
and its inner spirit is crucial. Although princes, presidents, and
kings and queens of this world lead countries and corporations,
the countries and corporations are beyond human control.
These persons choose or are chosen for a position in leadership,
but the position is embedded in a system that cannot be reduced
to the actions or personality of one individual. In Ephesians 6:12
Paul reminds us that "our struggle is not against enemies of
blood and flesh, but against the rulers, against the authorities,
against the cosmic powers of this present darkness, against the
spiritual forces of evil in the heavenly places."[4]

Our struggle then is with the "inner and outer manifestations
of political, economic, religious, and cultural institutions."[5] We
continue to wrestle with rulers but do so knowing our struggle is
also with the power and authority behind the person in authority—both the outer manifestation and the inner spirit.

President Clinton seemed not to understand Wink's message
about the powers and authorities in Ephesians 6:12. If he had
grasped the social nature of power structures and their inner
spirits, might he not have responded differently to the situation
in Guatemala? Following the May 25, 1993, coup that resulted in
the resignation of the current president, Jorge Serrano Elias, and
the election by Guatemala's Congress of a new president, former

102 Voices of the Voiceless

human rights ombudsman Ramón de Leon Carpio, Clinton was quick to show approval of the new administration. He made two proposals: first, that the United States release $6.5 million of the $12 million in military aid "stuck in the pipeline" since the 1990 massacre in Santiago Atitlán prompted a halt in military aid; second, that the United States give $10 million of economic support funds to Guatemala.

Both proposals ignored the powers and authorities at work in Guatemala: militarism, classism, and the resulting poverty of 87 percent of the population. U.S. military aid and joint military exercises with the Guatemalan government only make worse a tense situation. Clinton's support for the new president did not look beyond the election and performance of one man to the larger problem—a country torn by violence with an ever-widening gap between rich and poor and a military establishment that operates with impunity, no matter who is president. Although the new president made occasional peace initiatives, military and civil authorities did not alter their structures.

Wink and Daniel Day Williams both urge us first to acknowledge the social or corporate nature of the problem. In *The Demonic and the Divine*, Williams writes, "The denial of the demonic leaves us helpless before actual demonic social structures. We have no categories for understanding the exploiting character of social systems."[6] Wink's understanding of the powers and authorities would prompt Clinton to name militarism as the demonic social structure and to take incremental steps to convert it.

To recognize the powers and authorities at work in Guatemala and still show support for de Leon Carpio, Clinton and the U.S. Congress could have transformed funds for military aid and joint military training exercises into a fund for peace and reconciliation, money that would benefit all sectors of Guatemala and provide a much-needed incentive for peace. These funds could have rebuilt areas destroyed by the years of combat or retrain soldiers and guerrillas who lay down their guns. Second, in cooperation with the UN the U.S. could have supported mediation efforts between different sectors of Guatemalan society, particularly the military and the popular sector. Mediation could have settled land disputes between returning refugees and current landowners. Third, the United States, again with international cooperation, could have pushed for trials for those who have abused human rights. Such responses remain needed.

Powers and Authorities: Confronting Evil

Wink believes that we must confront fallen powers and authorities. But instead of confronting evil, our secular, scientific culture of the twentieth century denies the existence of evil and refuses to acknowledge the spirit world. Indeed, can any North American identify with the experience the ancient world called Satan? In the past fifteen years there has been a resurgence of belief in Satan, perhaps because of the evils of the modern world, but the image of Satan is limited to "a personal being whose sole obsessions would seem to be with sexual promiscuity, adolescent rebellion, crime, passion, and greed."[7] This image scarcely differs from the stories of Satan with red tights, a tail, and horns, the bogeyman who frightens children into good behavior. This Satan has much to do with correcting personal behavior through fear and terror but little to say to the social evils of racism, sexism, and corporate greed.

The Bible offers a corrective to contemporary images of Satan and an understanding of the evolution of the image of Satan. Like all language of the powers in the Bible, descriptions of Satan are imprecise. Throughout the Bible, however, the image of Satan only vaguely resembles the devil of popular culture. Originally biblical writings portray Yahweh as the source of good and evil. Gradually Yahweh is differentiated into two sides, light and dark, with angels as the light side and demons or Satan as the dark side.[8]

Satan's name appears only three times in the Hebrew Scriptures: in 1 Chronicles 21:1, Zechariah 3:1-5, and in the book of

Job. In the Old Testament Satan is portrayed as God's servant. Satan is a "fully credentialed member of the heavenly court" with an excessive zeal for justice.[9] In the book of Job, Satan acts as a prosecutor, eager to uncover injustice. Wink points out that Satan's excessive zeal for justice becomes entrapment as Satan uses tragedy to coax Job into rejecting God. Williams insists that the demonic powers (which would include Satan) try to separate love, power, and justice. Williams writes, "Justice without love lacks the most important ingredient of justice itself, compassionate openness toward the other."[10]

In some New Testament passages, Paul, Luke, and Matthew portray Satan as the servant of God. In the wilderness temptation account, Matthew 4:1-11 and Luke 4:1-13, Satan is the tempter who, led by God's Spirit, confronts Jesus with Jewish messianic expectations. In 1 Corinthians 5:1-5 and 1 Timothy 1:20 Satan is the servant of God whose function is to stop sinners from sinning and return them to God.

Although rabbinic Judaism acknowledges Satan as only the servant of God, in the intertestamental period and especially in the early church the Satan evolves into a purely evil enemy of God and father of lies.[11] In Mark 4:15 Satan prevents people from hearing the gospel and attempts to destroy the fragile young church in 2 Corinthians 2:11 and Ephesians 2:11.

Satan's transformation into the evil one provides an explanation for the problem of evil and suffering. Wink locates Satan's fall not in history but in the human psyche as Satan becomes the collective symbol of evil.[12] In a society plagued by poor self-images, Satan as the evil one denies God's blessing of humanity and feeds feelings of worthlessness and hopelessness. Wink suggests that "Satan is the real interiority of a society that idolatrously pursues its own enhancement as the highest good."[13]

Response

If Satan is the interiority of our society, then a proper response is to confront the evil in ourselves, both individually and collectively. To personalize the evil or ignore its existence simply allows evil more power over individual lives and the systems and structures of society. Instead, armed with the knowledge that God can transform any power and authority, we confront the powers of evil and death, bringing them into the light of God's love.

In the 1980s United States women in the peace movement engaged in actions to confront and unmask the collective evil of militarism. As they organized protests and demonstrations around the nuclear threat, the number of women in the peace movement grew dramatically. In November 1980, in one dramatic action, 2,000 women joined hands around the Pentagon to confront the evil of militarism. Women's Pentagon Action included theater presentations, sit-ins, and weaving together a seventeen-mile long peace ribbon around the Pentagon. One year later, 4,000 women repeated the action, demanding an end to the insanity of war, especially nuclear madness.

Powers and Authorities: Inner and Outer Nature

In *Unmasking the Powers* Wink addresses two contradictory views of the demonic. First, many people in the United States believe that psychopathology is the result of personal development malfunctions. Second, liberation theologians, Marxists, and social theorists reject the notion that a flawed personal psyche causes personal pathology, distress, and alienation.[14] Instead, capitulation to oppressive structures and systems of power causes personal pathology, distress, and alienation. The first group does not deny social influences but locates the primary cause in the individual. The second group locates the problem in the society where alienating ideologies and structures enslave people. The first group prescribes therapy, behavior modification, and lifestyle changes; the second group attempts social change, reform, or revolution. The first group situates demons in the inner realm; the second group finds the demonic in the outer realm.

Wink finds truth in both positions but only if they are held in tension.[15] Any definition of the demonic as internal to the exclusion of the external, or vice versa, distorts the truth and reality of the demonic. Furthermore, human nature cannot be restricted only to individual or social reality. Although individuals can never be completely understood without attention to their social matrix (environment), they are capable of self-transcendence, even in oppressive structures and systems. Individuals are tightly bound to political, economic, and social structures.

To correct the misperception of a separate inner and outer demonic, Wink emphasizes their unity.

> Like the thousands of smaller sewage pipes draining from every house in a city into the central main, our inner demons feed the outer. . . . Together they form a united front of hostility to the humanizing purposes of God.[16]

The outer demonic represents the inner spirit of suprahuman entities. The spirit of the corporate structure rejects its divine vocation, making its own goals the highest good. By gaining the willing consent from those in the system, the powers rule from within. Because of ambition, greed, self-interest, or group pride, individuals in the corporate structure participate in acts of oppression.

Wink's insistence on the unity of the demonic leads him to differentiate between three types of demonic manifestations: outer personal possession, collective possession, and inner personal possession. The story of the Gerasene demoniac in Mark 5:1-20 represents Wink's category of *outer personal possession*, which he defines as "the possession of an individual by something that is alien and extrinsic to the self."[17] Since communities cannot face their own evil, this community uses the demoniac as a scapegoat to place all their violence and collective madness. Thus outer personal possession is the personal pole of a collective demonism, unnamed and unconscious.

Wink names the *inner personal demonic* as the aspect of the self that is unintegrated but intrinsic to the personality.[18] Jesus refers to the inner personal demonic when he speaks of inner evil, the evil from the human heart. In Mark 7:14-15, 21-23 Jesus identifies evil thoughts, fornication, adultery, theft, murder, slander, pride, envy, foolishness, coveting, licentiousness, wickedness, and deceit. Wink holds that the inner demons are not intrinsically evil but are evil because of suppression.

Wink suggests that *collective possession* takes the form of mass psychosis. Instead of serving God, groups or nations serve a malevolent power, god, or demon. A mark of collective possession is "its explicit and avowed idolatry of the leader."[19] Unconsciously, a group or nation transfers allegiance from God to a mortal they have divinized. Furthermore, because of group pride nations or groups discern the collective possession in other groups or nations without awareness of their own possession. in the United States we recognize the injustice against Jews in the Holocaust and the evils of apartheid in South Africa without acknowledging our complicity in the scandal of homelessness, our explicit sexism in the paltriness of funding for research of women's health issues, or our responsibility for a foreign policy that supports ethnic cleansing in Guatemala.

Response

Above all, Wink insists that contemporary society recognize the demonic and respond to it. Contemporary literature and media, movies like *The Exorcist* and novels like Frank Peretti's *This Present Darkness*, picture demons as individualized grotesque representations of evil. This mythologized view excludes social manifestations of the demonic. Wink proposes an understanding of the demonic that includes the "crushing evils of our day—racism, sexism, political oppression, ecological degradation, militarism, patriarchy, homelessness, [and] economic greed."[20]

Inner Personal Demonic Possession. Response to the demonic hinges on the identity of the demon: is it inner or outer, personal or collective? Spiritual directors and other spiritual people can help discern the nature of the spirit. In the vast majority of cases of personal demons, the spirit manifests itself as an inner personal demon.[21]

Because of our resistance to the spiritual, contemporary Christians often deny the inner personal demon and project it onto another group or individual. From one end of the theological or political spectrum, Christians may demonize homosexuals, feminists, secular humanists. From another end they may demonize fundamentalists. Any group that represents "the other" may be demonized. By projecting the inner demonic onto "the other," we repress the inner demon and fail to deal with it on a personal level—giving the inner demon more power than it need have. By embracing what Carl Jung calls the "shadow side," we acknowledge the inner demonic as part of our selfhood under God's sovereignty rather than being consumed by fear. To acknowledge and transform the inner demonic, Wink suggests the tool of psychotherapy.[22]

Poor ladino and indigenous Guatemalans who have been the target of the counterinsurgency campaign of the military during the past twenty years regard the Guatemalan army as the source of violence and oppression. Family members tell story after story of sons and brothers who return to their villages changed persons after service in the army. Family members often refer to the changes as "brainwashing" or "turning my child into an animal." After military service, their sons and brothers demonstrate a greater propensity for violent solutions and often conspire with civil and military authorities against their friends and families.

Soldiers abducted seventeen-year-old Juan Sisay Morales and seven of his friends during the celebration of his village's patron saint.[23] Shoved into a truck with other men from his village and neighboring villages, the boys were transported several hours away to a military base in another department. In training, army officers taught Juan tactics of warfare and "facts" about his enemies. They taught that indigenous people, church leaders, and human rights workers are subversives and enemies of the government.

Through military training exercises and actual attacks, Juan learned that soldiers are rewarded for brutal behavior. At first Juan remembered what his parents had taught him: respect all life, pray even before you hoe the ground for planting or cut down a tree for firewood, and live peaceably with the world. Juan cried at night after burning a village. He felt nauseous when he saw a woman tortured. His hands trembled when he fired a shot. But he knew the penalty for disobedience. One of his friends had been shot and left for dead when he refused to torture a priest. In spite of an almost overwhelming sense of fear, Juan repressed the fear and doubts and nausea until he could shoot without trembling, rape a girl without thinking of his sister, and burn a village without remembering his village. Eventually his repression became habitual.

If Juan were to return to his village, his parents and friends would say that he had changed. Using Wink's category of the inner personal demonic, how could they respond to Juan? First, recognize the shadow side of Juan. To be a healthy person, every part of Juan must be recognized, accepted, and integrated. Second, remind Juan that he is loving and tender. During his years of military service, Juan repressed the tender part of himself because he perceived that it was unacceptable. Third, confront Juan with the evil that he has done and allow him to repent and to grieve. Hopefully through confrontation in a loving and familiar context, Juan will bring the part of him he has repressed during military service—the inner personal demonic—from the unconscious to the conscious.

Outer Personal Demonic Possession. Wink believes few cases of outer personal demonic possession actually exist, but if a case of outer personal possession emerges, he prescribes exorcism. He

grounds the practice of exorcism on Jesus' encounters with demons. Exorcism, as Jesus practiced it, is

> the act of deliverance of a person or institution or society from its
> bondage to evil, and its restoration to wholeness intrinsic to its
> creation. Exorcism is thus intercession for God's presence and
> power to liberate those who have become possessed by the pow-
> ers of death.[24]

Jesus, his disciples, and the early church did not practice sensa-
tional exorcisms; they simply but powerfully asserted the power
of God over the demonic.

In the rare case that an exorcism becomes necessary, Wink
recommends formation of an exorcism team including a psychi-
atrist or other mental health care professional and a Roman
Catholic priest. Although movies picture a lone priest waving a
cross as he dramatically struggles against the power of evil, it is
more effective to use a team of believers in the spirit world who
are grounded in commitment to Jesus Christ.

Collective Possession. Television, movies, and books often portray demonic possession as personal rather than collective. As a
society we are blind to the power of institutions and ideologies
over our attitudes and actions. Collective possession has more
power over persons, groups, and nations when unidentified.

To respond to collective possession Wink prescribes exorcism in the form of symbolic acts and social protests; the symbolic acts name and rebuke the demonic.[25] Symbolic acts and social
protests, acts like the Civil Rights Movement's March on Washington or protests against nuclear war, name such unconscious
ideologies as that of national security or white supremacy
groups which enslave individuals and nations.

The unmasking of collective possession may not occur with
one act. The welfare rights movement, led by African-American
women, was a movement of the poor persons in urban areas
during the turbulent years of the 1960s. Not content to live in

debilitating poverty, women and others in this movement used disruptive actions to demand change. Welfare mothers took over schools to protest inadequate education of their children and led campaigns to inform welfare recipients of their rights. Throughout the welfare rights movement, act after act, in the form of marches, demonstrations, boycotts, and mass meetings, unmasked the demons of classism and racism, collective possessions entrenched in U.S. society.

At its peak, the National Welfare Rights Organization involved 25,000 people and resulted in significant changes in programs for poor people, including creation of Medicaid and Medicare, to provide free health care for poor people and elderly people. Decades later the entire welfare system is under attack. New analysis of, and response to, collective possession may be needed.

In Guatemala in September 1993, representatives of the Communities of Population in Resistance, CPRs, exposed the demon of militarism in an act of exorcism they called "an exposition of horrors." Following a 250-mile journey from clandestine communities in the jungle to Guatemala City, 600 representatives of the CPRs gathered in the Central Plaza across from the National Palace to publicly disclose the terror of the past ten years. Surrounded by crosses with the names of the thousands killed, the exposition of horrors displayed children's drawings of the massacres and the remains of bombs from government air attacks on civilian communities.

North American churches have helped expose collective possession through the activities of Witness for Peace. One hundred and fifty representatives of North American churches traveled to Nicaragua in July 1983 to expose the demon of U.S. militarism and to stand in solidarity with Nicaraguans. With the support of the Nicaraguan government and the nongovernment agency Evangelical Committee for Aid and Development (CEPAD), the North American group interviewed supporters and opponents of the Sandinista revolution, visited hospitals and housing projects, attended church services and Christian base community meetings—all to discover the truth about U.S. involvement in Nicaragua.

The North Americans traveled to the border town of Jalapa, scene of frequent *contra* attacks and kidnappings of more than 300 persons earlier in 1983. Jalapa residents joined hands with the North Americans for a vigil with prayers and petitions. The North Americans prayed for forgiveness for the U.S. government's support for the contras and for the killings and kidnappings funded by U.S. dollars. After the third petition, a Nicaraguan *campesino* answered, *"Están perdonados"*—You are forgiven.[26]

Over and over on the trip, Nicaraguans told the North Americans, "You are signs of hope for us."[27] Besides offering hope to the Nicaraguans, one North American reported that

> Those of us who were present were challenged by the faith of Nicaraguans and were indicted by their cries for help. . . . Our presence in the war zone was a source of great comfort to the Nicaraguan people, and offered some degree of protection for them while we were there. We decided that we should make this presence permanent and that we should do so in a very public and visible way both to express solidarity with the victims of our foreign policy and to try to raise that policy for public debate.[28]

Before the group left Nicaragua, they created the foundation for Witness for Peace, an ecumenical grassroots organization determined to unmask U.S. policy toward Nicaragua, provide eyewitness reports to churches, and stand in solidarity with Nicaraguans. Within three months of returning to the United States, Witness for Peace formed a coordinating committee and opened five regional offices and a central office in Washington, D.C., with plans for rotating teams of U.S. citizens to visit Nicaragua. Their hope was that the presence of U.S. citizens in Nicaragua would curb aggression toward the Nicaraguan people and cause the U.S. government to reexamine its foreign policy toward Nicaragua.

Regardless of the form of possession, the mission of the church is to raise consciousness and to reject a worldview that excludes the demonic or an understanding that ignores social, economic, and political dimensions of the demonic. A prophetic church can help persons grasp the unity of the demonic as they realize that evil is experienced individually and as systemic, social, and institutional.

Domination System: Violence

Wink uses the expression *domination system* to identify "what happens when an entire network of powers becomes integrated around idolatrous values."[29] Institutions turn from their divine vocations and are characterized by greed, authoritarianism, violence, and everything contrary to life. The fallen powers have control of the institution for the present; their grasp is strong and seemingly impenetrable.

The domination system is grounded in the myth of redemptive violence. Rooted in the Babylonian creation story, the myth of redemptive violence chronicles the triumph of order over chaos by means of violence. Paul Ricouer contends that in the Babylonian creation myth, creation itself is an act of violence; there is no good God who approves of creation. The younger gods murder Tiamat, the elder mother god; out of her corpse the world is formed. Not only does evil exist before good, but evil exists before humanity and the rest of creation. Since humans are created out of violence, there is no possibility of peaceful coexistence; humans are doomed to violence, conflict, and evil. Instead of peace, proponents of the myth of redemptive violence speak of order imposed by a hierarchical and violence-based system.

In the Bible the domination system is known best by the words "world" or *kosmos* and "flesh" or *sarx*. Although kosmos means world, universe, creation, and the planet earth, kosmos in the New Testament also refers to "the human sociological realm that exists in estrangement from God."[30] A good God created the world and the world is fallen but it is also capable of redemption. Wink translates *kata sarx* as "dominated existence."[31] Although sarx generally is translated as flesh or the physical materials of the human body, those translations do not capture the strength of the "self in its alienated form." Wink says that sarx refers to "the pursuit of the values of the domination system.[32] Regardless of the word used to name the domination system, one fact is clear: the domination system that emphasizes hierarchies, violence, inequality, and greed contrasts starkly with the vision of the reign of God articulated by Jesus Christ.

An Alternative Vision: The Reign of God

Although the domination system appears to have total control of the institutions and individuals of the world, the pain of injustice and oppression is not the final word. God offers an alternative vision to the domination system—the reign of God. Wink defines the reign of God as

> a domination-free order characterized by partnership, interdependence, equality of opportunity, and mutual respect between men and women that cuts across all distinctions between people. This egalitarian realm repudiates violence, domination hierarchies, patriarchy, racism, and authoritarianism: a total system detrimental to full human life.[33]

The reign of God was a major focus of Jesus' ministry on earth; in fact, Jesus' movement offered a foretaste of the reign of God on earth. Jesus' ethic was primarily an ethic of the reign of God. Through Jesus' teaching, his relationships with outcasts, his values and actions, Jesus demonstrated that God is breaking into history. Jesus offered a glimpse of the reign of God—of what is to come if persons participate in the kind of world that Jesus offers. In his first sermon, Jesus read Isaiah's messianic and jubilee passage, identifying himself with the values of the reign of God. For Jesus, the reign of God has social and personal dimensions; it is universal and nondiscriminatory. Knowing humanity's proclivity to self-centeredness and group-centeredness, Jesus did not identify the reign of God with one political or economic system, or one ethnic group or class.

Ultimately, Jesus was executed because of his rejection of the domination system. Wink asserts that Jesus represented the most unendurable threat ever placed against the domination system.[34] Throughout the Gospels, the writers describe how Jesus threatened existing systems of power and influence and shattered stereotypes. Jesus' punishment, crucifixion—a crime reserved for subversives and thieves—indicates the seriousness of his threat to the power system. Although the New Testament authors later spiritualized the meaning of the crucifixion, his followers comprehended the meaning of the cross. Jesus' teaching and practice exemplify the reign of God, particularly his treatment of nonviolence.

Nonviolence

In the Magnificat, Mary announces the values of the reign of God. The reign of God is characterized by peace with justice, the restoration of right relationships, and freedom from domination. In his teaching and implementation of the reign of God, Jesus implements the words proclaimed by Mary, words alive with the power of nonviolence.

For some, nonviolence signifies the absence of violence. The nonviolence that Jesus practiced represented much more. Jesus practiced active nonviolence. Jesus' nonviolence, drawing on

> a power seldom recognized by oppressor and oppressed alike—a power integral to the new reality of God's reign. . . . Its heart is the refusal to mirror evil, to let one's responses be determined by what one deplores.[35]

In the Sermon on the Mount Jesus counsels followers to practice radical nonviolence by walking the second mile with a soldier's pack, by turning the other cheek after the first cheek is hit, by giving both a shirt and a cloak when a cloak is requested. By practicing active nonviolence, followers embody the character of the kingdom of God.

Throughout the Gospels, both Jesus' words and actions encourage the practice of nonviolence. Jesus did not advocate violence or conflict. Before his apostles left for their preaching mission, Jesus told them to greet everyone with *shalom* or peace. He instructed them to offer no resistance or retaliation. In the Sermon on the Mount he affirmed peacemaking and said that those who seek peace and pursue it reflect God's character. On his last visit to Jerusalem Jesus spoke about peace. When the soldiers arrested Jesus, Jesus rebuked Peter for his use of the sword and refused the option of violence.

Jesus' practice and teaching of nonviolence were strong enough to elicit a radical response from his followers. During the first three centuries of Christianity, all believers were pacifists. In fact, Christians were excommunicated for participation in the army. Tertullian was clear that "Christ in disarming Peter, unbelted every soldier."[36] Origen insisted, "For we no longer take up sword against nation nor do we learn war any more having become children of Peace for the sake of Jesus."[37] The credo of the early church—Jesus is Lord—relativized human authority. The citizenship of early Christians was in heaven, not on earth. Caesar might have been their ruler but Jesus was their Lord.

For Jesus the cross was the ultimate symbol of nonviolence. In the Roman and Jewish world, the cross was a symbol of violence—not a symbol of religious significance. Through 2,000 years of post-crucifixion Christianity, however, the cross has lost its shock value. The Roman government used punishment by crucifixion as a deterrent for crime. Wink maintains that rather than compromise with a violent and evil system, Jesus chose death on the cross.[38] Throughout time religious authorities had taught that domination and violence resided in the natural order. Jesus revealed the falsity of this myth through his life and his teachings about the reign of God; he revealed that domination did not exist in the fabric of the natural order. Because of the danger his claims presented to the status quo, religious authorities conspired with the Romans for Jesus' death.

Because of his experience on the cross, Jesus identifies with victims of violence. Wink declares that

> In his cry from the cross, "My God, my God, why have you forsaken me?" he is one with all doubters whose sense of justice overwhelms their capacity to believe in God; with every mother or father who cradles the lifeless body of a courageous son or daughter; with every Alzheimer's patient slowly losing the capacity of recognition.[39]

Those who endure the daily tragedies of substance abuse or live with the memories of torture discover a fellow sufferer in Jesus. Jesus' mystical identification with the poor and oppressed in Matthew 25 became a lived reality on the cross. God, through Jesus, suffers with those who suffer.

Response

Since powers and authorities are God's creations, Wink's solution for oppressive powers is to call the fallen powers back to their created purpose. Although his prescription includes resistance, Wink prefers the term "engaging the powers" instead of resisting, confronting, or overcoming the powers. Wink's predisposition toward nonviolence and his conviction that the reign of God is a domination-free order lead him to propose nonviolent strategies and tactics for engaging the powers.

Wink cautions not to respond to evil with evil, even with the best of intentions, since evil actions induce imitative or mirroring reactions.[40] The power of violence is so great that "even its use to destroy a flagrant enemy can recoil against the users and make them over into the likeness of the enemy."[41] Martin Luther King Jr., said that violence is impractical because it is "a descending spiral ending in destruction for all. The old law of an eye for an eye leaves everyone blind."[42]

The only way to break the spiral of violence is through non-violent engagement. Since violence causes more violence, non-violent action is the best way of overcoming exploitation and domination. Wink states that Jesus loathes both passivity and violence as responses to evil.[43] What Wink calls Jesus' third way, "militant nonviolence," offers a vigorous response to violence.

Wink asserts that contemporary culture lacks the capacity to imagine a culture of nonviolence. Through historical studies from elementary school through higher education, people have learned only the history of violence—with scarce attention to nonviolent actions or movements. As a result of years in the domination system, we have learned so little about nonviolence that we cannot imagine a world without violence. To correct this deficiency Wink suggests that we feed our imagination by offering a revisionist history that tells stories of nonviolent action. Drawing on Gene Sharp's *The Politics of Nonviolent Action*, he presents a short history of nonviolent actions from 1350 B.C.E. to 1992.[44] The stories of "people-power" stimulate the collective imagination of people and encourage more nonviolent actions.[45]

In the Guatemalan context, instead of pretending that only the armed resistance opposes oppressive powers and principalities, proponents of nonviolent action must tell countless stories of the popular movement courageously resisting a culture of repression. The story of Santiago Atitlán offers one example. Guatemalans call Santiago Atitlán *pueblo de paz*, the people of peace and the town of peace.

The story of the only town in Guatemala without a military presence began in 1980 when the military built a permanent base two kilometers outside the city. For the next ten years the military rained terror on the people. The Tzutuhil Indians who live in Santiago Atitlán report that every family lost at least one family member to the repression. A U.S. priest and several catechists were assassinated. Young boys and men were forced into military service, women were raped, church leaders and members of agricultural cooperatives were "disappeared." People were harassed, tortured, and killed.

On the night of December 2, 1990, soldiers shot one man and tried to kidnap another. The church bell rang out and in one hour between five and fifteen thousand women, men, and children gathered. The mayor and committee of resistance proposed a plan—to march to the base and demand an explanation. They were clear that the march would be nonviolent—no stones, sticks, or guns. They marched the two kilometers from the center of town to the base along a narrow dirt road. The crowd was so great that by the time the first people reached the base, others were beginning to line up at the plaza.

When the mayor said *"Buenas noches"* (good evening) to the guard, shots echoed through the silence. Soldiers opened fire on the crowd, killing eleven boys and men, wounding twenty-two people. In the midst of their grief, people were propelled into action. More than 20,000 Tzutuhil Indians put their thumbprints on a petition asking for the army's removal from Santiago Atitlán. The mayor and surviving members of the committee of resistance delivered the petition to the president of Guatemala and contacted international human rights groups and the media.

In ten days, the army base was dismantled and soldiers left town. A presidential decree promised a town with no military presence. Today at the massacre site corn, cotton, and bananas grow. The resistance committee has become the peace and justice committee. The mayor and committee lead monthly town meetings following the ecumenical worship service to remember those who died.

In the United States and England, women have been at the forefront of the peace movement. To demonstrate their opposition to war and steadfast support of peace, women organized the Greenham Commons Women's Peace Camp in England and the Seneca Falls Women's Peace Encampment in Seneca Falls, New York.

Greenham Commons Peace Camp began in 1981 when members of "Women for Life on Earth" organized a 125-mile march from South Wales to Greenham Commons to protest NATO's decision to place 96 cruise missiles at Greenham Commons, a U.S. Air Force base in England. The small group of women did not realize the impact of their march and their determination to remain at Greenham Commons until the missiles were removed. From 1981 until the missiles were removed in 1991, thousands of women from England and throughout the world maintained a permanent presence to protest militarism and to track the cruise missile convoys.

Like Greenham Commons, Seneca Falls Peace Encampment was established to create an alternative community based on peace and justice and to stop the deployment of missiles. When the U.S. government announced the scheduled deployment of cruise and Pershing II missiles at the Seneca Army Depot in 1983, women peace activists staged protests and other nonviolent acts of confrontation with the military at Seneca Falls. In addition to acts of protest, women set up a nonviolent system of governance that embodied feminist values.

Although protests, boycotts, and other techniques are effective in the struggle against oppressive powers, it is not enough to plan and implement nonviolent action without attention to the spiritual dimension of any action. Wink insists that the struggle against evil can make us evil. Battles against evil do not occur only in busy streets or in crowded offices but in the psyche. Individuals engaged in social justice movements must not neglect the spiritual warfare of struggle against the evils in our souls. Individual and corporate prayer, meditation, and Bible study must constitute an integral part of the response to evil. Wink writes that prayer "involves the great socio-spiritual forces that preside over so much of reality."[46] Indeed prayer becomes a form of social action. Civil disobedience strategies can change institutions, but without attention to the inner spirituality of the institution, the change will involve only the outer shell. For conversion and transformation of the power, the inner spirituality and the outer structure must be addressed in conjunction with political actions.

The Sanctuary movement in the United States offers an example of churches, firmly grounded in prayer and Bible study, responding to growing numbers of refugees from Central America. The movement began in Tucson, Arizona, where Pastor John Fife and the members of Southside Presbyterian Church listened to Central American refugees' stories about death squads, torture, and the persecution of the church. They responded by gathering weekly to pray for the people of Central America. Soon their prayer vigils grew to include persons from other faith traditions as well as their own congregation. Out of the prayer group they organized the Tucson Ecumenical Task Force for Central America, representing 65 Protestant and Roman Catholic churches, and designed programs to meet the needs of the growing refugee community.

At first the group functioned under the boundaries of the law by working for improved conditions in detention centers and raising money for refugees' legal fees. After recognizing that the Immigration and Naturalization Service deported almost all refugees, regardless of any danger to their lives when they returned home, the task force decided that to save the lives of refugees, they must help refugees avoid capture and deportation.

The elders of Southside Presbyterian Church and Fife first voted to bring Salvadoran and Guatemalan refugees to their church for asylum. Each week Fife introduced the refugees during the worship service and asked them to share their stories with the congregation. After the refugees told why they had come to the United States, Fife said to the congregation, "Your government says that these people are illegal aliens. It is your civic duty when you know about their status to turn them in to INS. What do you think the faith requires of you?"[47] After two months of prayer, Bible study, and discussion, church members voted to publicly declare their church a sanctuary for Central American refugees.

At the same meeting, they wrote letters to other congregations throughout the country, inviting them to receive a Central

American family into the sanctuary of their church on March 24, 1982, the anniversary of Archbishop Oscar Romero's assassination. Four churches became Sanctuary churches on March 24, and several cities began religious task forces focused on Central America.

The Sanctuary movement has grown to include Jewish and Christian congregations throughout North America as well as people of conscience not affiliated with a church or synagogue. Through churches, religious task forces, and refugee centers, people minister to refugees from Central America, work for asylum, and oppose unjust government immigration policies. Churches involved in the Sanctuary movement have discovered that they minister to the poor and oppressed through political action and direct involvement with refugees. Leaders like Fife and the members of Southside Presbyterian Church translate their faith into concrete, effective acts of civil disobedience because of their commitment to Jesus Christ.

Domination System: Inequality

In the temptation account and other words to the disciples Jesus draws on a new image of power. Power and domination have been based on economic status, gender, and political authority. Jesus rejects power as domination and exploitation. In fact Wink identifies Jesus as "an egalitarian prophet who repudiates the very premises on which domination is based: the right of some to lord it over others by means of power, wealth, shaming, or titles."[48] No longer will we be entrenched in hierarchical and patriarchal relationships based on domination and inequality. Jesus invites us to be servants-to-each-other, friends, and colleagues.

Perhaps the greatest areas of inequality, both in the first-century world and today, are economic inequality and the domination and exploitation of women. Wink focuses so sharply on the domination of violence that he emphasizes economic injustice much less clearly. Richard Horsley has criticized him for that. Therefore in this section I examine economic inequality and women's inequality, first in Jesus' day, then in twentieth-century Guatemala and the United States. Since I believe that Jesus rejects power based on economic or gender inequality, I also examine Jesus' words and practices. They are brimming with liberating insights for Guatemalan women and women in the United States. As a sign of the *basileia* (reign of God), I offer examples of Guatemalan and United States women's groups and individuals struggling against economic imperialism, working for gender justice, and charting new pathways in economic and gender relations.

Economic Inequality

In *Jesus and the Spiral of Violence*, Richard Horsley notes that biblical scholarship has tended to focus on cultural and religious dimensions, ignoring or underemphasizing the economic situation.[49] To address the neglect of economic injustice in contemporary biblical scholarship, he pays special attention to the economic exploitation of Palestinian Jews. During the first century C.E., Jewish priestly aristocracy and Herodian client-kings collaborated with Roman civil authorities to control Palestinian Jewish society. Their control was two-pronged—political and economic. As with other modern and ancient countries, the initial conquest occurred with military force but economic measures were used to support the civil and religious regimes and to maintain political control.

Roman political authorities and Jewish religious authorities imposed tolls, taxes, tributes, and tithes that severely weakened an already fragile agrarian society. The majority of farmers in Palestine barely grew enough for their families' needs. As small farmers, their

> margin for increase of output was very limited. Thus whether the cause was exploitative governmental officials, drought, or con-

quest, the productive base of the rulers was subject to serious damage. . . . Because of bad harvests or unusual demands for trib- ute, taxes, or tithes, already-marginal peasant families would fall into debt.[50]

The double exploitation by civil and religious authorities, com- plicated by drought and poor harvests, forced peasants first to fall into debt, then to sell their ancestral lands. After the sale of their lands, former landowners worked as day laborers or tenant farmers.

Jesus entered a world of poverty, hunger, and despair. As more and more peasant farmers fell into the spiral of poverty, the gap between rich and poor increased. Although all Jewish Palestinians experienced poverty (except for the high priest aris- tocracy), women were particularly vulnerable to poverty and hunger. Elizabeth Schüssler Fiorenza declares,

> In the first century—as today—the majority of the poor and starv- ing were women, especially those women who had no male agen- cies that might enable them to share in the wealth of the patriar- chal system.[51]

With growing poverty and no meaningful participation in political, economic, or religious structures, the common people of Palestine grew increasingly hopeless. Disheartened by the se- vere drought in the late 40s C.E., with no relief aid from civil or religious authorities, more people turned to banditry to supple- ment incomes. But more than merely robbing to feed families, social banditry served as a symbol of protest and resistance for the Jewish peasants who supported and protected the bandits. The bandits served much like Robin Hood, acting as a "champi- on of justice" by taking from the rich to feed the poor.[52] Josephus reports that one Italian bandit announced, "Tell your masters that if they would put a stop to banditry, they must feed their slaves."[53] The wide support of social banditry indicates the ex- tent of hopelessness and despair brought on by years of poverty. With banditry, either as participants or protectors, Jewish peasants were provided with an opportunity to resist an unjust order. As a form of social protest, social banditry was a precursor for the peasant revolts of 66-70 C.E.

Like first-century Jewish Palestine, Guatemala is a country divided by poverty, hunger, and despair. In fact, in the past ten years the inequality of resource and income distribution has grown from 79 percent in 1980 to 87 percent in 1987.[54] Three factors contribute to the impoverishment of Guatemala. First, the obvious militarization of the country drains economic resources; rather than spend needed funds for education, health care, and social services, economic resources are used to control the civil population.

Second, international development funds, particularly U.S. Agency for International Development (US AID) funds, benefit economic elites in Guatemala and foreign investors, rather than the majority poor. US AID has provided technical assistance and financial support to expand the *maquila* industry, an industry that has grown from six factories in 1984 to 350 factories in 1993. Although the maquilas employ 70,000 workers and generate more than $350 million in profits, Guatemala scarcely benefits from the arrangement. Foreign individuals and corporations own 60 percent of the maquilas. In a country where $7 to $8 per day is needed to supply basic shelter, food, and other necessities for an urban family, maquila workers are paid from $1.50 to $3.00 per day.

Third, because of external debt and a desire for economic growth, Guatemala is held captive by structural adjustment policies of international financial institutions, particularly the International Monetary Fund and the World Bank, and US AID's export-oriented development model. The Guatemalan government and US AID have encouraged small-scale producers to grow "nontraditional exports." Guatemala has become an international leader in the production and export of "nontraditional exports," replacing the corn and beans used to feed its own population.

Unfortunately, "becoming a leader" does not translate to greater wealth for the Guatemalan people. Since most Guatemalan farmers cannot afford the initial payment for seeds, fertilizer, pesticides, and equipment necessary for the new crops, they buy on credit from an export company, often a subsidiary of a transnational corporation like Del Monte or Standard Fruit Company. AVANSCO's studies show that when a U.S. buyer purchases a Guatemalan cantaloupe, the Guatemalan farmer earns one cent.[55] This model of development does not lead to economic growth, especially economic growth for the farmers who participate in this program.

Wink reminds us that every ideology has an inner spirit as well as an external structure. Economic justice is no exception. During the Reagan administration, economic inequality soared. With the promise of economic growth for all (much like Louisiana governor Huey P. Long's promise of "a chicken in every pot"), Reagan cut domestic spending and personal income taxes, giving the largest cuts to those in upper income brackets. The middle and lower classes watched powerlessly as Reagan economic policies and a global recession led to joblessness and poverty with reduced government job training and poverty programs to act as a safety net.

Throughout the world women and children are most vulnerable to economic inequality. Violence against women takes the form of gender inequity in employment and earnings. Hannelore Schroder reports that

> Women constitute half the world's population, perform nearly two-thirds of its work hours, receive one-tenth of the world's income and own less than one-hundredth of the world's property. Consequently, the other half of the world, men, perform only one-third of working hours, but receive nine-tenths of the world's income and own more than ninety-nine-hundredths of the property in the world.[56]

Whether in the rice paddy in Japan, the factory in Indonesia, or the bank in Singapore, women are working, but their jobs are frequently jobs of low skill with inadequate compensation.

The situation in the United States may not be as bleak as the global situation, but women still struggle with poverty due to unemployment, underemployment, inadequate salaries, and limited job opportunities. The dramatic increase in women's poverty in from the mid-1960s to 1980 is commonly referred to as "the feminization of poverty." The National Advisory Council on Economic Opportunity announced in 1981 that

> All other things being equal, if the proportion of the poor in female-householder families were to continue to increase at the same rate as it did from 1967 to 1978, the poverty population would be composed solely of women and their children before the year 2000.[57]

By 1980, two out of three adults living below the poverty level were women and more than one-third of families headed by females were poor.

Women's poverty is linked to employment. Even when employed full-time, women earn only 61 percent of men's salaries.[58] Not only are women's salaries less than men's in the United States, but females are channeled into certain jobs. Over 80 percent of women work in sales, service, clerical, crafts, light manufacturing, or similar jobs, jobs with "low status, little security, weak unionization, and few fringe benefits."[59] Although many professions are opening to women, some are still male-dominated. For example, less than 5 percent of sports reporters and broadcasters, firefighters, airline pilots and navigators, and construction workers are women.[60]

The economic crisis of the 1980s resulted in fear, suspicion, insecurity, and greed for women and men. North Americans grew increasingly suspicious of foreign business interests, believing foreigners had stolen "the American dream." Their suspicions led to greater prejudice, hate crimes, and the growth of white supremacy groups. In rural areas and urban poor neighborhoods, victims of poverty internalized their own oppression instead of acting to change their circumstances. Plagued by lack of self-worth, women and men lack the confidence to fight injustice. The urban poor live in ghettos surrounded by crime and drug and alcohol abuse and often feel survival takes all the energy they have.

Gender Inequality

The world of first-century Palestine confined women and children to a narrow sphere of influence. In Judaism, women were despised and labeled greedy, lazy, vain, and frivolous. Eliezer, a first-century rabbi, comments, "Rather should the words of the Torah be burned rather than entrusted to a woman. . . . Whoever teaches his daughter the Torah is like one who teaches her lasciviousness."[61] So great was the contempt for women that Jewish men daily thanked God that they were not created a Gentile, woman, or an ignorant man. In the synagogue, women were restricted to a special area and not permitted to read aloud or to participate in worship leadership.

In the larger society women suffered because of taboos and prohibitions in a patriarchal society. Women could not testify in court. Because of Jewish purity laws, women were considered unclean.

> Not only was woman secondary, but because of the superstition about menstrual blood and the earthiness of childbirth, she was ritually unclean, having to spend great periods of her life in seclusion.[62]

Rabbis did not speak to women in public, even their wives and daughters. Instead of attending school like Jewish boys, Jewish girls were confined to the home.

In addition to the economic injustice experienced by 87 percent of the population, Guatemalan women suffer the additional injustice of physical, sexual, and psychological abuse. Peasant women are particularly vulnerable to abuse by police, soldiers, and other government agents. Often widows or daughters of "the disappeared," such women lack support systems for protection. Fermin Gomez accused soldiers of raping Indian girls in the highlands. "It would be difficult to find a girl of eleven to fifteen who is a virgin. Even seven-year-olds have been raped."[63]

Often women are interrogated, raped, and tortured in prisons, either when they visit the prisons to look for "disappeared" family members or when soldiers arrest them. A woman held in the prison in Rabinal for one month reported that she "was raped over 300 times, including twice by the lieutenant in charge, in front of her father who was tied up and held in the same room."[64]

Human rights activists, community organizers, religious women, and trade unionists who have not remained silent in the face of violence have been victims of physical and sexual abuse by police, soldiers, and other government agents. GAM member Maria Mejia was arrested by the army twice. On the first occasion she was tortured and raped. She has a "son conceived as a result of the repeated rapes" she was subjected to while imprisoned in the military barracks.[65] Ursuline Sister Diana Ortiz, primary school teacher in the highlands, was abducted, raped, and tortured for eight days until international pressure prompted her release.

In the United States sexual and economic exploitation of women is inextricably interwoven in the lives of women—especially battered women, immigrants, and poor women.

Advocates raise voices against the victimization of children through child abuse, but few express moral outrage at the victimization of women who are sexually exploited through prostitution. Few women or girls voluntarily choose prostitution, but are trapped into prostitution through lack of job skills, economic resources, or because of vulnerability due to drug and alcohol abuse. Men prey on young girls who are runaways or immigrant women with few job prospects and inadequate language proficiency. Once entrapped, the men who employ women and girls in prostitution usually keep the women in a state of perpetual slavery, both economically, physically, and emotionally.

Sexual exploitation and abuse also occur in the home through family violence. Like prostitutes, battered women often are reluctant to leave abusive situations for fear of reprisal to them or their children, because they have no other place to go or adequate economic resources, or because they hope their husband will reform. In addition, women internalize their oppression and believe they deserve the abuse for some action of their own.

When we talk about violence against women, it is important to remember that violence takes many forms, one of which is physical violence that tends to increase when male wage earners lose their jobs. In addition, women, especially single parents, suffer from economic violence because of low wages or increased costs of food, housing, health care, and affordable child care. During economic crises, many women must work at two or three jobs to support their families or depend on public assistance.

Anne Wilson Schaef notes that sexual and economic exploitation are by-products of a patriarchal society, which she compares to air pollution.[66] Just as air pollution permeates every pore of the human body and leads to disease and death, so gender inequality permeates the structures and systems of society and cripples the potential of women, both consciously and unconsciously. Little girls internalize societal messages about vocational choice and identity, often resulting in their being people-pleasers with poor self-esteem. Since in patriarchy women and girls tend to see men as innately superior, they need to be connected to, and often dependent, on a man to feel whole. This acceptance of male superiority and fear of being abandoned often leads to physical, psychological, and emotional abuse. Similarly, gender inequality can be seen in discrimination and inequity in employment, resulting in poor salaries, limited job opportunities, and harassment in the workplace.

Response: Economic Equality

In the peasant societies of first-century Palestine, religious and economic elites kept the poor captive through low wages, unemployment and underemployment, tithes, tribute, debt, and taxation. Jesus recognizes that economic inequality breeds classism and discrimination, and he places a priority on economic equality. Jesus grounds his ethic on the sufficiency of resources for all people, since God has provided an abundance of resources—but only if people share equitably.

Throughout the Bible the poor are lifted up for God's blessings as a sign that God's kingdom will not be ruled by those with economic power. Problems occur when greed becomes the motivating force behind actions, as illustrated by the eighth-century prophets' harsh words to those who exploit the economically disadvantaged. James affirms the prophets' warnings when he proclaims misery for the rich because they have cheated their workers. John the Baptist advises disciples to share with the needy. When Jesus speaks of the reign of God he uses imagery of common people, images of women cleaning or farming.

Only if we are ignorant or apathetic will we deny Jesus' concern for economic justice. Throughout Jesus' ministry he identified with the poor and needy. In Matthew 25 Jesus advocates ministry to the poor, hungry, and homeless. Jesus calls his disciples to the continual denial of their possessions and identification with the poor. In the Sermon on the Mount Jesus warns disciples not to rely on material goods for happiness but instead to seek God and God's justice. Likewise, Jesus challenges the rich young ruler to sell all his possessions and follow him. In his encounter with Zacchaeus, Jesus does not require him to give up his wealth. But in an act of joyful repentance, Zacchaeus gives half his possessions to the poor and agrees to restore four times the amount he has taken from taxpayers.

In *The Politics of Jesus*, John Howard Yoder concludes that Jesus proclaimed the Jubilee as "a visible, socio-political, economic restructuring of relations among the people of God."[67] Yoder finds in Jesus' message and ministry three prescriptions with economic implications: remission of debts, liberation of slaves, redistribution of capital. In the Lord's Prayer, the Sermon on the Mount, and the parables of the merciless servant and the unfaithful steward, Jesus proclaims a jubilee by "abolishing debts and liberating debtors whose insolvency had reduced them to slavery."[68] Instead of living a life of wealth and luxury, Jesus practiced voluntary poverty and encouraged his disciples to sell all that they had and give it as alms. Furthermore, it is clear from Jesus' teaching that the motive of the offering is as important as the offering itself. Jesus commended the generosity of the poor widow and condemned the ostentatious giving of the wealthy.

In Guatemala, CUC recognizes that economic inequality is a major form of oppression. Actions like CUC's February 1980 strike of cotton and sugar workers on the southern coast improve the economic situation for thousands of agricultural workers and offer hope for change. The strike began on one plantation with 750 workers. Within days, the strike included from 70,000 to 80,000 workers. The striking farm workers paralyzed agricultural operations for fifteen days. To end the strike, the government met CUC's demands to increase the minimum wage.

In the United States, women and minorities have more economic equality as a result of affirmative action. Affirmative action helps businesses and schools take positive actions to end discrimination and bias in hiring and admission. Affirmative action programs and policies acknowledge that gatekeepers exclude—or more commonly do not include—women and minorities in the process of hiring or doing business. Affirmative action means more than quotas or preferential treatment. These programs establish goals for the involvement of women and minorities at every level of company life, management as well as labor. Companies should make every effort to find highly qualified women and minorities for positions.

Despite thirty years of affirmative action and improvement in employment and earnings for women and minorities, problems remain. First, women and minorities still encounter the "glass ceiling" in the workplace. Although women now constitute nearly 40 percent of the workforce, they constitute less than 5 percent of senior managers.[69] Second, although salaries for women have risen during the past thirty years, equitable salaries remain a problem, with women earning 54 percent as much as men.

Third, in response to cries from angry white males whose earnings have declined in the past twenty years and who fear that they are the targets of reverse discrimination, Republican members of Congress have called for an end to, or at least reexamination of, affirmative action rules. Labor secretary Robert B. Reich has labeled the call to abolish affirmative action "the politics of resentment" but insists resentment against women and minorities is misplaced. Women and minorities must vote for politicians who support affirmative action as a way to bring equity and diversity to the workplace. Likewise, we can use our economic power individually and collectively to support businesses that practice affirmative action.

Response: Gender Equality

Although Jesus entered a world dominated by patriarchy, he liberated and empowered women in several ways. First, in a society where women did not study theology, Jesus discussed theology with at least two women, the Samaritan woman and Mary.

Second, women held important roles in the ministry of Jesus. Although none of the twelve apostles were female, Jesus included several women in his company of followers, women like Joanna, Mary Magdalene, and others who supported Jesus' ministry financially.

Third, in a society where women and men were segregated from the rest of society because of physical or social conditions, Jesus disregarded the social mores and treated individuals with dignity and respect. Jesus related respectfully and lovingly to prostitutes, adulterers, and physically ill women.

Fourth, instead of accepting traditional roles for women and basing their value on those roles, Jesus redefined the basis of women's value. No longer were women valued only for their ability to bear children. In Luke 11:27-28 Jesus reminded women of their responsibility to hear the Word of God and respond. At Pentecost both women and men received the Holy Spirit. Although many today would relegate certain spiritual gifts only to men, spiritual gifts were not gender-specific. Jesus treated women the way he did because "the restoration of women to their full humanity in partnership with men is integral to the coming of God's egalitarian order."[70]

In Guatemala GRUFEPROMEFAM (Grupo Feminino Promejoramiento Familiar, Women's Group for the Improvement of Family Issues) recognizes that women are oppressed through gender, class, ethnicity. The women in GRUFEPROMEFAM recognize economic, social, and political violence against women and design programs to increase women's participation in realms from which they have been excluded. During the March 8 celebration of the International Day of the Woman, their banner read, "We struggle for a real and participatory democracy." They also focus on human rights and have found that women express human rights differently than men.

GRUFEPROMEFAM believes that women have internalized their own oppression, and so they sponsor workshops for women in factories, schools, and businesses on self-image and domestic violence. In the growing maquila industry, women are targets of physical and sexual abuse. Realizing that women are desperate for the jobs to feed their families, managers force women to work long hours and coerce them to give sexual favors in offices and storage rooms.

Through conversations and workshops with female maquila workers, GRUFEPROMEFAM helps women to believe in themselves and to realize that they have the right to control their own bodies. As the result of conversations together, women in maquilas have discovered the power of collective action; their employer may harass one employee, but not all women.

Like the women in Guatemala, many women in the United States have internalized their own oppression and remain prisoners of a patriarchal system. But in spite of the power of the patriarchal system and a backlash to feminism, women act courageously to make changes in their own lives and in larger systems and structures of society.

Domination System: Despair

The power of social evils—racism, sexism, militarism, greed, poverty, environmental devastation—can lead Christians to despair. Indeed, often the powers of evil and destruction are so pervasive there seems to be no real reason for hope.

I experienced despair during the October 1991 Senate Judiciary Committee's televised hearings regarding Supreme Court nominee Clarence Thomas. As the hearings to investigate University of Oklahoma law professor Anita Hill's allegations regarding sexual harassment by Thomas progressed, my feelings of disbelief, fury, and despair grew ever stronger. Instead of treating this allegation of sexual harassment with the proper seriousness any such allegation deserves, the Senate Judiciary Committee allowed the proceedings to turn into a media circus and what one television broadcaster called "sheer bedlam."

During the long days of testimonies by Hill and seven other women, it was clear the charges merited serious investigation. The Republican senators responded to the testimonies of the women by choosing to blame the victim—painting Anita Hill as the villain, a political opportunist, and at the least someone with an overactive imagination. Instead of acknowledging the tragic consequences of the sexual harassment many women experience in the workplace, Republican Senator Orin Hatch labeled all perpetrators of sexual harassment "psychopathic sex fiends in insane asylums." Republican Senators Simpson and Specter

joined Hatch in proclaiming Thomas's innocence and vilifying
Hill. The Democratic senators on the Judiciary Committee were
silent and seemed cowed by Thomas's declaration of innocence.

My despair grew as I thought of the women who experience
sexual harassment as a reality in the workplace, women who are
powerless victims in the workplace and often must choose between submission to sexual advances and innuendoes or no job.
I thought of the women who will not dare confront an offender
—or even report sexual harassment after seeing Hill's treatment
by the Senate Judiciary Committee. I thought of the estimated 40
percent of American women who experience sexual harassment
at work and would take the Senate proceedings as evidence that
it is not worth the risk to tell their stories and hope for justice
and fair treatment.

Response: Confrontation and Conversion

Whether in Guatemala or in the United States, a church determined to confront injustice must resist the temptation to despair. Despair interprets the powers and authorities as evil with
no hope of redemption. The church must listen to Wink's re-
sounding refrain in *The Powers* trilogy: The powers are created
by God and are therefore capable of redemption. To those suffering the pain of oppression, this refrain gives hope and
strength to continue the struggle.

Instead of giving up on evil systems, the Christian community must resist evil while recalling structures and systems to their
original purpose. When Christian structures and systems are
perpetrators of injustice and oppression, an individual or group
must act as leaven to call the institution to repentance and a new
way of acting. Integrating social strategy with spiritual disciplines equips the church to engage both the inner spirit and political form of powers and authorities.

In *The Demonic and the Divine* Williams acknowledges the
power of the demonic, of what Wink calls the powers and principalities. Although Williams concedes that the demonic and di-

vine are integrally related, he refers to the demonic as implicitly and explicitly evil. To break the power of the demonic, he suggests public resistance, ritual, and reason. Williams urges people to resist the demonic with the courage of faith, in public and private gatherings. He suggests that citizens cooperate with "the slow process of history" to resist the demonic and create more justice.[71] Humans, created in the image of God, carry reason, love, and hope in them. Although some people and systems appear evil beyond redemption, faithful people with the power of the divine can transform the demonic power.

The actions of the French Huguenot village, Le Chambon, illustrate public resistance. From 1940 until 1945, the 3,000 villagers refused to obey the regulations issued by the French authorities and saved the lives of at least 2,500 Jewish refugees from France, Germany, and other European countries.

Second, religious ritual grounded in biblical tradition can unmask personal and social evils. Williams writes that "ritual reenacts the victory of the divine over the demonic."[72] In worship Christians name and identify the demonic, exposing demons to the collective memory of the church that has battled the demonic for centuries. Until the demonic is publicly acknowledged, Christians are powerless before oppressive social structures.

Third, reason combats the demonic by using criticism and analysis to dispel superstitions about personal demons. Instead of blindly accepting evils like sexism in the workplace, women can use critical thinking to probe causes and conditions of social evil, then use direct action to change unjust conditions.

To a world wounded by injustice the church brings a word of hope, hope that the world will not always be as it now is, hope that the domination system will end, hope that the systemic evils of racism, classism, patriarchy, and violence will be replaced in the reign of God by equality and nonviolence, by peace and justice. That hope is an eschatalogical one (ultimate destiny) that begins today as Christians bring in the reign of God, shouting, "The battle is won, even though the struggle is not over."[73]

5

Toward a Theory of Social Justice

You know very well
how they talk of justice,
they are very honorable, decent
but with their action
they plot the fall of the just
(and if it is a woman, with greater pleasure).[1]

You know to them
your name is just an abstract concept
and
this word "justice"
they can't stop using it
they print it in capital letters
on every manifest
and yet
they can't issue a statement to the press
that isn't designed to deceive us.[2]

IN poetry born in the context of oppression in Central America, Julia Esquivel and Ernesto Cardenal remind us of the use and misuse of justice. The poetry reflects the confusion and ambiguity concerning the meaning of justice in our society. Some think of justice as "equal opportunities for every individual to pursue whatever he or she understands by happiness."[3] For many, justice is merely synonymous with fairness. For others, it represents the justice or injustice of the courts.

We are in danger of reducing justice to individualistic understandings that fail to speak to social injustice. How can we recover a meaning of justice that will prompt women in North America and Latin America to understand the situation of oppression all around us—whether in Guatemala, Nicaragua, inner-city Boston, or Indian reservations in Arizona—and to respond with compassionate and liberating actions?

We do not begin our discovery of justice without resources. Within the Christian tradition, we have stories of those who struggled against injustice; our history is filled with heroines and heroes of faith, people like Clarence Jordan, Dorothy Day, Martin Buber, Muriel Lester, Peter Maurin, Sojourner Truth, and Martin Luther King Jr. The Bible contains justice-words and stories of justice; justice is mentioned 1,060 times.[4] The Hebrew and Greek words *tsedaqah, mishpat, dike,* and *dikaiosyne* often are translated as judgment and righteousness, words we do not normally associate with justice, but words included in the meaning of justice in the Hebrew Scriptures and the New Testament.

Stephen Charles Mott suggests that when we see "righteousness or judgment in the context of social responsibility or oppression, one can assume that justice would be a better translation."[5] Glen Stassen urges us to "turn from the English 'righteousness' to the Hebrew word *tsedaqah,* which really means community-restoring justice."[6] Elizabeth Achtemeier adds that in the Hebrew Scriptures the righteous person "preserved the peace and wholeness of the community, because he or she fulfilled the demands of communal living."[7]

Guatemalan women involved in the struggle for justice and human rights have not articulated a systematic definition of justice, but through their actions we see the shape and form of their justice. The women are concerned more with survival and with creating a more justice-filled world for their daughters and sons. Although I have focused on the past twenty years in Guatemala, the women of Guatemala will remind you that poor Guatemalans, indigenous and ladinos, have suffered political, economic, and cultural domination and marginalization for the past 500 years. Now, in large and small initiatives, in the public sector and in the private sector, Guatemalan women and their companions are demanding an end to the violence and oppression that they have experienced for 500 years. They are tired of the silence, tired of the injustice. Now, they are eager for the world to know their story, eager for a Guatemala with justice, peace, and human rights.

North American churches have not responded to situations of injustice within their own country or in the larger global community with appropriate compassion. In spite of a biblical tradition brimming with rich resources for justice and story after story of Christians in the modern period who acted for justice, today we are plagued with excessive individualism that prevents most Christians and churches from involvement in situations of injustice. Both in our personal lives and in our church experiences, we see this individualism most in our understandings of love and sin. An individualized understanding of sin leads Christians to focus on issues of personal morality, ignoring social, systemic, and structural sin. The blinders of individualism keep us from noticing the linkages between our personal actions and their systemic and structural roots.

Our understanding of love has been so corrupted by excessive individualism that we reserve love for our family and friends, for those like us. We respond with apathy, suspicion, or fear to "the other." An individualized understanding of love leads North American churches to pass budgets with greater amounts of money allocated for their own needs, to build bigger and more elaborate buildings, to give less to world hunger and missions. Individualism keeps persons and churches isolated and separate from each other. We are consumed by our own fears and sense of need, and thus we are not aware of the stranger or the neighbor in our midst. Our world grows smaller and smaller as increasingly we turn inward.

North American women must realize that the paralysis of individualism prevents us from acting together to alleviate injustice. We see injustice all around but feel powerless to respond. Clearly, Guatemalan women and other victims of injustice in the United States and throughout the world cry out for a response from North Americans as sisters and brothers, members of the same human family. They challenge us to move beyond submissive passivity and the paralysis of individualism to creative and life-giving justice-actions. Just as James spoke of a faith that feeds the hungry, our faith also must move us to action, to working together with victims of injustice as cocreators of peace and justice.

In this chapter I propose an understanding of justice which I hope will be helpful for Guatemalan women and North American women. A definition of justice that gives voice to the experience of oppressed people will help clarify and strengthen their claims for justice. Also, a new understanding of justice will help North Americans hear and understand the stories of the oppressed. With a renewed commitment to justice, North American women will be empowered to engage in actions to help Guatemalan women and other oppressed persons.

This definition of justice pays attention to domination and exclusion, particularly in the areas of gender, political, and economic injustice. Instead of searching for abstract and universal principles of justice, I look for dimensions of justice that are concrete and particular, drawing on historical narratives for their shape and substance. Similarly, an understanding of justice for Guatemalan and North American women must include a strong emphasis on specific, effective responses to the historical situation of injustice.

To build a definition of justice, I borrow from the writings of two ethicists, David Hollenbach and Karen Lebacqz; one theologian, Gustavo Gutiérrez; and one political theorist, Michael Walzer. Through them I look for hints of an understanding of justice that pays attention to issues of domination and oppression. All four see a strong role for social criticism and social change as a response to domination and oppression. Lebacqz, Gutiérrez, Walzer, and Hollenbach all identify themselves explicitly with particular communities and religious traditions. Hollenbach, Lebacqz, and Walzer are citizens of the United States; Gutiérrez is Peruvian. Gutiérrez and Hollenbach are Roman Catholic; Walzer, Jewish; and Lebacqz, a member of the United Church of Christ.

Justice is a major focus in the writings of all four, although Lebacqz, Hollenbach, and Walzer take greater care to define and describe their understandings of justice than Gutiérrez does. Lebacqz has written explicitly about women; both Walzer and Gutiérrez have written less about women but their writings are sympathetic to women's concerns and have been used by feminist authors. Hollenbach and Gutiérrez share a focus on human rights and the Roman Catholic tradition, two emphases that resonate with many Guatemalan women.

Gustavo Gutiérrez, Roman Catholic priest, educator, and theologian, helped introduce liberation theology to the English-speaking world with his 1973 book, *A Theology of Liberation*. Henri Nouwen writes about Gutiérrez,

> There is a little man in Peru, a man without any power, who lives in a barrio with poor people and who wrote a book. In this book he simply reclaimed the basic Christian truth that God became human to bring good news to the poor, new light to the blind, and liberty to the captives.[8]

Gutiérrez was born into a Peruvian *mestizo* family. He was trained in European theology at the University of Louvain and the Gregorian University. He returned to Rímac, a Lima slum, to minister in a working-class neighborhood and lead courses at the Bartolomé de las Casas Center. Justice is a recurring theme in his writings but one Gutiérrez does not clearly define. He offers no systematized theory of justice, no carefully delineated principles of justice. His picture of justice must be "caught" by readers; justice is implicit but not explicit in Gutiérrez.

David Hollenbach, a Catholic human rights theorist and professor of moral theology at Weston School of Theology, stresses participation and mutuality in justice. He has written three books: *Claims in Conflict: Retrieving the Catholic Human Rights Tradition; Justice, Peace, and Human Rights: American Catholic Social Ethics in a Pluralistic World;* and *Nuclear Ethics: A Christian Moral Argument.* Hollenbach is a Roman Catholic priest and a Jesuit. His two books on human rights offer a compelling and coherent interpretation of the change in the Catholic Church's position on global human rights, setting contemporary Catholic human rights theory in the context of 100 years of Catholic social teaching. For Hollenbach, justice is rooted in solidarity with all persons, especially the poor.

Karen Lebacqz, Protestant ethicist and professor of Christian ethics at the Pacific School of Religion, studied at Wellesley College and Harvard University. Ordained to the ministry in the United Church of Christ, she serves on the board of directors for the United Church of Christ AIDS Ministry in northern California. Besides her two books on justice, *Six Theories of Justice: Perspectives from Philosophical and Theological Ethics* and *Justice in an Unjust World,* Lebacqz has written two books on ministerial ethics for pastors and parishioners. Lebacqz writes explicitly about justice and injustice, with a bias for the poor and oppressed. She begins conversation about justice not with words about free exchange in a rational world, but with the experience of injustice in a world tainted by human sin. A Christian theory of justice must begin with the experience of injustice since "a mirror held up to our world reveals the rupture of justice and the reign of injustice."[9]

Michael Walzer, political theorist formerly at Harvard University and now at the Institute for Advanced Studies in Princeton, studied at Brandeis University, Cambridge University, and Harvard University. In addition to his work as professor of social science at the Institute for Advanced Studies, he serves as a contributing editor for *Tikkun* and *Dissent*. Walzer's books and articles reflect diverse interests and commitments; he has written about the Puritan Revolution, Jewish-Palestinian relations, the anti-Vietnam movement, social democracy, and the value of the community in discerning the shape of justice. Walzer envisions a plurality of justice systems, based on a social understanding of distributive justice and opposition to the injustice of domination. For Walzer, concentrations of economic power and political power represent threats to justice.

Theologians, ethicists, and philosophers write of the need for justice. In seminars and symposiums, articles and books, authors painstakingly describe justice—its shape and resulting behaviors. Unfortunately, in the desire to describe justice adequately, the same authors have sometimes ignored the pervasive injustice that creates havoc throughout the earth. Karen Lebacqz correctly suggests that the beginning place for a study of justice for mere humans, all perpetrators of some type of injustice, is injustice.

The Nature of Injustice

A. D. Woozley maintains that injustice is more morally interesting than justice. At the least injustice is "unfair discrimination between persons or groups in the distribution of advantages and disadvantages," but Woozley insists that this definition is merely the first step in the analysis of injustice.[10] The judgment of discrimination must be based on criteria relevant to the distribution of the advantages or disadvantages.

Woozley's second step moves readers toward what is offensive in the discrimination. He suggests a number of factors as a basis for examination of injustice but sees *conformity to rule* as the most important. Indeed this category has the greatest relevance for the human rights situation in Guatemala. Citizens have the right to expect justice either from the existence of rules, such as a constitution or the United Nations Declaration of Human Rights, or from positive morality, customs, or traditions. When rules are broken and discrimination and injustice occur, victims see others who are not relevantly different being treated better. The perpetrator of the discrimination, whether government official or business owner, implicitly denies that some persons, or in Guatemala's case, a majority of the citizens, possess rights and privileges that other citizens enjoy.

In his analysis of injustice, Barrington Moore connects moral outrage and the sense of injustice. Moore first looks at recurring situations that people universally recognize as unjust, then moves to historical examples of injustice. Authority figures create moral codes for the advantage of their group and to the detriment of minority groups. Moore locates injustice largely among the bottom members of the social order—people with no economic or political power, prestige, education, or influence.

Injustice and oppression occur primarily in three realms: authority and challenge to authority, the distribution of goods and services, and the division of labor. Within the realm of authority, Moore concludes that rulers, including all institutions of the state, are obligated to protect all citizens, maintain peace and order, and to contribute to material security.[11] Often injustice occurs when an imbalance of power or wealth exists and when those in authority inappropriately use violence against groups or individuals. Through the social and psychological domination by authorities, the victims of injustice learn to devalue themselves or to accept domination as a part of the natural order.

Given the reality of injustice in the world today, compassionate Christians and disciples from all religious traditions support a move from injustice to justice. In spite of definitions of justice and well-meaning people, the problem remains—how to move from the lived reality of injustice to justice. The world is on a collision course with injustice, environmental devastation and destruction, violence in families and society, economic exploitation, ethnic cleansing, and oppression of the powerless. Is all talk of justice grasping at straws? Or can we develop a better understanding of justice that will motivate North American women and men to respond to injustice?

In the Beginning: Injustice

The tapestry that is Karen Lebacqz's theory of justice contains various strands that represent injustice and suffering. Echoing liberation themes, she suggests that studies of justice begin appropriately with an exploration of the context of injustice. Woven throughout *Justice in an Unjust World* are portraits of injustice—quotes and stories of those who experience injustice as a daily reality. It is from those who suffer the daily victimization by oppressive structures and fallen systems that we learn best how to move from injustice to justice.

With a litany from victims of political, economic, sexual, racial, and ethnic injustice, Lebacqz paints a portrait that assails the senses. With the eyes of the heart we see Nicaraguan peasants grieving a son shot in the night and California farm workers struggling to make a living wage. We hear the slur of ethnic jokes and the cry of a woman who has been raped. We smell rotten food at garbage dumps as the homeless search for food. We feel the sting of blows on the back of a South African youth and the shame of a Korean woman forced to endure harassment to keep her job.

Gutiérrez also begins with the concrete experience of injustice. He agrees with Juan Luis Segundo that the world should not be the way it is. Gutiérrez rejects theology from above as the primary point of departure. He insists instead on beginning with the concrete situation of oppression. He begins with the concrete experience of injustice, which represents a radical shift for theology. Modern theology concerns itself with the critiques of religion that have risen in response to the advances of science and technology in a post-Enlightenment world. It embraces questions that are articulated by well-educated and technologically proficient people. Gutiérrez believes modern theology considers first unbelievers, persons in "a world come of age" who find faith in God difficult or impossible.

Beginning theology with the concrete experience of injustice prompts liberation theologians to consider first nonpersons, poor and oppressed persons from the underside of history. Gutiérrez asserts,

> in Latin America the challenge does not come first and foremost from nonbelievers but from nonpersons—that is, those whom the prevailing social order does not acknowledge as persons: the poor, the exploited, those systematically and lawfully stripped of their human status, those who hardly know what a human being is. Nonpersons represent a challenge, not primarily to our religious world but to our economic, social, political, and cultural world; their existence is a call to a revolutionary transformation of the very foundations of our dehumanizing society.[12]

· Justice as Participation

Throughout Guatemala, boys and girls, women and men, yearn for a country where they can experience justice as participation. But day after day, their marginalization reinforces the reality that there are two Guatemalas. In one Guatemala, well-fed children attend private schools, talk with classmates and teachers in their own language, and at the end of the day eat steak and potatoes in their homes with electricity and water. Their parents, usually educated at universities in Guatemala or the United States, work at jobs with substantial salaries and participate in political parties and neighborhood associations.

In the other Guatemala, children do not attend school, because there is no school or they are needed to work in the fields to supplement their family's income. Even if the children go to school, they probably have a teacher who does not speak their language, or they are crowded into a one-room school with 100 children and one teacher. At the end of the day, they eat tortillas and beans in their one-room home with a candle for lighting and no safe water. Their mother and father work in factories or coffee plantations or sell produce in the local market. They belong to no political party, neighborhood association, or union—the past fifteen years of repression have taught them the cost of membership in groups—whether human rights, union, or church groups. They vote, but only to avoid being labeled "guerrilla," a label that can lead to disappearance or death.

Marginalization leads to many forms of injustice in Guatemala. These include inadequate education, housing, and health care, dehumanizing poverty, poor land distribution, underemployment and unemployment, a corrupt judiciary, and an unrepresentative legislature. Guatemalans are silenced not because they cannot speak, but because they lack a meaningful voice in political, economic, and social structures. Structures of domination imprison them in a "culture of silence."

Marginalization occurs when persons are excluded from participation in their community. The Bible teaches inclusion, not exclusion; participation, not marginalization. Thus marginalization is an affront to biblical teachings on justice. In their pastoral letter on Catholic social teachings and the economy, the U.S. bishops write,

> Basic justice demands the establishment of minimum levels of participation in the life of the human community for all persons. The ultimate injustice is for a person or group to be actively treated or passively abandoned as if they were nonmembers of the human race.[13]

In countries throughout the world, marginalization takes different but often interlinking forms. When peasants are denied the right to vote, have their lands taken away without due process, or are harassed or tortured for political views, they experience political marginalization. When women or men work long hours for unjust salaries, are deprived of land due to unequal land distribution, or are unable to feed their families because of soaring inflation, they experience economic marginalization. When women are not given the opportunity to be educated, are refused jobs and equal salaries, or endure harassment and abuse to keep a job, they experience gender marginalization.

Hollenbach finds the answer for marginalization in participation in social life. In his explanation of the importance of *Pacem in Terris* for the Catholic human rights tradition, he distinguishes between three types of rights according to how they are actualized and institutionalized by different countries and cultures. These are personal, social, and instrumental rights. Figure 1 schematizes (makes a systematic arrangement for) the relationships between the rights.

Personal rights, such as those to bodily integrity, work, and religious belief, reflect basic needs of the individual. Social rights, such as the right to a living wage and decent working conditions, or the right to education, are personal rights that require social and communal mediation for their fulfillment. Instrumental rights, such as the right to a social security system or the right to religious freedom, are mediated through larger institutions that shape our social existence. *Pacem in Terris* illustrates the linkage of all three sets of rights and the Catholic Church's commitment to human dignity and human rights.

Not content merely to describe the rights and their inner relationships, Hollenbach acknowledges the likelihood of competing and conflicting claims and suggests that the primacy of the full set of social rights helps to settle judicially competing claims.

> Social rights, such as the rights to political participation, adequate food, health care, assembly, protection, etc., identify kinds of social interaction which are essential to human dignity. Without these, people can neither survive nor flourish.[14]

As the expressions of the obligations that society has to its members, social rights are necessary for human dignity. Social rights recognize that an individual is always a person-in-community and someone who depends on other members of society, or on the community itself, for sustenance and survival. Similarly, social rights affirm the interdependence and mutuality of human society.

Gutiérrez also concludes that social rights should be central in any human rights policy. During the Carter administration, foreign policy reflected concern for human rights, however imperfectly, but the human rights focus was dropped during the Reagan administration. In several countries, the new administration supported dictators who flagrantly violated human rights.

In countries supported by the Reagan administration, like Guatemala and El Salvador, where massacres conducted by the military terrorized populations, world opinion was fixed more on civil and political rights—suppression of freedom of associa-

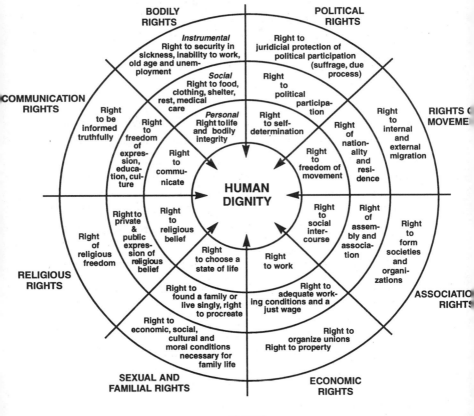

Figure 5

**Personal, Social, and Instrumental Rights:
An Interpretation of *Pacem in Terris* [14]**

tion and dissent, freedom of free speech and a free press—than on social and economic rights. When focus is exclusively on political rights, such as torture, the government and the world community think "that the human rights problem has been solved" when torture is abolished or lessened.[16] Gutiérrez calls us to recognize that the starvation of a child, a mother's death in childbirth, a family living in a garbage dump are all violent and inexcusable violations of human rights.

To provide guidance for deciding among social rights for human rights policies and competing claims, Hollenbach provides three strategic moral principles:

1. The needs of the poor take priority over the wants of the rich.
2. The freedom of the dominated takes priority over the liberty of the powerful.
3. The participation of marginalized groups takes priority over the preservation of an order which excludes them.[17]

Strategic moral principles provide empirical guidelines for prioritizing human rights claims and criteria for deciding which person or group has the most urgent need. Of course, the use of the principles presupposes a willingness to acknowledge that groups in the community or society are excluded because of economic status, political persuasion, ethnicity, or gender.

If Hollenbach's three principles are applied to *de facto* human rights policies in Guatemala, indigenous children will be educated in their own languages, factory workers will form unions and earn a living wage, widows will receive social security payments after the deaths of their husbands, and women in groups like CONAVIGUA and GAM will be encouraged to continue the struggle for human rights. If his three principles are applied to *de facto* human rights policies in the United States, migrant workers will receive a living wage and humane working conditions, single parents will find affordable childcare, and welfare mothers will not fear that their children will be placed in orphanages.

Similarly, Walzer strongly criticizes marginalization, exclusion, and domination. He recognizes that participation in all kinds of diverse communities is an integral part of the human experience and that our obligations differ, depending on the kind of group or community of which we are a member. Within the different "spheres of justice" different criteria should be used to govern the distribution of goods—never allowing the domination of one sphere by another.

Walden Bello reminds us that marginalization and abuse of human rights does not just happen only to individuals and groups but also to entire countries and regions. Human rights language must be used collectively—for poor nations as well as for individuals, for economic and social rights as well as for civil and political rights.[18] Denis Goulet affirms human rights for individuals and nations and broadens the principle to a concrete one of social justice: no wealthy nation should receive luxury needs until poor nations have their basic human needs met.[19] Basic human needs include political rights—such as the right to vote and participate in a political party—but also include the right to participate as an equal partner in the social and economic realm. All meaningful conversation about justice and human rights that does "not take into account the deep causes of the present conditions and the real prerequisite of building a just society [is] merely escapist."[20]

Participation rights encompass economic, political, gender, and cultural rights. The following four sections describe the shape of justice as participation for the economic, political, gender, and cultural dimensions of life.

Economic Justice

Gutiérrez's understanding of justice demands that the church must give a special preference to the poor and oppressed. The church's response to poverty becomes a litmus test for justice. In the past, the church has oppressed the poor and turned a blind eye as systems and structures oppressed the poor. The past cannot be undone but the church can make a new and fresh commitment to struggle with and for the poor.

The term *preferential option for the poor* became the unifying theme for the Third Consejo Episcopal Latinoamericano in Puebla, Mexico, in 1979. Gutiérrez and other liberation theologians, although key figures in Latin American religious life, were officially excluded from the Puebla meeting because of the "corrupting" influence of liberation theology. Eager to have their own "experts" and not just consultants hired by the conservative faction, progressive bishops rented a house outside the seminary grounds for Gutiérrez and 39 other theologians and social scientists. The group prepared 84 papers that the progressive bishops collected and presented at the meetings. Moises Sandoval estimates that 25 percent of the final document was written by Gutiérrez and others.[21]

With attention to the plight of women in poverty, the Puebla document acknowledged the changing face of poverty and the exponential growth of poverty in the ten years since CELAM II in Medellín. The bishops applauded organization by the poor and all efforts for social justice, especially in Christian base communities. In "A Missionary Church Serving Evangelization in Latin America," they announced "the need for conversion on the part of the whole Church to a preferential option for the poor."[22]

Gutiérrez writes convincingly of the need for this preferential option in writings beyond his Puebla contributions. He grounds the preferential option on the historical example of Jesus who was born poor, chose to live with the poor, and gave preference to the poor. In *The Power of the Poor in History*, Gutiérrez insists that Jesus "is proclaiming a kingdom of justice and liberation, to be established in favor of the poor, the oppressed, and the marginalized of history."[23]

The biblical grounding for the preferential option for the poor is not limited to the life and ministry of Jesus, for the entire Bible mirrors God's preference for the poor and oppressed. With this understanding it becomes the mission of the church to work for and with the poor, joining in the struggle for justice.

While Gutiérrez does not name one primary injustice, he focuses on the injustice of poverty. Identifying poverty as institutionalized violence, Gutiérrez calls it the "most murderous kind of violence" because poverty is accepted as part of the legal order. Through his eyes, we see the cyclical and structural nature of poverty. Aggravated by unjust political and economic structures, unemployment and underemployment, lack of education and heath care, poverty brings death and destruction to individuals, families, communities, and ethnic groups.

Gutiérrez considers defense of the rights of the poor a biblical mandate and the major focus of human rights. In fact, although he acknowledges the value of human rights in the liberal tradition, he contends Christians have a stronger grounding for human rights in the prophetic tradition of the Bible.

> Justice and rights cannot be emptied of the content bestowed on them by the Bible. Defending human rights means above all defending the rights of the poor. It is a prophetic theme, and one deeply rooted in the tradition of the church. . . . Our understanding of the true meaning, and biblical requirement, of the defense of human rights will originate with the poor of Latin American society. Here is where we shall begin to grasp that this task is an expression of the gospel proclamation, and not some subtle form of power-grabbing, or presenting a program as a political alternative in Latin America. The church does not receive its prophetic inspiration from adherence to a liberal program, but from its roots in a world of poverty.[24]

The defense of human rights, then, becomes much more than an optional program of social justice. Instead, because of God's concern for the poor, the struggle is integral to the mission of the church.

Gutiérrez clearly distinguishes between the liberal, bourgeois concept of human rights and the Christian understanding. Although the two traditions share some emphases and history, Gutiérrez believes the bourgeois understanding does not fit the Latin American setting because social equality never existed in Latin American societies.

> The Indians and the blacks were never really recognized as others,
> different and equal in status in their culture and religion. . . .
> Christianity always showed sensitivity to the poor, but was impla-
> cable and ethnocentric when confronted with cultural difference.
> The "other," the indigenous person, the black person, was regard-
> ed as the enemy, the pagan, the infidel.[25]

With its beginnings in the North American and French revolutions, the bourgeois understanding of justice and human rights
emphasizes individualism, universality, and equality.

An emphasis on human rights will translate to a better life for
all people, not just economic and political rights for the minority
business or military elite. In Latin America the poor have been
ignored as recipients of economic and political rights. At best,
they have been treated as second-class citizens.

A just human rights policy in Latin America and the United
States will have many results. They include support for measur-
able standards for progress in poverty programs; job training for
women leading to employment, especially in countries like El
Salvador, Guatemala, and Nicaragua where war has left a high
percentage of widows; loans to poor people that enables them to
provide their own basic needs; public assistance that empowers
persons in poverty; and agricultural assistance for poor farmers
that encourages local food production by small farmers instead
of export agriculture or agriculture dominated by agribusiness.

Political Justice

During former President Bush's whirlwind tour of five Latin
American countries in December 1990, he celebrated the end of
authoritarian politics in the region and commended the countries for their expressions of democracy. Bush was not wrong to
celebrate democratization, because democratic societies aid the
growth of peace. But perhaps he could have encouraged democratic societies that allow for greater participation of their citi-
zenry as well as societies that emphasize human rights, demilita-
rization, and equity.

The two main political justice issues in Guatemala and in other third world countries are national security ideology and human rights violations. Both are linked to discussions about democratization, and both demonstrate the connection between political justice and economic justice. National security ideology provides the rationale for repression, often in the form of massive abuse of human rights.

In national security ideology, the needs of the state are elevated above the needs of the individual or minority group because of a real or perceived crisis in national security. A small minority of the political, economic, or military elite maintains control not through popular support or consensus, but through coercion and repression. The state, nation, and military are seen as integrally related, almost synonymous. Therefore criticism and civil disobedience are not tolerated without serious repercussions—any criticism is regarded as unpatriotic. To protect against internal subversion and destruction of the state, the ruler or military often suspends political rights and freedoms to maintain control.

Margaret Crahan believes that national security doctrine has negative consequences for human rights. In her study of Latin American military-dominated countries espousing national security doctrine, she discovered that the concentration of power in the hands of a minority elite lessens popular participation in government and gives the military permission to use force, legally or illegally, to preserve order.[26]

Because of the flagrant use of torture in Guatemala, most conversation about human rights centers on the abuse of political rights. Although the entire population, except for the minority elite, is the target of state terrorism, it would be wrong to confine terrorism exclusively to political terrorism. Torture and political repression are inextricably linked to economic deprivation. Patricia Weiss Fagan of the Center for International Policy determined that countries which violate the civil and political rights of their citizens also do not respect their social and economic rights.[27] Alongside the abuse of political rights, countries like Guatemala enforce economic terrorism by not meeting the basic human needs of their population. This yields a population weakened by hunger, homelessness, and desperation. At the least justice as participation requires the empowerment of poor people so they can take part as equal partners in both the political and economic realm.

Gender Justice

At the June 1993 United Nations conference on human rights in Austria, the representatives could not reach consensus on one issue, women's rights. During a recent forum on AIDS, Mardge Cohen suggested that the campaign to supply women with condoms was misdirected since statistics on violence against women reveal their lack of power, whether in the home or the workplace. Women are not free to refuse sex, demand the use of condoms, or insist on their partner's fidelity. Women's poverty is on the rise; even if women work full-time, they average only 54 percent of what men earn.[28]

Although Hollenbach does not write specifically about women, his three priority principles have great relevance for gender justice. His first principle, "The needs of the poor take priority over the wants of the rich," relates to justice for women, since a majority of the poor in the United States and third world countries are women and children. His second and third principles argue for the priority of "the freedom of the dominated" and "the participation of marginalized groups"—two categories where women clearly fit the criteria. Since many women are poor, dominated, and part of marginalized groups, their needs should be considered when shaping government policies and programs or church policies and programs.

Lebacqz names exploitation as the primary form of injustice; domination and oppression grow out of exploitation. Especially sensitive to injustice against women, she names and describes the oppression and exploitation that women suffer—from the economic injustice of the feminization of poverty to the sexual injustice of rape, harassment, and other forms of violence against women. Her sensitivity to violence against women resonates with the experiences of Guatemalan women and women in the United States.

In the past twenty years since the beginning of Latin American liberation theology, Gutiérrez has made substantive progress in his support of women. Initially, like other liberation theologians, he concentrated on the marginalization and oppression of the poor, with scarce mention of the injustices suffered by women. Now he speaks of the double and triple oppression and marginalization of women. At his request, the first study commissioned by the Bartolemé de las Casas Center dealt with the oppression of women in Peru.[29] In 1988 Gutiérrez wrote, "We in Latin America are only beginning to wake up to the unacceptable and inhuman character of their [women's] situation."[30] Feminist theologians Elisabeth Schüssler Fiorenza, Carter Heyward, and Elsa Tamez speak with appreciation about his influence on their thought.

Even though he is part of a *machismo* culture and a church dominated by patriarchal dominance, Gutiérrez writes with sensitivity about women. Although he does not discuss sexism in the 1971 edition of *A Theology of Liberation*, he does acknowledge women's place in the struggle for liberation in Latin America, especially in Christian base communities. In the introduction to the revised edition, he corrects his previous error and writes briefly on the feminization of poverty. His strongest statement about women is in *Against Machismo*, Elsa Tamez's interviews with third world theologians.

> First, like any profound oppression, the oppression of women damages all of society in an intolerable way. Not only are women marginalized and oppressed, but also a sick human society results. . . . Second, not only must we be sensitive to the intolerable situation of women in society today, but we must also be sensitive to all that human society is losing because of this oppression. I'm

very much afraid that by speaking of their oppression we will approach women in a condescending way: "That poor little thing is
so marginalized and oppressed, we need to help her out." I think
we need to join in solidarity with women's demands because otherwise we miss out on too much ourselves.[31]

Gutiérrez and other liberation theologians must continue to include women's issues, particularly the double and triple oppression that women suffer in Latin America, when they discuss injustice.

Walzer's writings on justice have been commended and ap-
propriated by feminist authors. Feminist political theorist Iris
Marion Young shares his strong opposition to domination and
oppression and "adopts Walzer's threefold definition of justice
as life, liberty, and participation in community."[32] Believing that
contemporary theories of justice have not been sufficiently informed by the experiences of oppressed groups, she advocates
beginning a concept of justice with the experience of domination and oppression.[33] Young applauds Walzer for a definition of
justice that is concrete and particular, not universal and abstract.
She shares Walzer's commitment for justice structures that challenge structures of domination and exclusion so that every
group and citizen participates in public dialogues and democratic decision-making.

Similarly, Susan Moller Okin praises Walzer's *Spheres of
Justice* for its beneficial attention to women and gender and to injustice in the family. She believes the gendered division of labor
in the family puts women at a disadvantage. Some women experience as a trap a gendered system which gives them the major responsibility for childcare and housework. A just society requires family structures which do not trap women through in-
flexible gender expectations. But because the family has been
relegated to the private realm, social theorists have not dealt
with oppressive family structures. Walzer's insistence that the
family is a separate "sphere of justice," and his awareness of the
power imbalance between the sexes and pervasive discrimina-

tion gives Okin hope for justice in the family.[34]

Although appreciative of Walzer, Okin takes further than Walzer the feminist implications of the separate spheres criterion for justice. She maintains that gender is a serious threat to Walzer's complex equality, since many think that the gender situation is either just or unalterable. Although Walzer admits that women are defined by their position in the family, and the family structure must be reformed, he says that "the real domination of women has less to do with their familial place than with their exclusion from other places."[35] Okin is not blind to injustice in political, economic, and social life but believes that the present family structure is unjust. This injustice reinforces the injustice in other spheres.

Like Young, Okin appreciates Walzer's "radically particularistic principles of justice." She commends his definition of justice for its focus on "pervasive inequality and dominance. It has the potential to be a valuable tool for feminist criticism."[36] Feminist writings argue against objective, neutral, and universal pronouncements. Instead, feminists value subjective, personal, and contextual statements. Walzer comments, "The task of a social critic is precisely to touch the conscience. . . . You can't do that from a stance of turning your back; you have to do that as an insider."[37]

His identification of a social critic in *The Company of Critics: Social Criticism and Political Commitment in the Twentieth Century* as a "connected critic" who stands "inside the cave" resonates with women's experiences in social-change movements. Such social critics are women like Eleanor Roosevelt or Rigoberta Menchú, who are not detached and emotionally uninvolved but are intensely committed to social justice in spite of the costs.

Cultural Justice

Beginning with the invasion of Guatemala by Spain in 1523, indigenous Guatemalans have experienced marginalization and domination at the hands of political and economic elites. Hundreds of thousands of indigenous people died, first because of the cruelty of Spanish conquistador Pedro de Alvarado, then through the forced labor system and the introduction of European diseases by the Spaniards.

Today more than four million Guatemalans are indigenous, representing 60 percent of the Guatemalan population. Although they speak different languages and wear different *trajes*, or traditional dress, the 22 groups of Mayan Indians share similar religious practices, forms of economic cooperation, worldviews, and history. Even more important, they share the experience of oppression by the minority elite. Social and economic indicators testify to their oppression and marginalization. Certainly they are a significant majority of the 87 percent poor of Guatemala. In addition, while the life expectancy for a Guatemalan is 63 years, the life expectancy for an indigenous person is 44 years. Likewise, the illiteracy rate for Guatemalans is 49 percent but for indigenous persons, 77 percent.[38]

Since the conquest, indigenous Guatemalans have struggled to survive and maintain their identities as separate communities and cultures, and yet be part of the Guatemalan culture. Throughout the years, they have been denied political, economic, and social rights.

> Today what makes the victims [indigenous people] suffer most is the fact of not being recognized, the fact that their cultures are despised, their languages banned in schools, their religions still persecuted by the churches and their feasts mocked.[39]

Although the constitution promises them equality, they have been excluded from participation in party politics, since the government has not legalized political parties that represent the interests of poor and indigenous people since 1954. Susanne Jonas insists, "In this situation that approaches *de facto* apartheid, issues of ethnic identity and democratic rights for the indigenous majority of the population have become central."[40] Guatemala today is a multicultural nation, yet the political and economic elite have not included the majority indigenous population in political, economic, and social structures of society.

Glen Stassen sees two principles of Walzer's understanding of justice as having particular relevance for cultural justice: "Domination is always wrong; and persons and communities must always be respected."[41] In Guatemala's case, the indigenous population has been dominated since the conquest by Spain. The form of domination has changed through the years: In the 1970s and 1980s, the military used political violence to subdue the population. Today, although there is still excessive political violence, the form of domination is economic through an export-based economy and austerity measures that cripple the poor. Clearly, indigenous persons and communities are not respected. In Guatemala, many ladinos use racist expressions like *no seas indio* (don't be an Indian) or *es más estúpido que un indio* (he or she is dumber than an Indian). They characterize Indians as lazy, dirty, barbaric, and untrustworthy.

Walzer emphasizes three rights: to life, liberty, and community. *The right to life* includes the negative right not to be robbed of life, and the positive right to the goods of life. When applied to Guatemala, the negative dimension of this right means that indigenous persons would no longer be denied access to health care, education, or political parties because they are indigenous. No longer would they fear being abducted and tortured by the military. The positive dimension to this right would guarantee all Guatemalans, whether indigenous or ladino, basic human needs and the opportunities to pursue their own vocational interests.

The right to liberty consists of "the negative right not to be robbed of basic personal liberties" and "the positive right to participate in decision-making and value-creating."[42] For indigenous Guatemalans, the negative right means that they no longer need fear participation in voluntary associations, whether church group or agricultural cooperative. They would be able to form or join a union without fear for their lives. The positive freedom of participation would enable indigenous Guatemalans to become cocreators of Guatemalan society and to participate actively in business, politics, education, or any other dimension of Guatemalan life.

The right to community is seen most clearly in Walzer's writings on membership. This includes the negative right not to be excluded from a community and the positive right to have and to defend a community. The application of the negative right means that indigenous persons would not have to fear reprisals for participation in the political life of their city or department. Walzer affirms the positive right of membership in a particular community in *Spheres of Justice.*

> We are (all of us) culture-producing creatures; we make and inhabit meaningful worlds. Since there is no way to rank and order these worlds with regard to their understanding of social goods, we do justice to actual men and women by respecting their particular creations. . . . Justice is rooted in the distinct understandings of places, honors, jobs, things of all sorts, that constitute a shared way of life. To override those understandings is (always) to act unjustly.[43]

As a result of the positive right, indigenous persons in Guatemala—whether Mam, Tzutuhil, or Quiché—would have a voice in their own culture and community and as members of a culture within Guatemala would have a voice in Guatemala.

Walzer's right to membership can be seen explicitly in his essay about social critic Randolph Bourne. While many early twentieth-century North Americans were calling for the assimilation of immigrants into the dominant culture, he affirmed a multicultural society. Bourne's vision of the United States was filled with the richness of cultural diversity. He criticized U.S. citizens who repressed their cultural identity and challenged his contemporaries to build an open, democratic, cooperative society that valued diversity.

Bourne's "beloved community," like Martin Luther King Jr.'s

similar vision, represents a radically inclusive vision of the United States, one that celebrates the presence and participation of cultures within the larger culture. Swedish-Americans, Irish-Americans, African-Americans, and members of other immigrant groups are "pluralist citizens." Walzer defines such a citizen as "one who receives protection and shares in the ruling and being ruled, not in spite of plural memberships, but because of them."[44] Bourne was a true cultural pluralist; he celebrated foreign-sounding names, different cultures, and diverse languages.

In Guatemala, Bourne would discourage the assimilation of indigenous cultures into the ladino culture. Instead, drawing on his vision of "the beloved community," he would encourage ladinos not to be threatened by the different dress, language, and customs of the indigenous population, but to celebrate the richness of the different cultural groups. Certainly Bourne, as described by Walzer, would applaud the statement of the delegates at the Second Continental *Encuentro*: "Only when [the governments] recognize our rights as a community and as indigenous peoples, taking into account our cultures, can we say that we have begun to construct a true democracy."[45]

Of course, Guatemala is different in one respect from the United States. In Guatemala indigenous groups form the majority of the population; the immigrant groups in the United States constitute a much smaller percentage of the population. Still, I suspect that Walzer's Bourne would celebrate the existence of a country with at least 22 different cultural groups and encourage all Guatemalans to work together to shape "the beloved community."

In the revised edition of *A Theology of Liberation*, Gutiérrez addresses two aspects of injustice (in his words, two aspects of poverty) not given sufficient attention in his earlier writings: racism and sexism. He confesses that the first edition only addressed the economic and social aspects of poverty, ignoring racism and sexism. Repudiating the idea that Latin America is free of racism, Gutiérrez acknowledges the marginalization of black and indigenous populations and applauds their efforts to gain human rights and respect.

Two factors have helped indigenous Guatemalans participate in the struggle for human rights. First, during the 1970s the Catholic Church, influenced by liberation theology, served as a vehicle for lay leadership training and development through Catholic Action groups and Christian base communities. Also in the late 1980s, after the election of a progressive archbishop, Próspero Penados del Barrio, the church became more outspoken on human rights and social justice—thus gaining more credibility with poor and indigenous persons.

Second, as devastating as the years of military violence in the highlands were, the blatant ethnic oppression served as a catalyst for many indigenous persons to enter the popular movement and for members of the larger popular movement to be advocates for and with the indigenous population. The popular sector is the only part of Guatemalan society that reflects the multiculturalism of Guatemala's population. Today a majority of the members of CUC, GAM, and CONAVIGUA are indigenous, and the indigenous population is well represented at all levels of leadership in organizations in the popular movement.

Justice as Radically Historical Narrative

Lebacqz, Walzer, and Gutiérrez reject a justice that is an ahistorical, abstract, individualistic, universal mathematical formula of fairness or a legal transaction. Instead, they demand a justice that is concrete, specific, and historically particularistic. Justice and injustice are radically historical—an act of injustice today cannot be isolated from its social and historical context.

Lebacqz constructs her framework for justice on the foundation of narrative—the meaning of justice is embedded in biblical stories combined with stories of suffering and struggle in contemporary society. Since human justice is a response to our relationship with God, a Christian theory of justice must attend to biblical images of justice as a window to God's response to injustice. Refusing to reduce biblical narrative to neat propositional formulas, Lebacqz draws on biblical stories to form building blocks for a theory of justice.

Since the Bible has been used as a tool of oppression by conquistadores in South America, Afrikaners in South Africa, and slave owners in the United States, Lebacqz demands a new hermeneutic, one with historical consciousness that looks at Scripture from the perspective of the poor and oppressed. For Lebacqz biblical remembrance, always from the perspective of the oppressed, is the ground where justice must be built. With this understanding of biblical remembrance, she examines several biblical texts that demonstrate God's and the community's response to injustice.

Gutiérrez first calls for a reconstruction of history to include the poor and marginalized. Written from the perspective of the dominant powers, history does not include the voices and experiences of the oppressed. Justice demands a history that recovers the forgotten voices—voices of women and girls, indigenous and black people, slum dwellers and domestic servants, farmers and factory workers.

Oppression and exploitation of Latin America began with the economic and political conquest and colonization by Spain and Portugal in the fifteenth and sixteenth centuries. Instead of claiming political imperialism or economic greed as motives for the conquest, the "new lands" ostensibly were conquered for spiritual reasons. According to the colonizers, the spiritual poverty of the newly discovered territory made necessary the salvation of the pagan indigenous peoples. The church justified any violence or plunder deemed necessary by conquering armies as a missionary impulse. Serving the interests of the conquering armies and the church, priests like Juan Ginés de Sepúlveda became apologists for the conquest. He argued that Indians were inferior human beings and natural slaves.

In prudence, talent, virtue, and humanity they are as inferior to the Spaniards as children to adults, women to men, as the wild and cruel to the most meek, as the prodigiously intemperate to the continent and temperate, that I have almost said, as monkeys to men.[46]

Therefore, wars to formalize this distinction were legitimate and necessary for the salvation of the Indians.

However, even in the midst of theological justification of injustice against the Indian population, priests like sixteenth-century Bartolomé de las Casas refuted Sepúlveda's theses and condemned violence against the Indians. In a world where the church identified more with the conquistadores than with poor Spaniards and Indians, Las Casas courageously condemned perpetrators of violence and church leaders who justified violence. Gutiérrez commends him for his commitment to the Indians through his ministry to them and his theological work refuting Sepúlveda and other apologists. An advocate of social justice who viewed the Indians more as poor persons than as pagans to be subjugated, Las Casas proclaimed that the salvation of those who exploited Indians was in jeopardy, for "it is impossible for anyone to be saved who does not observe justice."[47]

Gutiérrez praises Las Casas for beginning a theology for the marginalized. Confronting religious and political structures that defended the privileged regardless of the cost in the human lives of Indians and poor Spaniards, Las Casas practiced "theology from the underside"—theology that considers first the marginalized and oppressed of society. By identifying the persecuted and murdered Indians with Christ, he viewed Christ as one of the marginalized. In fact, Las Casas saw "Jesus Christ, our God, scourged, afflicted, and crucified, not once, but millions of times."[48]

Like Lebacqz, Gutiérrez grounds his understanding of justice on God's participation in human history, particularly through the example of Jesus, who confronted the religious and political authorities and was executed as a subversive. From Jesus' involvement in history, we see that history is the location of our encounter with God. Gutiérrez emphasizes that history should not be separated into the sacred and secular—God participates in the whole of human history. With this grounding, the church should be involved wherever injustice exists.

Lebacqz criticizes contemporary theories of justice for their lack of attention to the historical particularity of justice—justice is inextricably tied to historical liberation. In *Six Theories of Justice*, she bemoans the fact that Rawls and Nozick propose theories of justice derived from logically formulated propositions instead of justice grounded in a particular historical context with attention to injustice.

Walzer's concept of reiteration, or reiterative morality, is crucial for justice as radical historical narrative. Instead of basing justice on universal foundations, he argues for a concept of justice that is community-based and grounded in a particular community's historical narrative. In an essay on Martin Buber, Walzer insists that we understand others by reiterating our self-understanding. Reiteration articulates the history and vision of a particular community, giving the community insight into its own identity and helping it to understand and find a place in the larger community. In an article commending Walzer's reiterative justice, Stassen writes, "Reiteration functions both to get us to walk in the shoes of another community, and also to confirm truths we see in our community when others reiterate them."[49]

Walzer's use of reiteration can be seen most clearly in *The Company of Critics*:

> Each authentic critic Walzer studies not only identifies with her or his society, as Walzer argues, but also has a reiterative identification with a second or third community—often a marginalized community within the larger society.[50]

In his essay on Breyten Breytenbach, Walzer contrasts Breytenbach's reiterative morality with the fraudulent universalism of the communists. Although Breytenbach, an Afrikaner critical of apartheid, advocated a unified and participatory South Africa with majority black rule, he still urged white militants to work within their own communities for transformation.

Similarly, Buber suggested binationalism as a creative solution for the Arab-Jewish conflict in Palestine because he was convinced that both Arabs and Jews had legitimate claims to citizenship in Israel. Instead of the polarization that occurs with group egotism, Buber recommends that his fellow Zionists try to understand the position of Palestinians: "We know that . . . we have genuine national unity and a real nationalist movement; why should we assume that these do not exist among the Arabs?"[51] Reiteration for Buber involves listening with his heart to the story of his own people and to the story of Arab sisters and brothers, then responding with small but concrete initiatives that build trust between Arab and Jew.

In *Exodus and Revolution* and *Revolution of the Saints*, Walzer points to the value of the historical community in discerning the shape of justice. In *Exodus and Revolution*, he approaches the Exodus as a story that is part of Western cultural consciousness, a revolutionary response to injustice and oppression that is part of the history of Jewish people. Instead of repressing the memory of the injustice that they suffered in Egypt, the Hebrew people are encouraged to remember the Egyptian experience and to act justly, not as their Egyptian taskmasters acted.

How the remembering of their experience shaped the actions of the Israelites explains the impact of what the authors of *Habits of the Heart* call communities of memory. Bellah insists that communities are more than free-standing groups of people isolated in time and space; they are shaped and formed by their past. He explains,

> A community is involved in retelling its story, its constitutive narrative, and in so doing, it offers examples of the men and women who have embodied and exemplified the meaning of the community. . . . The stories that make up a tradition contain conceptions

of character, of what a good person is like, and of the virtues that define such character. But the stories are not all exemplary, not all about successes and achievements. A genuine community of memory will also tell painful stories of shared suffering that sometimes creates deeper identities than success. . . . The communities of memory that tie us to the past also turn us toward the future as communities of hope. They carry a context of meaning that can allow us to connect our aspirations for ourselves and those closest to us with the aspirations of a larger whole and see our own efforts as being, in part, contributions to a common good.[52]

Guatemalans in the popular sector realize that remembrance is crucial to social change. Frustrated by the lack of women's stories in Guatemalan history taught in schools, the women in GRUFEPROMEFAM opened a documentation center with the sole purpose of recording the history of women who have struggled for justice. Through scarce written resources and oral histories, they have given voice to women like Mama Maquín, who led a nonviolent protest and was martyred by the army. In addition to collecting the stories, they tell them in workshops and use the stories to empower women so they may act for justice.

In spite of the fact that the majority of Guatemala's population is indigenous, schools have not taught the history of indigenous people. The history taught children and adults has largely been a colonial history. The quincentenary of Columbus's arrival to the Americas provided the occasion for the Guatemalan popular sector, including both indigenous and ladinos, to educate Guatemalans about their history.

In 1989, Guatemalans joined indigenous people from countries throughout North, Central, and South America in the campaign of 500 Years of Indigenous, Black, and Popular Resistance. Although the main goal was to bring together indigenous peoples, early in the campaign leaders became convinced that the campaign must include not only indigenous but all peoples. At the Second Continental Gathering of the campaign in Quetzaltenango, Guatemala, in October 1991, Rigoberta Menchú challenged the delegates to tell each other their oral histories. By retelling their stories, they can link the past with the present.

> Here we are, in the place where indigenous people were killed, where women were killed, where children were killed, and where elders were killed. Each of them represented a dream, a dream of the future. All of our dead can live today if we have the will to learn from the past experience and the present experience for the future. . . . Let us dance while building a diverse culture and a vision which accepts the cultural diversity of this old land which is ours.[53]

Through the telling of stories, whether through song, religious ceremony, or history, the participants celebrated unity in diversity and together determined never to be silenced again.

Women in the United States can share in a community of memory by letting their voices ring out with the stories of women—stories largely unknown because women's stories have not been told. To offer remedial education to boys and girls, men and women, women must tell their stories and the stories of their foremothers—horrible stories of women who were tortured, drowned, and burned in the witch trials; inspirational stories of religious women who faithfully served God and ministered to the poor; empowering stories of women who served as role models and pathfinders.

Justice as Praxis

Gutiérrez and other liberation theologians owe a great debt to Brazilian educator Paulo Freire for his critical work on conscientization and praxis. Freire defines praxis as reflection and action to transform the world.[54] Instead of separating action from reflection, he believes that reflection and action are tightly woven together, since all true reflection presupposes action. Freire insists that praxis as reflection and action must be directed at unjust structures of society in need of transformation; otherwise, the action disintegrates into empty words or activism.

Borrowing Freire's understanding of praxis, Gutiérrez also emphasizes an active response to injustice. In fact, praxis *is* the response to injustice—it is not sufficient merely to acknowledge the presence of injustice.

> Theology in Latin America today will be a reflection in, and on, faith as liberation praxis. . . . It will be an understanding of faith from a point of departure in real, effective solidarity with the exploited classes, oppressed ethnic groups, and despised cultures of Latin America, and from within their world.[55]

He is not naive about the cost of work for justice—the struggle for justice led Jesus to the cross. The kind of justice that Jesus practiced, a costly justice, roots out evil structures and systems and builds a new world where God's love is expressed and domination abolished.

Gutiérrez is clear that the mission of the church is not to survive but to serve the weakest members of society, the poor and oppressed. In fact, we become more truly church when we "defend and protect the poor, who are the privileged members of the kingdom; otherwise, there is a contradiction of the very essence of the ecclesial community."[56] We do this by protecting human rights, struggling against powerful interests, and rejecting all forms of violence, whether that of institutions, terrorists, or repression in the name of battling terrorism.

Justice as praxis demands that we resist sin, the ultimate cause of injustice and oppression, by participating in liberation. For Gutiérrez, sin is related to the three dimensions of liberation: liberation from unjust economic and social structures, human liberation throughout history, and liberation from sin.[57] Although he emphasizes the social dimension of sin because the Christian community has paid too little attention to it, Gutiérrez does not ignore the personal dimension of sin. Individuals and groups participate in unjust structures and willingly reject God and neighbors. Resisting sin begins with awareness of personal action and participation in oppressive structures that exploit individuals, ethnic groups, and social classes.

Likewise, built into Lebacqz's approach to injustice is an active response. Along with Gutiérrez, she does not merely acknowledge injustice. To note exploitation without participating in liberation is to affirm injustice by passivity. Instead, she calls Christians to participate in liberation by relentless resistance, rebellion, and redress.

A response from U.S. churches to the situation in Guatemala begins with confession and repentance. We must acknowledge that our country has provided Guatemala with equipment and expertise to cause death and destruction. In addition to the millions of dollars of covert aid through the CIA, from 1981-1990 the U.S. government provided Guatemala with more than $33 million in military loans and grants and weapons valued at $26 million. The administration projected $15 million in military sales for 1993.

Furthermore, our present refugee policy, although reformed in 1980 to emphasize humanitarian considerations, is influenced by foreign policy interests and powerful lobbies like Jewish resettlement organizations and the Indochinese lobby. As a result refugees from countries like Guatemala, where the United States supports the government, rarely are granted asylum. In 1992 only 7 percent of Guatemalans who applied for political asylum in the United States received it.[58] The United States admits little more than 1,000 refugees annually from Africa, a region with four million refugees and much political violence and hunger.

Walzer's mutual aid principle presents a helpful corrective to the refugee policy of the United States, as does his emphasis on hospitality to the stranger. U.S. history strikes familiar chords with the history of the Israelites, for we have been both the "Egyptian taskmasters" oppressing Native Americans and African-Americans and the "Israelite slaves" oppressed by the British. Walzer challenges us to translate our experiences with oppression into just action and mutual aid. The Jewish tradition of remembering the Exodus offers a reminder to citizens of the

United States. The greater the distance from our beginnings as immigrants, the more we forget to identify with those in need. Just as the Israelites' experience in slavery helped shape their moral code, so our experiences as immigrant, oppressor, and the oppressed can help shape a positive and humanitarian immigration policy.

The American Baptist Church found a way to challenge the injustice of the U.S. refugee policy toward Central America by bringing a lawsuit against the Immigration and Naturalization Service.[59] Disturbed by the low rates of political asylum in the 1980s and the knowledge that Guatemalans refused asylum were sent back to Guatemala, perhaps to their deaths, attorneys for the American Baptist Church challenged the basis for asylum adjudications. The INS settled the lawsuit by acknowledging that asylum decisions were based on foreign policy decisions rather than on the law. Now all Guatemalans denied asylum during the past ten years are entitled to new reviews of their cases.

Guatemalans and women in the United States can respond best to their situation of repression and injustice through people power and nonviolent direct action, as seen in the examples of CUC, CONAVIGUA, and GAM. A movement for nonviolent social change through people power begins with a critical awareness of the problem. For people to organize, they must be actively aware of their problems. This happened prior to the beginning of GAM, when women gathered at morgues to identify bodies and began to talk about why their relatives were missing. Another crucial element of a nonviolent social change movement is the articulation of the vision of a new society. Workers involved in the struggle for justice and human rights must be able to imagine a better world, a world without the injustices they now suffer.

Justice as Solidarity

Implicit in Lebacqz's response to injustice is a priority on solidarity, placing her conclusions on justice close to those of liberation theologians, as well as Hollenbach and James McGinnis. For McGinnis, justice has four components: first, the right of every person to sufficient life goods; second, the right to human dignity; third, the right to participation—which includes political and economic rights; and fourth, the right to solidarity—the duty to promote these rights with and for others.[60] For McGinnis, as well as for Lebacqz, Walzer, and Gutiérrez, solidarity means working with people to change political, economic, and cultural situations and structures that victimize people.

The church stands in a unique position to act in solidarity with the people of Guatemala and others who suffer violations of human rights. Guatemalans, like Olga Rivas of GRUFEPROMEFAM, want North Americans to act in solidarity with them.

> We may be poor and need financial resources, but our greater need is for women from the United States to stand with us in the struggle, to tell us their difficulties and victories, and let us tell them ours, and to know that together we become strong.[61]

Voluntary associations, like churches and other groups, are important in the advocacy of human rights. Charles Harper, director of the Human Rights Resource Office for Latin America for the World Council of Churches, explains,

> In every single case where there's been effective, persuasive, persistent work on human rights, there has been involvement by the churches—not just the hierarchies, but the members, the young people, the local pastors. There's a growing maturity to this involvement, so that across Latin America you find dozens of little church-related committees doing their part for human rights in the name of Jesus Christ.[62]

Churches have articulated a creed claiming the image of God in every person, God-given rights to existence, and a special understanding of what it means to be human. With this creed, churches can make human rights claims based on their understanding of moral responsibility for their own life, family, society, and the larger global community.

Churches must affirm a creed that places human rights as a priority, and then design programs, ministries, and activities to reflect the priorities in their creed.

> If the biblically-based religious communities of the West are to maintain the social-ethical leadership and prophetic witness which they have, at their best, demonstrated in the past, they must undertake a clear assessment of rights.[63]

Instead of relegating advocacy and activity of human rights to professional agencies and organizations, churches can act as advocates for human rights and make coalitions with other groups interested in human rights education and advocacy.

Although Stackhouse acknowledges that churches have oppressed persons and have failed to provide moral leadership, he insists that they also have demonstrated a positive impact on human rights. In countries like Nicaragua and the former East Germany, churches created a social space in society for voluntary associations. In Burma, American Baptist churches support peace talks between the government and the insurgents. In El Salvador, the Mennonite Church funds international workers to support Baptist youth who declare themselves conscientious objectors. In Chile and El Salvador, the Catholic Church set up a national office on human rights to monitor the human rights situation and pressure the government for an end to human rights violations.

The women of Guatemala challenge North Americans to act in solidarity with them as they work for justice and human rights, making the connections between the Christian faith and the situation of injustice that Rigoberta Menchú makes.

We began studying [the Bible] more deeply and . . . came to a conclusion. That being a Christian means thinking of our brothers [and sisters] around us, and that every one of our Indian race has a right to eat. . . . It is not God's will that we should live in suffering, that God did not give us that destiny, but that people on earth have imposed this suffering, poverty, misery, and discrimination on us. . . . We have understood that being a Christian means refusing to accept all the injustices which are committed against a humble people who barely know what eating meat is, but who are treated worse than horses. . . . We feel it is the duty of Christians to create the kingdom of God on earth among our brothers [and sisters].[64]

Solidarity begins with the recognition that all of us—women and men, North Americans, Central Americans, Africans, and Asians—are children of the living God. We have lived too long separated by barriers of language, gender, culture, and geography, isolated and afraid of "the other." Especially those of us who are Christians must recover a definition of justice that empowers us to act for justice. With a definition of justice that emphasizes participation and political, economic, gender, and cultural rights, citizens in Guatemala and Christians in North American churches can struggle against dehumanizing marginalization and violations of human rights. Our struggle is fueled by our historical consciousness and biblical remembrance, always remembering the voices of those who are oppressed. As connected critics we work for social change in a thousand small steps, rejecting apathy and individualism for passionate and compassionate actions for peace and justice.

6

Conclusion

SEVERAL years ago Elise Boulding designed a workshop, Imaging a World Without Weapons, to help people visualize a world with peace and justice. She believed that hopes, wishes, and dreams for the future are necessary for justice, and thus she guides participants to form images of a future world where problems that concern them have been solved. Boulding asserts that what happens as the result of this kind of work is that we perceive connections that we normally do not see and develop images of strategies we have never thought of. Imagination becomes a tool for social change as persons visualize a future with peace and justice, then proceed to implement their vision in incremental steps.

Throughout this book, we have seen a glimpse of the vision of Guatemalan women for a world with peace and justice. In this chapter I will comment on their vision of a world with justice. I will explore how their vision may help them in their context and also help North American women engage in creative actions to end their own situations of injustice and to act in solidarity with oppressed persons everywhere.

Guatemalan Women and the Struggle for Justice

Rigoberta Menchú and the women of GAM and CON-AVIGUA represent the women in Guatemala who struggle for human rights and justice through church groups and human rights groups. Like women in El Salvador, Nicaragua, Chile, and Brazil, they have been tireless in their commitment to solidarity and struggle.

Perception of Threat

Guatemalan women's perception of the threat shapes their actions and attitudes. Women and other oppressed persons respond to the situation of injustice through the lens of empirical evidence of injustice and their perception of the situation.

Genocide through poverty and militarism. Poor and indigenous Guatemalan women have firsthand experience of ethnic and class genocide through poverty and militarism. Like the women of Israel who grieved over Jepthah's daughter and Rachel weeping over her children, Guatemalan women mourn the deaths of loved ones. Like Faustina, a Jacalteco refugee, they have witnessed massacres and been subjected to torture. As mothers must have trembled while Herod's soldiers hunted for baby Jesus, so Guatemalan mothers hid their babies while· soldiers searched for the Communities of Population in Resistance hidden in the jungles of the Sierra. The massacre victims in the highlands, the members of CPRs in the Sierra, and other indigenous persons who have been targeted for repression—their crime is only their ethnicity, only that they are different. They speak different languages and wear different clothes. They are part of the 22 groups of Mayan Indians who have lived in Guatemala for hundreds of years, long before the conquistadores from Spain. That is their offense.

Because the largely ladino government is threatened by the indigenous population and because the military elite cannot conceive of a pluralistic state, government specialists developed the doctrine of cultural domination. A 1981 article in *Revista Militar*, Guatemala's military magazine, explains the logic.

> It urges the *ladinoization* of the Ixil population in such a way that it
> ceases to exist as a cultural subgroup. What is meant . . . is that
> they become Spanish speakers, that their distinctive clothing and
> all other external features that differentiate them as a group be
> suppressed.[1]

With the doctrine of cultural domination, the military justified
violence against indigenous persons as necessary for the good of
the state, for national security. At the very least, indigenous persons were to be assimilated into the ladino culture. But beginning with the regime of General Lucas García, the assimilation
took the form of extermination or ethnic cleansing. Colonel
Marco Antonio explains the government's desire to exterminate
the indigenous cultures to the School of Ideological Warfare in
1984.

> The existence of twenty-three ethnic groups demonstrates that we
> are not integrated; we lack a national identity. Who better than the
> men in uniform to project ourselves to every last corner of the Fa-
> therland bearing the message of nationalism.[2]

As a result, indigenous persons have been targeted for repression since 1978.

Poor ladino and indigenous Guatemalans also suffer from
economic exploitation. Economic and social indicators testify to
the severity of poverty, but Guatemalan women do not need
World Bank figures or statistics from UNICEF to educate them
about poverty. Instead of quoting statistics on maternal morbidity and infant mortality, they see mothers and babies die at birth
because of poor nutrition and health care. Instead of reading
about hunger and malnutrition, they see children with bloated
stomachs and discolored hair, listless because they eat one meal
of beans and tortillas each day. They see men who labor in the
cotton fields of the fincas on the southern coast, women who
sew shirts in the hot and dirty maquilas, and children who beg in
the city streets. Whether they see the faces of the poor in Communities of Population in Resistance or in Mexican refugee

camps, on the hillsides of rural Guatemala or on a city street, they realize intuitively that poverty is dehumanizing.

Walter Wink's work on the inner and outer nature of the powers and authorities offers a helpful addition to Guatemalan women's analysis of the threat. Wink's work reminds us to look beyond economic and political violence to what hundreds of years of oppression have done to the inner spirit of poor and indigenous Guatemalans. Not only have Guatemalans suffered from hunger and malnutrition, harassment and torture, but after living with evil and oppression they have changed their own behavior to survive. They have internalized the oppression and evil, often cooperating with the powers and authorities.

Granted, much of the cooperation occurred at gunpoint, as in the sixteenth century when landowners forced Guatemalans to work on their plantations, or in the twentieth century when soldiers forced thousands of indigenous Guatemalan men to serve in civil defense patrols, turning against their own families and neighbors. But as a result of their internalization of oppression, poor and indigenous Guatemalans disregard their own potentialities as political or economic actors, indeed, even as human beings. Poor and indigenous Guatemalans often are silent and passive, accepting the majority culture's stereotype of them as stupid peasants. Because the oppression exists inside them as well as in external structures and systems, the liberation of poor and indigenous Guatemalans must address both the inner and outer nature of the evils that they have internalized, the damage to their personal and collective psyches as well as the evils in structures and systems of Guatemalan society.

Climate of fear. Women's experience of legitimate loss of their husbands, fathers, and children by death, disappearance, or forced military service has created fear. The loss has changed the family structure—instead of traditional family structures, women became the heads of households. The loss has removed an economic partner and the link to the outside world. The loss has also removed the translator of the outside world for indigenous women isolated by language and culture. But more than an economic partner or a translator of the ladino culture, the loss has removed a loved family member. As a result of the loss, women have felt fears—fears that soldiers could kill their children, fears that they could not provide for the economic needs of the family, fears that they were not strong enough to sustain the family emotionally, and fears that soldiers could abduct and torture them, thus robbing their children of their remaining parent.

Poor and indigenous persons have also experienced fear because of the climate of fear—fear spread throughout villages and towns like a plague as neighbors disappeared, family members were killed, and stories of massacres and relocations became common knowledge. During the ten years of army occupation in Santiago Atitlán, one woman said, "Although people talked about the problems in whispers late at night, if at all, fear was so strong that you could touch it." Fear kept peasants from planting and harvesting their crops in the country, or from being outside their homes at night. Often they kept fears locked inside. Not talking about the violence only heightened the fear and sense of dread. The knowledge that there was nothing (apparently) that they could do to stop the "monster" made matters worse.

The scandal of silence. The culture of silence was two-pronged: within Guatemala and in the international community. Within Guatemala, women have kept silent because of their restricted space in the private sector—their domain has been home and family. But women and other victims of injustice have also kept silent because of the fear of repression. This is not an imaginary fear; the public persona of many women—their husbands, fathers, sons—have been killed, disappeared, or taken by the army.

The violence of the late 1970s and early 1980s and the growth of the popular movement presented women with a choice: silence for the safety of their children, with economic survival through crafts, cooking, domestic service, farm labor. Or breaking the silence and saying *no* to the injustice perpetrated by the army and paramilitary death squads that terrorize the countryside.

But the culture of silence is not confined to Guatemala. Throughout the world, the mainstream media did not report the extent of violence and human rights abuse occurring in Guatemala. The silence of the international community prompts Guatemalans, especially Guatemalans in human rights and church groups, to feel dismay and discouragement, as if no one cares that poor and indigenous persons are being exterminated, both by the violence of poverty and the violence of guns and armies. Julia Esquivel puts it well.

> Why is so little known
> of Guatemala's
> crucifixion?
>
> Why do the delegations
> and the newspapers
> and the important people
> worry zealously
> over Argentina and Chile
> over Haiti and the Philippines
> over El Salvador and Honduras?
>
> Why not over Guatemala?
>
> You know, my friend,
> our little wounded Guatemala,
> land of widows and orphans,
> our sister homeland
> is only a woman.
> Now do you understand?[3]

Beverly Harrison speaks of silence as the enemy of authentic change.[4] Silence reinforces the status quo and masks injustice. Whether the silence is within Guatemala or in the larger global community, it is equally harmful.

Means of Social Change

In Guatemala, a country with more injustice than justice, more violence than peace, persons in the popular sector use a variety of methods for social change. First, direct action, what Hollenbach calls education of the heart, has been an effective means of social change in Guatemala. Direct action has been proven good and necessary in addressing the effects of economic exploitation and political oppression, but it is not a long-term solution for Guatemala's problems. Religious groups and private relief agencies have opened orphanages and soup kitchens to serve the estimated 100,000 street children the war has left roaming Guatemala City, Quetzaltenango, and other cities. Guatemalans and groups from the United States help build houses with Habitat for Humanity. In Santa Apolonia, a small village in Chimaltenango devastated by army attacks, members of the School Sisters of Saint Francis operate an orphanage for abandoned children and work with the women of the village in agricultural projects and a weaving cooperative.

Second, almost all groups in Guatemala affirm the efficacy of political change through collective action. From the weekly pots-and-pans protest in front of the Public Ministry office to parades of women and children carrying pictures of their disappeared relatives, GAM utilizes collective action as its primary method of social change. Until the formation of GAM, women tried to work individually for social change, with little success. Likewise CUC uses mass meetings, demonstrations, boycotts, and protests to force the government and private employers to listen to their demands. Their February 1980 strike involving 70,000 farm workers paralyzed agricultural operations for two weeks and forced the government to increase the minimum wage.

The women of CONAVIGUA also depend on collective action for political change. They have been particularly effective with parades and demonstrations, like the parades involving thousands of Guatemalans on Father's Day and International Day of Women in 1989, and their recent demonstration in front of the National Congress for alternative social service instead of military service.

Third, mainline Protestant churches and the Catholic Church have been both partners and catalysts in the movement for social change in Guatemala. In 1840 Marx said that religion was the opiate of the people—and if a religion doesn't concern itself with social concerns, it may be just that. Martin Luther King Jr. insisted that any religion concerned with souls and not concerned with "the slums that damn them, the economic conditions that strangle them, and the social conditions that cripple them is dry-as-dust religion."[5] Especially Presbyterian, Mennonite, Methodist, and Catholic churches have demonstrated their concern for social, economic, and political conditions in Guatemala.

In repressive societies like Guatemala, where freedom of movement and the freedom to organize do not exist, churches have provided alternative social structures and leadership training. Through Bible study and religious training, Guatemalans have "caught" the biblical emphasis on justice. Christians like Rigoberta Menchú discovered in the Bible and their religious tradition a grounding for their involvement in social change that continues to empower and motivate them.

Although the struggle for human rights has resulted in the deaths of hundreds of catechists, priests and nuns, and other Christians, the church continues to be a voice for human rights and justice. Protestant and Catholic clergy groups as well as ecumenical groups like APGC (Permanent Assembly of Christian Groups) monitor the human rights situation to educate Guatemalans. In addition to the work of churches in Guatemala, church groups in the United States and Canada act in solidarity with Guatemalan churches through sister church relationships, work projects, and mission trips. Through programs like the Church Women United's 1993 World Day of Prayer that focused on Guatemala, Christian women throughout the world gather to hear the stories of Guatemalan women and to pray about their situation.

Fourth, although legal action, change through the courts, exists in some countries as an effective means of social change, it has been effective in only a few cases in Guatemala. Because of the corruption of the judiciary through bribery and the intimidation through death threats and murders, change through the courts has been minimal. On at least one occasion, GAM submitted 900 habeas corpus petitions to the courts to prompt the investigation of the deaths and disappearances of thousands of Guatemalans. Although the courts did not investigate claims, the 900 petitions brought important media attention to Guatemala.

Likewise on April 12, 1995, Boston federal district judge Douglas Woodlock ordered former minister of defense General Hector Gramajo to pay $47.5 million to Sister Diana Ortiz and seven Guatemalans. Gramajo directed a campaign of terror against Ortiz, an Ursuline nun from Kentucky, and thousands of Guatemalans in the 1980s. Again, although the plaintiffs may never receive the monetary settlement, this case received substantial media attention in Guatemala and the United States and unmasked the violence of the Guatemalan military.

Furthermore, Guatemalans work for social change by acting in solidarity with international nongovernmental organizations and church groups. International accompaniment was so important that the refugees made it one of the seven conditions of the January 1993 refugee return. The role was filled by citizens of the United States, Sweden, Canada, and other countries, representing Witness for Peace, Peace Brigades, church groups, and human rights groups. During the refugee return, international relief organizations provided essential food and humanitarian assistance. Nongovernmental organizations also provide seed money for building schools and clinics. The United Nations High Commission on Refugees provides meager food supplies.

But most important, the presence of internationals provides a measure of security against future massacres. The army, which claims to be the instrument of justice and peace, surely would commit no violence while internationals are present to witness their crimes. Also, since the mainstream media rarely report on Guatemala, international groups also function as communication to the outside world and an alternative media source.

Guatemala: A World with Justice

Guatemalans are empowered by their dreams and hopes for a world with justice. They are wise enough to realize that the battle for justice will take time and persistence. They may not know justice, but they live in the hope that their children will experience peace and justice. After years of violence, they know justice is costly; the hundreds of martyrs who have died in the struggle for it testify to the costliness of justice. They have learned to celebrate victories, however large or small, and to share with each other their vision of a new Guatemala. In the following three sections, I describe the shape of justice for Guatemalan women involved in the struggle.

Justice as Participation

For Guatemalan women, justice is best experienced as participation. Instead of the economic, political, cultural, and gender marginalization they have endured for five hundred years, they struggle for a country where they can enjoy the full set of rights. Archbishop Oscar Romero of El Salvador said it best.

> To take seriously the preferential option for the poor means striving to understand and denounce the mechanisms that generate poverty; uniting our efforts with those people of good will in order to uproot poverty and create a more just and fraternal world; supporting the aspirations of laborers and peasants, who wish to be treated as free, responsible human beings. They are called to share in the decisions that affect their lives and their future, and we encourage all to improve themselves; defending their fundamental right to freely create organizations to defend and promote their interests, and to make a responsible contribution to the common good.[6]

In a Guatemala with justice as participation, *all* Guatemalans are full partners in society and Guatemala is richer because of their contribution to society.

With social and economic rights, all citizens of Guatemala will have access to employment with just wages. Since in Guatemala only 35 percent of the economically active population is fully employed, jobs with living wages must be created. Unlike the present effort to manage inflation by controlling wages but not prices, adding to the number of poor and hungry in Guatemala, the government must provide for the basic human needs of all citizens. Furthermore, although Guatemala is crippled with external debt, concern with justice should preclude reducing debt through cutting education and social services. Instead of economic policies designed to benefit the private sector and foreign interests, economic policies must also consider the needs of the 87 percent poor.

Gender equality begins with the education of children, educational programs that do not reinforce current patterns of machismo and sexism but educate for equality. With gender rights, the women and girls of Guatemala will no longer live in fear of sexual harassment and rape in the workplace, nor will women suffer discrimination in salaries or job opportunities. In a Guatemala with justice, women will have access to all jobs. They will be able to form unions for collective bargaining. In marriages, women will be equal partners with men under law; their husbands will not have the right to molest or abuse them.

Justice as participation translates to equity in political and civil rights. Guatemalans will be able to participate fully in existing political parties and to create parties that reflect the needs of the poor. A Guatemala with freedom of expression, freedom of movement, and freedom to organize will remove the need for insurgents since all persons will be able to act within the political process without fear of reprisal. In the new Guatemala, persons will be free to express opposition opinions in the press without fear of censorship. Similarly young boys and men will not be forced to serve in the military or civil defense patrols, nor will they fear being tortured or killed.

In a Guatemala with justice, indigenous persons will share the same rights as ladinos. They will be able to develop their own cultures within the larger Guatemalan society without fear of extermination or assimilation. History books will be rewritten to include the history of indigenous cultures, and children will learn their history in schools with bilingual education. Guatemala will develop a truly pluralistic society where all ethnic groups are respected and given equal rights and privileges.

A New Image of Power

Justice for women in Guatemala draws on a new image of power—power as vulnerability and participation. In their homes and in the structures and systems of Guatemalan society, women have experienced power as domination, as coercion used to control and manipulate. Throughout the history of their country, they have seen the devastating effects of unbridled power—whether that power resided in the National Palace, army barracks, or the office of a transnational corporation. Now women are envisioning a new practice of shared power, power with instead of power over.

CONAVIGUA's structure illustrates shared power. Instead of a president, the organization has a national coordinating council in Guatemala City and regional councils in small towns and villages throughout Guatemala. Granted, one reason for shared power in their national and local structures is its practicality. The violence of the early 1980s destroyed a generation of leaders in unions and human rights groups, and organizations with one or two leaders are easy targets for repression. But the reasons for shared power are deeper than pure practicality. Shared power demonstrates desire for mutuality and a common vision.

Even in groups like CUC, with a charismatic leader like Rigoberta Menchú, leadership and vision are shared. Groups

190 Voices of the Voiceless

like GAM, CUC, and CONAVIGUA are not the possession of one leader but are "owned" by the group, by all who struggle together to articulate a common vision and devise wise strategies of action.

The Dangerous Memory of Suffering

An important motif in Guatemalan women's understanding of justice is suffering. They realize that suffering because of injustice is woven into the fabric of Guatemalan life. A Guatemalan peasant put it clearly, "It's not just that we've been suffering since 1977—we've been suffering for 500 years." Although Guatemalans like former president Cerezo label the women in GAM "masochistic" for not forgetting the past, poor and indigenous Guatemalans in the popular movement are telling their story with a new fervor.

Guatemalans and other victims of injustice keep the dangerous memory of suffering alive as a reminder that the injustice that once happened can happen again. Although they celebrate victories, they need never forget that men still are abducted and forcibly recruited by the military, human rights workers still receive death threats and harassment, women in factories still are beaten and sexually abused, and children still live with poverty and malnutrition. Their memories of suffering and oppression empower them to continue to act for justice, even when situations seem hopeless.

North American Women: Partners in Justice

What will prompt North American women, especially Christian and Jewish women, to engage in justice-actions in response to situations of injustice, whether at home or abroad? How can women be empowered to participate in justice-actions? The next two sections describe the barriers to justice-actions with attention to correctives within our faith tradition and to stories of individuals who act for justice and human rights.

Barriers to Justice-Actions

In spite of countless biblical texts affirming the importance of social justice, many Christians still question the centrality of justice in the mission of the church. They see the mission of the church as evangelism and worship; justice-actions are the domain of private relief organizations and government agencies. The mission of the church is justice and evangelism—both are integral and arise out of love for fellow human beings. In *Biblical Ethics and Social Change*, Stephen Charles Mott states that both evangelism and the implementation of justice "arise spontaneously out of love for our fellow human beings who are hurt, who need us, and whose need we feel within us," and both are the mission of the church.[7] Ron Sider adds,

> It is time for evangelicals to refuse to use sentences that begin with "the primary task of the Church is . . ." regardless of whether the sentence ends with evangelism or Bible teaching or social concerns. They are all integral, necessary aspects of the Church's task.[8]

Many Christians do not consider or become involved in social action because their theology or church practice leads them to believe that social improvement happens as you change people one by one. These people believe change happens at the individual level through education and gradual improvement of circumstances. Others believe individuals change through religious conversion, then in turn change the social order.

Often individual Christians and churches do not involve themselves in social justice because their priorities prevent their having time or financial resources to commit to a project or issue or they lack knowledge and understanding about the problem and do not realize their ability to act for change. They want change to happen but do not want to be troublemakers or to disturb the status quo. Change of attitude tends to happen slowly or not at all, unless someone is personally involved in an issue.

Another barrier to justice-actions is excessive individualism.

This results in churches that are self-centered and foster a private spirituality that isolates religion from the rest of life. The authors of *Habits of the Heart* describe the conflict and contradiction between a purely private spirituality and wholistic religion influencing all of life with implications for public and political actions.[9] Even with an emphasis on private spirituality, Parker Palmer sees within American religion and biblical religion the materials for transformation—dormant, perhaps, but there nonetheless.

> Perhaps the most important ministry the church can have in the renewal of public life is a "ministry of paradox": not to resist the inward turn of American spirituality on behalf of effective public action, *but to deepen and direct and discipline that inwardness in the light of faith* until God leads us back to a vision of the public and faithful action on the public's behalf.[10]

Prophets like Palmer discover resources for renewal within the faith tradition and call the church to justice-actions.

Feminists offer a new vision as a corrective for rampant individualism in U.S. society. Feminists reject individualism and private spirituality for a spirituality that is wholistic and connected with relational ways of praying, knowing, living, and acting. Instead of a church that is private, esoteric, otherworldly, and separate from the rest of life, feminist spirituality insists instead that morality is not a private but a social affair. Feminists envision Christian spirituality as eating together, sharing together, experiencing God's presence together, and "proclaiming the gospel as God's alternative vision for everyone, especially those who are poor, outcast, and battered."[11]

A Cloud of Witnesses

We have a "cloud of witnesses," individuals who show us how to make the connection between personal and corporate faith and actions for social justice. One such advocate for justice is Muriel Lester, an English Baptist in the early twentieth century. Although raised with the economic and educational privileges of wealth, as an adult she espoused voluntary poverty and used her financial resources to fund social service agencies in the poorest part of London. She maintained that Christian discipleship was radical and costly; in her classes at Loughton Union Church, she taught that Christians must do "Jesus Christ the honor of taking him seriously, of thinking out his teachings in daily life, and then acting on it, even if ordered by police, prelates, and princes to do the opposite."[12] Convinced that ministry with and to the poor demanded residency requirements, Lester, her sister, and brother moved to a small house in a poor neighborhood of East London.

Lester took Jesus Christ seriously which led her into a life of activism grounded in her Christian faith. Part of her work with the poor in London involved advocacy for women and children's rights. She also joined Fellowship of Reconciliation during World War I and served as traveling secretary for International Fellowship of Reconciliation. She organized chapters in Africa, Latin America, India, and China. In London, she participated in protests against the war and conscription for military service and for women's suffrage and humanitarian famine relief.

Charles Liteky demonstrated his commitment to peace and human rights through creative actions. In a letter to President Reagan on July 29, 1986, Charles Liteky returned and renounced his Congressional Medal of Honor as a sign of his strong opposition to U.S. military policy in Central America.

> There are a lot of us Americans who do not care to be counted among the oppressors of the world and we intend to let the government you lead know it by way of a series of nonviolent protests that will end when you stop the killing, the raping, the torturing, and the kidnapping of poor people in Central America. . . . Some morning I hope you wake up and hear the cry of the poor riding on a southwest wind from Guatemala, Nicaragua, and El Salvador. They are crying, "Stop killing us."[13]

As a veteran of the Vietnam War, Liteky had seen the tragic effects of militarism. With other veterans he joined the movement against militarism in Central America.

Considered the drum major for justice, Martin Luther King Jr. was aware of racial discrimination and moved beyond awareness to action, actions to alleviate the oppression and discrimination suffered by millions of African-Americans. Understanding the connection between the gospel message and the church's actions, he taught that our faith commitment should result in an absolute refusal to accept injustice as the norm.

> There are some things within our social order to which I am proud to be maladjusted. I never intend to adjust myself to segregation and discrimination. I never intend to adjust myself to mob rule. I never intend to adjust myself to the tragic effects of the methods of physical violence and to tragic militarism. I call upon you to be maladjusted to such things.[14]

King calls us not to become adjusted to racism, sexism, poverty, militarism, and other injustices prevalent in Guatemala and the United States. Like King, our response should be activism, not passivity.

Sojourner Truth, Oscar Romero, Dorothy Day, Marian Wright Edelman, the Sojourner community, the Koinonia community, and the women of Guatemala also remind us that faith and action are integrally related, two strands of the same thread. We find in these people and others Christians who are not willing or able to divorce vocation from public involvement; they affirm that faith calls for transformation of all that is not just in the world.

Conclusion

As this book has described, there is in Guatemalan women a practice of justice that seems remarkable in a country where poor and oppressed persons have been marginalized for five hundred years. Although their actions have increased the justice, there are still too many disappearances and deaths, too many clandestine cemeteries with bodies of loved ones, too many children and old ones buried in the mountains because of hunger and disease, too many children without parents, too many parents without jobs. Their struggle will not end until justice reigns.

Likewise, the struggle of women in the United States must not end until justice reigns. Women's experience is marked by years of systematic exclusion from social and political spheres. This exclusion can make us bitter and vengeful. Or we can respond with compassion and understanding for any person who experiences alienation and oppression. At the least, women must engage in politics of resistance—vowing to refuse to accept policies, doctrines, and systems that exclude and marginalize persons. Instead, we can use our creative imagination to dream of different structures and systems and to work with other sisters and brothers to solve the problems of our communities and world.

From the women of Guatemala we learn that participation is crucial for justice and social change. Because they are Christians and mothers, Guatemalan women engage in actions to end injustice, but they were effective only after they participated in collective action. Before they joined public actions, Guatemalans quietly and individually protested disappearances and deaths, rising prices and unjust wages, and ethnic oppression. Now groups like CUC, GAM, and CONAVIGUA testify to the power of joining together in the struggle for peace. Despite the dangers, throughout Guatemala people are participating in human rights groups, artisan and agricultural cooperatives, and church groups committed to justice.

Inspired by the story of women in Guatemala, people of faith in North America can act together for justice. North Americans are not callous, uncaring individuals. Most are eager to serve God. They are genuinely concerned about world needs. But most do not work in programs to meet basic human needs nor do they engage in advocacy to end social problems. North American women in churches and synagogues must articulate a broader vision, a vision that includes people of all economic groups and ethnic backgrounds as equal partners. We must engage in a ministry that transcends racial and class barriers with human rights as a central concern. We must affirm the validity of political activity as a tool for implementing human rights.

In the conclusion to *Exodus and Revolution*, Walzer summarizes the lessons of the Exodus, lessons helpful for Guatemalans and North Americans with a passion for justice.

> first, that wherever you live, it is probably Egypt; second, that there is a better place, a world more attractive, a Promised Land; and third, that the way to the land is through the wilderness. There is no way to get from here to there except by joining together and marching.[15]

Walzer's words are an ever-present reminder that the way to the promised land is through struggle. All of us—Guatemalans, North Americans, Bosnians, South Africans, and more—must join in solidarity to reach that land as cocreators of justice. We struggle together, confident that we follow the God of justice, secure that God empowers us for the journey.

Notes

Chapter 1

1. Guatemalans refer to the years from 1944-54 as their springtime. In 1944 masses of Guatemalan people overthrew the military dictator, General Jorge Ubico, in a nonviolent revolution. During the next ten years the country experienced social and economic reform—land reform, a Bill of Rights, health programs, literacy campaigns, and a social security law.

2. United Nations Children's Fund, *The State of the World's Children 1991* (New York: Oxford, 1991).

3. National Economic Planning Council, SEGEPLAN 1990, quoted in "Human Rights Facts," Guatemala Human Rights Commission/USA.

4. UNICEF, *The State of the World's Children 1991*.

5. World Bank, *Social Indicators Report, 1990*, quoted in "Human Rights Facts," Guatemala Human Rights Commission/USA.

6. Lindsay Gruson, "Political Violence on the Rise Again in Guatemala, Tarnishing Civilian Rule," *New York Times International*, June 28, 1990, p. 3.

7. When Spaniards invaded Guatemala in the sixteenth century, interbreeding between Spanish men and Indian women produced a third group of people, referred to as *ladina* or *ladino*. Today the term often refers to a privileged minority of people with mixed Indian and Spanish blood.

8. Marieclaire Acosta, quoted in Jennifer G. Schirmer, "Those Who Die for Life Cannot Be Called Dead: Women and Human Rights Protest in Latin America," *Feminist Review*, 32 (Summer 1989), 4-5.

9. Marysa Navarro, "The Personal Is Political: Las Madres de Plaza de Mayo," in *Power and Popular Protest: Latin American Social Movements*, ed. Susan Eckstein (Berkeley: University of California Press, 1989), p. 253.

10. Ibid.

11. Karen Lebacqz, *Justice in an Unjust World* (Minneapolis: Augsburg Publishing House, 1987), p. 11.

Chapter 2

1. W. George Lovell, *Conquest and Survival in Colonial Guatemala: A Historical Geography of the Cuchumatán Highlands 1500-1821* (Montreal: Queen's University Press, 1985), p. 38.

2. Jim Handy, *Gift of the Devil: A History of Guatemala* (Toronto, Ont.: Between the Lines, 1984), p. 20.

3. Severo Martinez Paláez, *La Patria del criollo* (San Jose, Costa Rica: Editorial Universitaria Centroamericana, 1979), p. 535.

4. Bernal Diaz del Castillo, quoted in J. H. Elliot, *Imperial Spain: 1469-1716* (Hammondsworth, England: Pelican Books, 1976), p. 65, quoted in Lovell, *Conquest*, p. 75.

5. A hacienda is an estate, usually with a mixed economic base of agriculture and ranching. A finca is a large farm, possibly a cotton or coffee plantation.

6. The French demographer Channu, quoted in Handy, *Gift*, p. 19.

7. Lovell, *Conquest*, p. 153.

8. Handy, *Gift*, p. 51.

9. In the highlands, labor contractors loaned small amounts of money to peasants in exchange for their participation in debt bondage. Their contracts were sold to finca owners for harvesttime. The contracts, often with usurious interest rates, were controlled by landowners or foremen.

10. Handy, *Gift*, p. 63.

11. *Time*, June 26, 1944, p. 45, quoted in *Liberation Ethics*, by John Swomly Jr. (New York: Macmillan, 1972), p. 69. Also, Pedro Stanfield, "Guatemala: When Spring Turned to Winter," in *Relentless Persistence: Nonviolent Action in Latin America*, ed. Philip McManus and Gerald Schlabach (Philadelphia: New Society Publishers, 1991), p. 17, and Gene Sharp, *The Politics of Nonviolent Action*, part one, *Power and Struggle* (Boston: Extending Horizon Books, Porter Sargent, 1973), p. 90.

12. Sharp, *Politics*, p. 91.

13. Historians differ on the classification of the 1954 action. The military action was planned and funded by the United States government. Stephen Kinzer and Stephen Schlesinger gathered evidence for U.S. involvement using the U.S. Freedom of Information Act. The "official" leader of the action was Castillo Armas, a disgruntled Guatemalan. In *Bitter Fruit: the Untold Story of the American Coup in Guatemala*, Kinzer and Schlesinger refer to the action as a CIA-sponsored invasion. Suzanne Jonas, Walter LeFeber, other Latin American historians, agree that the action was a CIA-sponsored invasion.

14. Jean-Marie Simon, *Guatemala: Eternal Spring—Eternal Tyranny* (New York: W. W. Norton, 1987), p. 21.

15. Maria Monteforte Toledo, *Guatemala: Monografia sociologica* (Mexico City: n.p., 1959), pp. 47-50, quoted in Handy, *Gift*, p. 107.

16. Until 1944 peasants owning less than ten acres were required to work 100 days of unpaid labor each year. Until the early twentieth century peasants were required to carry the wives of military officers and landowners on their backs. Simon, *Eternal*, p. 21.

17. Schlesinger, *Bitter*, p. 40.

18. Ibid.

19. The company's own declaration of value listed the value of the land as $627,000. Ibid., p. 27.

20. José Aybar de Soto, quoted in Handy, *Gift*, p. 119.

21. Stanfield, "Guatemala," p. 25.

22. John Foster Dulles had been legal counsel and Allen Dulles served on the board of trustees of the United Fruit Company. Both brothers owned stock in the United Fruit Company.

23. Catholic Action groups, a grassroots movement, were organized by Spanish priests in the 1930s and grew with the advent of liberation theology. The groups focused on local organizing and the integration of the gospel and social justice. Catholic Action members were often the target for repression in the 1970s and 1980s.

24. Ojo por Ojo (An Eye for an Eye) and Mano Blanca (The White Hand) were two of the most powerful death squads. They were known for the fear and intimidation they created among the general populace. Handy, *Gift*, p. 160.

25. Ibid., p. 167. Colonel Carlos Arana Osorio was called Jackal of Zacapa because of his ruthless counterinsurgency campaign in the provinces of Zacapa and Chiquimula from 1966-1970. Under the guise of wiping out communism, he killed an estimated 10,000 noncombatants in order to assassinate 300-500 guerrillas. Simon, *Eternal*, p. 25.

26. Handy, *Gift*, p. 257.

27. Simon, *Eternal*, p. 179.

28. Ibid., p. 180.

29. The June 1982 Oxfam America report, coauthored by Shelton H. Davis, entitled "Witnesses to Political Violence in Guatemala: The Suppression of a Rural Development Movement," quoted in Shelton H. Davis, "Introduction: Sowing the Seeds of Violence," in *Harvest of Violence: The Mayan Indians and the Guatemalan Crisis*, ed. Robert M. Carmack (Norman, Okla.: University of Oklahoma Press, 1988), p. 23.

30. Ibid.

31. Rios Montt's church was affiliated with Gospel Outreach Church of Eureka, California, and strongly supported by the Christian Broadcasting Network in Virginia. Handy, *Gift*, p. 270.

32. Schlesinger, *Bitter*, pp. vi-vii.

33. Juan J. Linz, *The Breakdown of Democratic Regimes: Crisis, Breakdown, and Reequilibration* (Baltimore: The Johns Hopkins University Press, 1987), p. 5.

34. Susanne Jonas, "Contradictions of Guatemala's Political Opening," in *Democracy in Latin America: Visions and Realities*, ed. Susanne Jonas and Nancy Stein (New York: Bergin and Garvey, 1990), p. 65.

35. Lillian Hellman, *Pentimento* (Boston: Little, Brown, and Co., 1973), p. 3.

36. Ximena Bunster-Burotto, "Surviving Beyond Fear: Women and Torture in Latin America" in *Women and Change in Latin America*, ed. June Nash and Helen Safa (South Hadley, Mass.: Bergin and Garvey, 1986), p. 317.

37. From 1960 until 1985 Guatemala was considered a classic counterinsurgency state. Jonas suggests that the transition with Cerezo's regime is from military counterinsurgent state to civilian counterinsurgent state. Jonas also points out that the counterinsurgency state is (and has been) a project of both the military and the ruling coalition. Jonas, *Battle*, p. 171.

38. Ibid.

39. The distribution of the land was a response to Father Andrés Girón's *pro tierra* (for land) movement. Cerezo's government divided the land but gave no supplies, technical assistance, credit, housing, or medical care.

40. Figures 1-3 are from Comisión de Derechos Humanos, *1981-1991: Diez años de impunidad: Extrajudiciales en Guatemala* (Mexico City: Comisión de Derechos Humanos, 1991). This report lists names (when known) and date of death or disappearance. Figure 4 is from Grupo de Apoyo Mutuo Por el Aparecimiento Con Vida de Nuestros Hijos, Esposos, Padres, y Hermanos, *Nos une la esperanza de su regreso* (Guatemala City: GAM, 1986). This book contains accounts of "Los Desaparecidos," with photographs, information on victims, spouses and children, brief biographical sketches, and details of disappearances.

41. Jonas, "Political Opening," p. 77.

42. Letter from John Nelson, Guatemala coordinator for Witness for Peace, Guatemala City, Guatemala, August, 1992.

43. "Guatemala," *The Defense Monitor*, 21, no. 5 (1992), 5.

44. Dr. Orlando García, "Tortured Women: Stories of Political Terror," quoted in Jennifer Tisdale, "Abuse of Women in Today's Guatemala," *Guatemala Bulletin*, 10, no. 4 (1993), 6.

45. The Guatemalan National Office on Women, quoted in Tisdale, "The Abuse of Women," p. 7.

46. 1991 U.S. State Department Human Rights Report on Guatemala.

47. "Guatemala," *Defense Monitor*, p. 5.

48. During an interview with Rodolfo Robles, one of the top labor leaders in Guatemala, he shared the dangers of union involvement. He has been threatened repeatedly by the military. On one occasion he was abducted but managed to escape his captors. During our conversation, the police just one block away opened fire on a crowd of farm workers protesting poor salaries and working conditions. They injured six people, two of whom were children.

49. Archbishop Prospero Penados del Barrio, quoted in "Human Rights," p. 35.

50. Simon, *Eternal*, p. 166.

51. Handy, *Gift*, p. 280.

52. Fried, *Rebellion*, p. 24.

53. Gernot Kohler, "Global Apartheid," in *Toward a Just World Order*, ed. Richard Falk, Sam Kim, and Saul Mendlovitz (Boulder, Colo.: Westview Press, 1982), p. 317.

54. Davis, *Harvest*, p. 33.

55. United Nations Development Programme (UNDP), *Human Development Report 1991* (New York: Oxford University Press, 1991). The Human Develop-

ment Index (HDI) evaluates countries based on income levels, life expectancy, health, and education.

56. Ibid.

57. Richard Hough, et al., *Land and Labor in Guatemala: An Assessment* (Washington, D.C.: Agency for International Development, 1982), pp. 1-2.

58. Jonas reports that "prices have almost quintupled since the mid-1970s." Jonas, "Contradictions," in *Democracy*, p. 75.

59. Jonas, *Battle*, p. 110.

60. Ibid., p. 183.

61. Francesca Miller, *Latin American Women and the Search for Social Justice* (Hanover, N.H.: University Press of New England, 1991), pp. 242-243.

62. UNICEF, *The Invisible Adjustment: Poor Women and the Economic Crisis* (Santiago, Chile: UNICEF, The Americas and the Caribbean Regional Office, 1989), p. 12.

63. The terms, *maquila* and *maquiladora* are used interchangeably to refer to Latin American factories, usually foreign owned, that produce goods for export. In the Guatemalan context, the goods produced are clothing for markets in the United States.

64. U.S./Guatemala Labor Education Project, *The Phillips-Van Heusen Campaign: A Struggle for Justice and Basic Rights in the Global Economy* (Chicago: U.S./Guatemala Labor Education Project, December, 1991), p. 3.

65. U.S./Guatemala Labor Education Project, "The Phillips-Van Heusen Campaign," p. 2.

66. Ricardo Falla, "Struggle for Survival in the Mountains: Hunger and Other Privations Inflicted on Internal Refugees from the Central Highlands," in *Harvest of Violence: The Mayan Indians and the Guatemalan Crisis*, ed. Robert M. Carmack (Norman, Okla.: University of Oklahoma Press, 1988), p. 244.

67. Davis, *Harvest*, p. 10.

68. Simon, *Eternal*, p. 235.

69. Simon, *Eternal*, p. 236.

70. Handy, *Gift*, p. 280.

Chapter 3

1. Only 9 percent of women complete secondary school. Women's illiteracy rate is the highest in the hemisphere. Even the Guatemalan civil code discriminates against women. In a marriage, the husband is the legal representative and can dispose of joint property. The code specifies that the female is in charge of child care and other domestic responsibilities. The husband can legally forbid the wife to participate in activities outside the home. Jennifer Tisdale, "Abuse of Women in Today's Guatemala," *Guatemala Bulletin*, 10, no. 4 (December 1992), 6.

2. Rigoberta Menchú, *I, Rigoberta*, trans. and ed. Elisabeth Burgos-Debray (New York: Verso, 1984), pp. 120-121.

3. Adolfo Perez Esquivel, quoted in "Rigoberta Menchú Tum: Symbol of Peace and Reconciliation Wins Nobel Peace Prize," *Central America Report*, 12, no. 6 (December 1992), 1.

4. Ibid.

5. Jean-Marie Simon, *Guatemala: Eternal Spring—Eternal Tyranny* (New York: W. W. Norton & Company, 1987), p. 9. Menchú, *I, Rigoberta*, p. 160. Susanne Jonas, *The Battle for Guatemala: Rebels, Death Squads, and U.S. Power*, Latin American Perspectives Series, no. 5 (Boulder, Colo.: Westview Press, 1991), pp. 127-128. The expropriated land was located in what is called "the Zone of the Generals." This land was expropriated after the discovery of oil. General Lucas, the new president in 1978, owned 78,000 acres near Panzós.

6. Arturo Arias, "El movimiento indígena en Guatemala: 1970-1983," in *Movimientos populares en Centroamérica*, ed. Daniel Camacho and Rafael Menjívar, (San José, Costa Rica: EDUCA, 1985), pp. 102-103. Passage translated by Susanne Jonas in Jonas, *Battle*, p. 132.

7. Douglas Farah, "Indian from Guatemala Wins Nobel Peace Prize," *The Washington Post*, Saturday, October 17, 1992, sec. A, p. 1.

8. Tim Golden, "Exiled Indian from Guatemala Awarded the Nobel Peace Prize," *The New York Times*, Saturday, October 17, 1992, sec. A, p. 1, and "Rigoberta Menchú Tum: Symbol of Peace and Reconciliation Wins Nobel Peace Prize," *Central America Report*, 12, no. 2 (December 1992), 1.

9. John Reed, "The Dictatorship Has Taught Me the Road," *Latin American Perspectives*, 18 (Fall 1991), 96-103.

10. Reed, "The Dictatorship," p. 96.

11. Sharp defines nonviolent action as "a technique by which people who reject passivity and submission, and who see struggle as essential, can wage their conflict without violence." Gene Sharp, *The Politics of Nonviolent Action* (Boston: Porter Sargent, 1973). These methods are discussed in chapter 3 and chapter 8.

12. Sharp, *Nonviolent Action*, p. 537.

13. Jean-Marie Simon, "In Search of the Disappeared: Guatemalan Women Resurrecting Democracy," *Multinational Monitor*, (October, 1986), p. 7.

14. Allan Nairn and Jean-Marie Simon, "Bureaucracy of Death," *The New Republic*, 194 (June 30, 1986), p. 14.

15. Interview with Rosalina Tuyuc, member of the National Coordinating Council of CONAVIGUA, Quetzaltenango, Guatemala, June 29, 1992.

16. CONAVIGUA, "CONAVIGUA 1988," 1988, pp. 5, 12.

17. CONAVIGUA, "Introductory Statement," 1988, p. 8.

18. Rosalina Tuyuc, quoted in a letter received from Jenn Rader, Witness for Peace worker, February 12, 1993.

19. Rosalina Tuyuc is a member of the national coordinating council of CONAVIGUA. CONAVIGUA, "Violations," p. 4.

20. Martin Luther King Jr. *Why We Can't Wait* (New York: Harper & Row, 1963), pp. 82, 87.

21. Frances Fox Piven and Richard A. Cloward, *Poor People's Movements: Why They Succeed and How They Fail* (New York: Vintage Books, 1979), pp. 3-4.

22. Charles D. Brockett, "The Structure of Political Opportunities and Peasant Mobilization in Central America," *Comparative Politics* (April 1991), pp. 253-274. Brockett borrows Henry A. Landsberger and Cynthia N. Hewitt's definition

of peasant as "any rural cultivator who is low in economic status and political status," from "Ten Sources of Weakness and Cleavage in Latin American Peasant Movements" in *Agrarian Problems and Peasant Movements in Latin America,* ed. Rodolfo Stavenhagen (New York: Doubleday Anchor Books, 1970), p. 560. For Guatemala, the peasant, though once a "rural cultivator" because of displacement and unequal land distribution, may be rural or urban, indigenous, or ladino.

23. Brockett, "The Structure of Political Opportunities," p. 254.

24. Douglas MacAdam, *Political Process and the Development of Black Insurgency 1930-1970* (Chicago: University of Chicago Press, 1982), p. 43. Note that MacAdam and others write of the political process model and the structure of political opportunities using Western industrialized countries as models. See also Frances Fox Piven and Richard A. Cloward, *Poor People's Movements* and Sidney Tarrow, *Struggling to Reform: Social Movements and Policy Change during Cycles of Protest,* Western Societies Paper no. 15 (Ithaca, N.Y.: Cornell University, 1983) and Sidney Tarrow, *Democracy and Disorder: Social Conflict, Protest and Politics in Italy, 1965-1975* (New York: Oxford University Press, 1989).

25. McAdam, *Political Process,* p. 37.

26. Ibid., p. 44.

27. Ted Gurr, "The Political Origins of State Violence and Terror: A Theoretical Analysis," in *Government Violence and Repression,* ed. Michael Stohl and George A. Lopez (New York: Greenwood Press, 1986), p. 66.

28. Gordon Bowen, "The Political Economy of State Terrorism: Barrier to Human Rights in Guatemala," in *Human Rights and Third World Development,* ed. George W. Shepherd Jr. and Ved P. Nanda (Westport: Greenwood Press, 1985), p. 104.

29. Morris and Herring, "Theory and Research," p. 168.

30. Pamela Oliver, "Bringing the Crowd Back In: The Nonorganizational Elements of Social Movements," in *Research in Social Movements, Conflict and Change,* vol. 11. (Greenwich, Conn.: JAI Press, 1989), p. 18.

Chapter 4

1. Walter Wink, *Naming the Powers: The Language of Power in the New Testament,* The Powers, vol. 1 (Philadelphia: Fortress Press, 1984), p. ix.

2. Walter Wink, *Unmasking the Powers: The Invisible Forces That Determine Human Existence,* The Powers, vol. 2 (Philadelphia: Fortress Press, 1986) p. 69.

3. Walter Wink, *Naming,* p. 100.

4. Ephesians 6:12, The New Revised Standard Version Bible.

5. Wink, *Naming,* p. 78.

6. Daniel Day Williams, *The Demonic and the Divine,* ed. Stacy A. Evans (Minneapolis: Fortress Press, 1990), p. 22.

7. Wink, *Unmasking,* p. 9.

8. Ibid., p. 11.

9. Ibid., p. 13.

10. Williams, *The Demonic,* pp. 13-14.

11. Ibid., p. 14.

12. Ibid., p. 24.

13. Ibid., p. 25.

14. Ibid., p. 41.

15. Ibid, p. 42.

16. Ibid., p. 43.

17. Ibid.

18. Ibid., p. 52.

19. Ibid., p. 51.

20. Walter Wink, *Engaging the Powers: Discernment and Resistance in a World of Domination*, The Powers, vol. 3 (Minneapolis: Fortress Press, 1992), pp. 9.

21. Wink, *Unmasking*, p. 57.

22. Ibid., p. 53.

23. Juan's story is a composite of stories that I heard during three trips to Guatemala.

24. Wink, *Unmasking*, p. 59.

25. Ibid., p. 67.

26. Joyce Hollyday, "A Shield of Love," *Sojourners*, 12, no. 10 (November 1983), 13.

27. Ibid.

28. Jim Wallis, "Witness for Peace," *Sojourners*, 12, no. 10 (November 1983), 3.

29. Wink, *Engaging*, p. 9.

30. Ibid., p. 51.

31. Ibid., p. 62.

32. Ibid.

33. Ibid., p. 107.

34. Ibid., p. 110.

35. Ibid., p. 140.

36. Tertullian, *On Idolatry*, 19.3; *The Chaplet*, 11.4, quoted in Wink, *Engaging*, pp. 210, 383.

37. Origen, *Against Celsus*, 5.33 and 3.8, quoted in Wink, *Engaging*, pp. 210 and 382.

38. Wink, *Engaging*, p. 141.

39. Ibid, p. 142.

40. Wink draws on the language of René Girard, who believes that through mimesis violence turns into the very thing it opposes. Wink, *Engaging*, pp. 90-91, 195, 201.

41. Ibid., p. 198.

42. Martin Luther King Jr., *The Words of Martin Luther King Jr.* (New York: Newmarket Press, 1987), p. 73.

43. Walter Wink, *Violence and Nonviolence in South Africa: Jesus' Third Way* (Philadelphia: New Society, 1987), p. 14.

44. Gene Sharp presents 198 different kinds of nonviolent actions with examples and descriptions in each category in *The Politics of Nonviolent Action*. Gene

Sharp, *The Politics of Nonviolent Action* (Boston: Porter Sargent, 1973).

45. In *Peace Works*, David Cortright tells the stories of peace activists in North America and Europe during the 1980s and how their grassroots actions helped end the Cold War. David Cortright, *Peace Works* (Boulder, Colo.: Westview Press, 1993). Glen Stassen tells more "people-power" stories in *Just Peacemaking*, particularly the story of churches and the Peace Movement in East Germany and the story of the Freeze Campaign. Glen Stassen, *Just Peacemaking: Transforming Initiatives for Justice and Peace* (Louisville, Ky.: Westminster/John Knox, 1992).

46. Wink, *Engaging*, p. 309.

47. Joyce Hollyday and Jim Wallis, "Conspiracy of Compassion," *Sojourners*, 14, no. 3 (March 1985), 17.

48. Wink, *Engaging*, p. 112.

49. Richard Horsley, *Jesus and the Spiral of Violence: Popular Jewish Resistance in Roman Palestine* (San Francisco: Harper & Row, 1987), p. 6.

50. Ibid., p. 246.

51. Elizabeth Schüssler Fiorenza, *In Memory of Her: A Feminist Reconstruction of Early Christian Beginnings* (New York: Crossroad Publishing Co., 1983), p. 141.

52. Horsley, *Jesus*, p. 37.

53. Josephus, *Dio Cassius*, 77.10.

54. These figures represent the percentage of Guatemalans living below the poverty level, according to CEPAL (Economic Commission for Latin America). Both CEPAL and USAID report that the number of people living in extreme poverty (unable to feed their families a minimum number of calories) has grown from 52 percent in 1980 to over 66 percent in 1987 to 72 percent in 1990. Susanne Jonas, *The Battle for Guatemala: Rebels, Death Squads, and U.S. Power*, Latin American Perspectives Series, no. 5 (Boulder, Colo.: Westview Press, 1991), pp. 177-178.

55. Out of the $1.00, seventy-nine cents goes to the U.S. broker, shipper, wholesaler, and retailer; nine cents goes to the international shipper; two cents to the Guatemalan exporter; five cents for the chemicals, seeds, and fertilizers. AVANSCO/PACCA, "Growing Dilemmas: Guatemala, the Environment, and the Global Economy" (Austin, Tex.: AVANSCO/PACCA, 1992), p. 3.

56. Hannelore Schroder, "The Economic Impoverishment of Mothers Is the Enrichment of Fathers," in *Women, Work, and Poverty*, ed. Elisabeth Schüssler Fiorenza and Anne Carr, (English language ed.), and Marcus Lefebure (Edinburgh: T. and T. Clark, LTD, 1987), p. 10.

57. Jackie M. Smith, ed. *Women, Faith, and Economic Justice* (Philadelphia: Westminster Press, 1985), p. 48.

58. National Conference of Catholic Bishops (NCCB), *Economic Justice for All: Pastoral Letter on Catholic Social Teaching and the U.S. Economy* (Washington, D.C.: National Conference of Catholic Bishops,1986), p. 88.

59. Ibid, p. 88.

60. Patricia Aburdene and John Naisbitt, *Megatrends for Women* (New York: Villard Books, 1992), pp. 80-81.

61. Eliezer, quoted in *Foremothers* by Nunnally-Cox, p. 99, and Wink, *Engaging*, p. 362.

62. Sheila Collins, *A Different Heaven and Earth* (Valley Forge, Pa.: Judson Press, 1974), p. 65.

63. Fermin Gomez, "Violence in Guatemala," *Guatemala Human Rights Commission/USA*, 8, no. 1 (March 1990), 3.

64. Americas Watch, *Guatemala: A Nation of Prisoners* (New York: Americas Watch, 1984), p. 111.

65. Nineth de Garcia quoted in "Six Years in Military Barracks," *Enfoprensa: Information on Guatemala*, year 5, no. 10 (Washington, D.C.: Enfoprensa/USA, March 13, 1987), p. 3.

66. Anne Wilson Schaef, *Women's Reality: An Emerging Female System in a White Male Society* (New York: Harper & Row, 1985), p. 4.

67. John Howard Yoder, *The Politics of Jesus* (Grand Rapids, Mich.: Eerdmans Publishing Company, 1972), p. 39.

68. Ibid., p. 74.

69. "Men Still Reign in Corporate World," *Courier-Journal*, March 16, 1995, A-1.

70. Wink, *Engaging*, p. 134.

71. Williams, *The Demonic*, p. 17.

72. Ibid., p. 21.

73. Wink, *Engaging*, p. 324.

Chapter 5

1. Julia Esquivel, "A Trembling," in *The Certainty of Spring: Poems by a Guatemalan in Exile*, translated by Anne Woehrle (Washington, D.C.: Ecumenical Program on Central America and the Caribbean, 1993), p. 60-61.

2. Ernesto Cardenal is a poet, priest, and former Minister of Culture during the Sandinista government in Nicaragua. Ernesto Cardenal, "Lord It's Incredible," in *Psalms*, trans. Thomas Blackburn, et al. (New York: Crossroad, 1981), p. 59.

3. Robert Bellah, et al., *Habits of the Heart: Individualism and Commitment in American Life* (New York: Harper & Row, 1985), p. 25.

4. Glen Stassen, "The Struggle against Injustice: Narrative of our Time," forthcoming in *Theology without Foundations*, ed. Nancey Murphy, Mark Nation, and Stanley Hauerwas (Nashville: Abingdon Press).

5. Stephen Charles Mott, *Biblical Ethics and Social Change* (New York: Oxford University Press, 1982), p. 59.

6. Glen H. Stassen, *Just Peacemaking: Transforming Initiatives for Justice and Peace* (Louisville: Westminster/John Knox, 1992), p. 72.

7. Elizabeth R. Achtemeier, "Righteousness in the Old Testament," *Interpreter's Dictionary of the Bible*, vol. 4 (Nashville: Abingdon Press, 1962), pp. 80ff.

8. Henri Nouwen, *Gracias!* (New York: Harper & Row, 1983), pp. 174-175.

9. Karen Lebacqz, *Justice in an Unjust World* (Minneapolis: Augsburg Publishing House, 1987), p. 11.

10. A. D. Woozley, "Injustice," in *Studies in Ethics*, American Philosophical Quarterly Monograph Series 7 (Oxford: Basil Blackwell, 1973), p. 110.

11. Moore speaks of the obligation of protection as protection from foreign powers. Barrington Moore, *Injustice: The Social Bases of Obedience and Revolt* (New York: Macmillan, 1978), pp. 21-22. In the years since *Injustice* was written, the number of wars and violent incidents within the borders of countries has grown, expanding the obligation implicit in his definition to include protection from forces within a country as well as protection from foreign powers.

12. Gustavo Gutiérrez, *The Truth Shall Make You Free* (Maryknoll, N.Y.: Orbis Books, 1990), p. 7.

13. National Conference of Catholic Bishops (NCCB), *Economic Justice for All: Pastoral Letter on Catholic Social Teachings and the U.S. Economy* (Washington, D.C.: National Conference of Catholic Bishops, 1986), p. 77, quoted in David Hollenbach, *Justice, Peace, and Human Rights: American Catholic Social Ethics* (New York: Crossroad, 1990), p. 82.

14. Adapted from the Yale Task Force on Population Ethics (D. Cristiansen, et al.), "Moral Claims, Human Rights, and Population Policies," *Theological Studies*, 35 (1974), p. 102, quoted in Hollenbach, *Claims in Conflict: Renewing and Retrieving the Catholic Human Rights Tradition* (New York: Paulist Press, 1979), p. 98.

15. Ibid, p.198.

16. Gustavo Gutiérrez, *The Power of the Poor in History* (Maryknoll, N.Y.: Orbis Books, 1983), p. xiv.

17. Hollenbach, *Claims*, p. 204.

18. Ismael García, *Justice in Latin American Theology of Liberation* (Atlanta: John Knox Press, 1982), pp. 89-90.

19. Goulet's work hinges on three categories of needs: subsistence and survival needs, enhancement needs, and luxury needs. Goulet's call for all nations to focus first on subsistence needs before meeting luxury needs would require nations to redistribute their wealth, or as Goulet says later in the book, "practice voluntary austerity." While I agree with Goulet's statement, "There is no justification for allowing a few wealthy societies to use a disproportionate share of the world's resources for the satisfaction of luxury needs while the needs of the masses are unmet," I realize that much of the First World would be threatened by the implementation of Goulet's categories, especially those who follow the Protestant work ethic and a capitalism that rewards the few at the expense of the many. Denis Goulet, *The Cruel Choice* (New York: Atheneum, 1973), pp. 236-248. See also Michael Walzer, *Spheres of Justice: A Defense of Pluralism and Equality* (New York: Basic Books, 1983), pp. 64-67, 75-76, 79-83.

20. Gustavo Gutiérrez, *A Theology of Liberation: History, Politics, and Salvation*, 2nd ed., trans. Sister Caridad Inda, John Eagleson, and Matthew J. O'Connell (Maryknoll, N.Y.: Orbis Books, 1988), pp. 136-137.

21. Robert McAffee Brown, *Gustavo Gutiérrez: An Introduction to Liberation Theology* (Maryknoll, N.Y.: Orbis Books, 1990), p. 38.

22. Puebla # 1134-1165, *Puebla and Beyond: Documentation and Commentary,*

ed. John Eagelson and Phillip Scharper, trans. John Drury (Maryknoll, NY: Orbis Books, 1979), quoted in Brown, *Gutiérrez*, p. 59.

23. Ibid., p. 15.

24. Gutiérrez, *Power*, pp. 211-212.

25. Leonardo Boff and Virgil Elizondo, eds. *1492-1992: The Voice of the Victims* (London: SMC Press, 1990), p. viii.

26. Margaret E. Crahan, "The State and the Individual in Latin America: An Historical Overview," in *Human Rights and Basic Needs in the Americas*, ed. Margaret E. Crahan (Washington, D.C.: Georgetown University Press, 1982), p. 118.

27. Patricia Weiss Fagan, "The Links between Human Rights and Basic Needs," *Background* (Center for International Policy), Spring, 1978, p. 4, quoted in Hollenbach, *Claims*, p. 192.

28. Children's Defense Fund, *The State of America's Children 1991* (Washington, D.C.: Children's Defense Fund, 1991), p. 25.

29. Brown, *Gutiérrez*, p. 208.

30. Gutiérrez, *A Theology*, 2nd ed., p. xxii.

31. Elsa Tamez, *Against Machismo* (Oak Park, Ill.: Meyer-Stone, 1987), p. 41, in Brown, *Gustavo*, p. 72.

32. Glen Stassen, "Michael Walzer's Situated Justice," in *The Journal of Religious Ethics*, 22, no. 2 (Fall, 1994).

33. Iris Marion Young, *Justice and the Politics of Difference* (Princeton, N.J.: Princeton University Press, 1990), pp. 3, 6.

34. Susan Moller Okin, *Justice, Gender, and the Family* (New York: Basic Books, 1989), p. 111.

35. Walzer, *Spheres*, pp. 240-241, quoted in Okin, *Justice*, p. 114.

36. Okin, *Justice*, p. 9.

37. Michael Walzer, *The Company of Critics: Social Criticism and Political Commitment in the Twentieth Century* (New York: Basic Books, 1988), pp. 149-151, quoted in Stassen, "Narrative."

38. United Nations Development Programme, *Human Development Report 1991* (New York: Oxford University Press, 1991), p. 120, and World Bank Development Tables, 1991.

39. Boff and Elizondo, eds., *1492*, p. viii.

40. Susanne Jonas, *The Battle for Guatemala: Rebels, Death Squads, and U.S. Power* (Boulder, Colo.: Westview Press, 1992), p. 9.

41. Ibid., p. 9.

42. Stassen, "Situated," p. 12.

43. Walzer, *Spheres*, p. 314.

44. Michael Walzer, *Obligations: Essays on Disobedience, War, and Citizenship* (Cambridge, Mass.: Harvard University Press, 1970), p. 227. See also Michael Walzer, "Pluralism in Political Perspective," in *The Politics of Ethnicity*, ed. Ann Orlov, Stephen Thernstrom, and Oscar Handlin (Cambridge, Mass.: Harvard University Press, 1982), pp. 1-28.

45. Michael Mann, "To Celebrate Columbus or Not to Celebrate: Is That the Question?" Brown Bag Lunch Series, Kroc Institute for International Peace Stud-

ies, Notre Dame, Indiana, January 23, 1992, p. 24.

46. Pablo Richard, "1492: The Violence of God and the Future of Christianity," in Boff, *1492*, p. 62.

47. Bartolomé de las Casas, *Del unico modo de atraer los pueblos a la verdadera religión* (Mexico City: Fondo de Cultura Económica, 1942), p. 545, quoted in Gutiérrez, "God from the Underside of History," in *Power*, p. 195.

48. "Historia de las Indias," in *Obras escogidos* (Madrid: BAE, 1958), p. 356, quoted in Gutiérrez, *Power*, p. 196.

49. Stassen, "Narrative."

50. Ibid.

51. Martin Buber, *A Land of Two Peoples: Martin Buber on Jews and Arabs*, ed. Paul R. Mendes-Flohr (Oxford: Oxford University Press, 1983), p. 91, quoted in Walzer, *The Company*, p. 67.

52. Bellah, et al., *Habits*, p. 153. See also chapter 15, Alasdair MacIntyre, *After Virtue* (South Bend, Ind.: University of Notre Dame Press, 1981).

53. Rigoberta Menchú, quoted in Conference Statement, Second Continental Gathering, Quetzaltenango, Guatemala, October 1991.

54. Paulo Freire, *Pedagogy of the Oppressed*, trans. Myra Bergman Ramos (New York: Herder and Herder, 1971).

55. Gutiérrez, *Power*, p. 60.

56. Ibid., p. 23.

57. Gutiérrez, *A Theology*, 2nd ed., p. 103; Gutiérrez, *The Truth*, p. 14.

58. The 7 percent rate is an improvement over the 1 percent approval rate of the 1980s. Shannon Salinas, "TPS Campaign for Guatemalans," in *Guatemala Bulletin*, 2, no. 4 (1993), 10.

59. The lawsuit, *American Baptist Churches v. Thornburg*, was a major catalyst for the improved acceptance rate for Central American refugees. Salinas, "TPS," p. 10.

60. James McGinnis, *Bread and Justice: Toward a New International Economic Order* (New York: Paulist Press, 1979), p. 10.

61. Interview with Olga Rivas, coordinating council, GRUFEPROMEFAM, July 27, 1992.

62. "Supporting Brothers and Sisters in the Struggle," *One World*, no. 112 (1986), 28-29.

63. Max Stackhouse, *Creeds, Societies, and Human Rights: A Study in Three Cultures* (Grand Rapids, Mich.: Eerdmans, 1984), p. 3.

64. Rigoberta Menchú, *I Rigoberta Menchú: An Indian Woman in Guatemala*, ed. Elisabeth Burgos-Debray, trans. Ann Wright (London: Verso, 1984), pp. 132, 134.

Chapter 6

1. Patricia K. Hall, "Military Rule Threatens Guatemala's Highland Mayan Indians," *Cultural Survival Quarterly*, 10, no. 2 (1986), 48-52.

2. Sean F. Reardon, "An Overview of Awareness of Indigenous Rights in Guatemala," p. 8, quoted in Michael Mann, "To Celebrate or Not to Celebrate: Is

That the Question?" Brown Bag Lunch Series, Kroc Institute for International Peace Studies, Notre Dame, Indiana, January 23, 1992, p. 30.

3. Julia Esquivel, "Why" in *The Certainty of Spring: Poems by a Guatemalan in Exile*, translated by Anne Woehrle (Washington, D.C.: Ecumenical Program on Central America and the Caribbean, 1993), pp. 22-23.

4. Beverly Harrison, *Making the Connections: Essays in Feminist Social Ethics*, ed. Carol S. Robb (Boston: Beacon Press, 1985), p. 243.

5. Martin Luther King Jr., quoted in "The Testimony of Scripture and of Martin Luther King Jr.," *Baptist Peacemaker*, 12, no. 3-4 (Fall/Winter, 1992), 16.

6. Oscar Romero, *Voice of the Voiceless: The Four Pastoral Letters and Other Statements* (Maryknoll, N.Y.: Orbis Books, 1990).

7. Stephen Charles Mott, *Biblical Ethics and Social Change* (New York: Oxford University Press, 1982), pp. 122-123.

8. Ronald J. Sider, review of *The Evangelical Renaissance* by Donald G. Bloesch, *Christianity Today*, 18 (1974), 1161.

9. Bellah, et al., *Habits of the Heart: Individualism and Commitment in American Life* (New York: Harper & Row, 1985), p. 248.

10. Parker Palmer, *Company of Strangers: Christians and the Renewal of American Public Life* (New York: Crossroad, 1981), p. 155, [emphasis in original].

11. Elisabeth Schüssler Fiorenza, *In Memory of Her: A Feminist Theological Reconstruction of Christian Origins* (New York: Crossroad, 1983), p. 345.

12. Muriel Lester, *It Occurred to Me* (New York: Harper and Brothers, 1937), p. 42.

13. Charles Liteky, personal letter and Congressional Medal of Honor left at the Vietnam Wall, Washington, D.C., July 29, 1986; on display at the National Museum of History, Washington, D.C., October, 1993.

14. King, "The Testimony," p. 16.

15. Michael Walzer, *Exodus and Revolution* (New York: Basic Books, 1985), p. 149.

A Select Bibliography

Books

Aburdene, Patricia and John Naisbitt. *Megatrends for Women.* New York: Villard Books, 1992.

Adams, Richard N. *Crucifixion by Power: Essays on the Guatemalan National Social Structure, 1944-1966.* Austin: University of Texas Press, 1970.

Alinsky, Saul D. *Rules for Radicals.* New York: Vintage Books, 1971.

Alvarez, Sonia E. "Women's Movement and Gender Politics in the Brazilian Transition." In *The Women's Movement in Latin America: Feminism and the Transition to Democracy.* Ed. Jane S. Jaquette. Boston: Unwin Hyman, 1989.

Americas Watch. *Persecuting Human Rights Monitors: The CERJ in Guatemala.* Washington, D.C.: Americas Watch, 1989.

_____. *Closing the Spaces: Human Rights in Guatemala; May 1987-October 1988.* New York: Americas Watch, 1988.

_____. *Guatemala: A Nation of Prisoners.* New York: Americas Watch, 1984.

_____. *Guatemala: The Group for Mutual Support.* New York: Americas Watch, 1985.

_____. *Getting away with Murder.* New York: Americas Watch, 1991.

_____. *Messengers of Death: Human Rights in Guatemala November 1988-February 1990.* New York: Americas Watch, 1990.

Amnesty International. *Guatemala: Human Rights Violations under the Civilian Government.* New York: Amnesty International Publications, 1989.

_____. *Guatemala: The Human Rights Record.* London: Amnesty International Publications, 1987.

_____. *Women in the Front Line: Human Rights Violations against Women.* New York: Amnesty International, March 1991.

Arias, Arturo. "El movimiento indígena en Guatemala: 1970-1983." In *Movimientos populares en Centroamérica.* Ed. Daniel Camacho and Rafael Menjívar. San José, Costa Rica: EDUCA, 1985.

Asamblea Nacional Constituyente. *Constitución política de la República de Guatemala.* Guatemala: Jimenez and Ayala, 1985.

Bellah, Robert, et al. *Habits of the Heart: Individualism and Commitment in American Life.* New York: Harper & Row, 1985.

Boff, Leonardo, and Virgil Elizondo, eds. *1492-1992: The Voice of the Victims.* London: SMC Press, 1990.

Bowen, Gordon. "The Political Economy of State Terrorism: Barrier to Human Rights in Guatemala." In *Human Rights and Third World Development.* Ed. George W. Shepherd Jr., and Ved P. Nanda. Westport: Greenwood Press, 1985.

Brown, Cynthia. *Human Rights in Guatemala: No Neutrals Allowed.* New York: Americas Watch, 1982.

_____, ed. *With Friends like These.* New York: Pantheon, 1985.

Brown, Robert McAfee. *Gustavo Gutiérrez: An Introduction to Liberation Theology.* Maryknoll, N.Y.: Orbis Books, 1990.

Bulmer-Thomas, Victor. *The Political Economy of Central America since 1920.* Cambridge: Cambridge University Press, 1987.

Bunster-Burotto, Ximena. "Surviving Beyond Fear: Women and Torture in Latin America." In *Women and Change in Latin America.* Ed. June Nash and Helen Safa. South Hadley, Mass.: Bergin and Garvey, 1986.

Caldwell, Dondeena. *If Quetzals Could Cry.* New York: Friendship Press, 1990.

Cardenal, Ernesto. "Lord It's Incredible." In *Psalms.* Trans. Thomas Blackburn, et al. New York: Crossroad, 1981.

Children's Defense Fund. *The State of America's Children 1991.* Washington, D.C.: Children's Defense Fund, 1991.

Comisión para la Defensa de los Derechos Humanos en Centroamérica. *Situación de los derechos humanos en Centroamérica:*

Informe anual, Mayo 1989/ Mayo 1990. San José, Costa Rica: CODEHUCA, 1991.

Cortright, David. *Peace Works*. Boulder, Colo.: Westview Press, 1993.

Crahan, Margaret, "The State and the Individual in Latin America: An Historical Overview." In *Human Rights and Basic Needs in the Americas*. Ed. Margaret E. Crahan. Washington, D.C.: Georgetown University Press, 1982.

_____. "National Security Ideology and Human Rights." In *Human Rights and Basic Needs in the Americas*. Ed. Margaret E. Crahan. Washington, D.C.: Georgetown University Press, 1982.

Davis, Shelton H. "Introduction: Sowing the Seeds of Violence." In *Harvest of Violence: The Mayan Indians and the Guatemalan Crisis*. Ed. Robert M. Carmack. Norman, Okla.: University of Oklahoma Press, 1988.

_____. "State Violence and Agrarian Crisis in Guatemala." In *Trouble in Our Backyard: Central America and the United States in the Eighties*. Ed. Martin Diskin. New York: Pantheon Books, 1984.

_____, and Julie Hodson. *Witness to Political Violence in Guatemala*. Boston: Oxfam America, 1982.

Elliot, J. H. *Imperial Spain: 1469-1716*. Hammondsworth, England: Pelican Books, 1976, p. 65. Quoted in *Conquest and Survival in Colonial Guatemala: A Historical Geography of the Cuchumatán Highlands 1500-1821*, by W. George Lovell. Montreal: Queen's University Press, 1985.

Ellis, Marc H. and Otto Maduro, eds. *The Future of Liberation Theology: Essays in Honor of Gustavo Gutiérrez*. Maryknoll, N.Y.: Orbis, 1989.

Esquivel, Julia. "Christian Women and the Struggle for Justice in Central America." In *Speaking of Faith: Global Perspectives on Women, Religion, and Social Change*. Ed. Diana L. Eck and Devaki Jain. Philadelphia: New Society, 1987.

_____. "A Trembling." In *The Certainty of Spring: Poems by a Guatemalan in Exile*. Trans. Anne Woehrle. Washington, D.C.: Ecumenical Program on Central America and the Caribbean, 1993.

_____. "Why." In *The Certainty of Spring: Poems by a*

Guatemalan in Exile. Trans. Anne Woehrle. Washington, D.C.: Ecumenical Program on Central America and the Caribbean, 1993.

Falla, Ricardo. "Struggle for Survival in the Mountains: Hunger and Other Privations Inflicted on Internal Refugees from the Central Highlands." In *Harvest of Violence: The Mayan Indians and the Guatemalan Crisis*. Ed. Robert M. Carmack. Norman, Okla.: University of Oklahoma Press, 1988.

_____. "We Charge Genocide." In *Guatemala: Tyranny on Trial*. Ed. Susanne Jonas, et al. San Francisco: Synthesis, 1984.

Fiorenza, Elisabeth Schüssler. *In Memory of Her: A Feminist Theological Reconstruction of Christian Origins*. New York: Crossroad, 1983.

_____. "The Politics of Otherness." In *The Future of Liberation Theology: Essays in Honor of Gustavo Gutiérrez*. Maryknoll, N.Y.: Orbis, 1989.

Foster, George. *Culture and Conquest: America's Spanish Heritage*. Viking Fund Publication in Anthropology, no. 27. New York: Viking Press, 1960.

Fried, Jonathon, et al. *Guatemala in Rebellion: Unfinished History*. New York: Grove Press, 1983.

Galeano, Eduardo. *Guatemala: Occupied Country*. New York: Monthly Review Press, 1969.

García, Ismael. *Justice in Latin American Theology of Liberation*. Atlanta: John Knox Press, 1987.

Goldston, James A. *Shattered Hope: Guatemalan Workers and the Promise of Democracy*. Boulder, Colo.: Westview, 1989.

Goulet, Denis. *The Cruel Choice*. New York: Atheneum, 1973.

Guatemalan Human Rights Committee in Mexico. "Legislación en materia de derechos humanos." In *Guatemala:Violación y defensa de los derechos humanos*. Mexico City, Mexico: Comisión de Derechos Humanos, 1991.

Gurr, Ted. "The Political Origins of State Violence and Terror: A Theoretical Analysis." In *Government Violence and Repression*. Ed. Michael Stohl and George A. Lopez. New York: Greenwood Press, 1986.

_____. *Why Men Rebel*. Princeton, N.J.: Princeton University Press, 1970.

Gutiérrez, Gustavo. *The God of Life*. Trans. Matthew J. O'Connell. Maryknoll, N.Y.: Orbis, 1991.

_____. *Hablar de Dios desde el sufrimiento del inocente*. Lima: Instituto Bartolomé de Las Casas, 1985.

_____. *The Power of the Poor in History*. Trans. Robert R. Barr. Maryknoll, N.Y.: Orbis, 1983.

_____. *Teología desde el reverso de la historia*. Lima: Centro de Estudios y Publicaciones, 1977.

_____. *A Theology of Liberation: History, Politics, and Salvation*. Trans. and ed. Sister Caridad Inda and John Eagleson. Maryknoll, N.Y.: Orbis, 1988.

_____. *A Theology of Liberation: History, Politics, and Salvation*. 2nd ed. Trans. Sister Caridad Inda, John Eagleson, and Matthew J. O'Connell. Maryknoll, N.Y.: Orbis Books, 1988.

_____. *The Truth Shall Make You Free*. Trans. Matthew J. O'Connell. Maryknoll, N.Y.: Orbis Books, 1990.

_____. *We Drink from Our Own Wells: The Spiritual Journey of a People*. Maryknoll, N.Y.: Orbis Books, 1984.

_____, and Richard Shaull. *Liberation and Change*. Ed. Ronald Stone. Atlanta: John Knox Press, 1977.

_____, et al. *Reflexion sobre la teología de la liberación*. Iquitos, Perú: Centro de Estudios Teológicos de la Amazonia, 1986.

Hamill, Hugh M. Jr., ed. *Dictatorship in Spanish America*. New York: Alfred A. Knopf, 1965.

Handy, Jim. *Gift of the Devil: A History of Guatemala*. Toronto, Ont.: Between the Lines, 1984.

_____. "Insurgency and Counterinsurgency in Guatemala." In *Sociology of Developing Societies in Central America*. Ed. Jan L. Flora and Edelberto Torres-Rivas. New York: Monthly Review Press, 1989.

Harrison, Beverly. *Making the Connections: Essays in Feminist Social Ethics*. Ed. Carol S. Robb. Boston: Beacon Press, 1985.

Hellman, Lillian. *Pentimento*. Boston: Little, Brown, and Co., 1973.

Heyward, Carter. "Doing Theology in a Counterrevolutionary Situation." In *The Future of Liberation Theology: Essays in Honor of Gustavo Gutiérrez*. Maryknoll, N.Y.: Orbis, 1989.

Hollenbach, David. *Claims in Conflict: Retrieving and Renewing the Catholic Human Rights Tradition*. New York: Paulist, 1979.

_____. *Justice, Peace, and Human Rights*. New York: Crossroad, 1988.

Horsley, Richard. *Jesus and the Spiral of Violence: Popular Jewish Resistance in Roman Palestine*. San Francisco: Harper & Row, 1987.

Hough, Richard, et al. *Land and Labor in Guatemala: An Assessment*. Washington, D.C.: Agency for International Development, 1982.

Immerman, Richard H. *The CIA in Guatemala: The Foreign Policy of Intervention*. Austin: University of Texas Press, 1982.

Jonas, Susanne. "Contradictions of Guatemala's Political Opening." In *Democracy in Latin America: Visions and Realities*. Ed. Susanne Jonas and Nancy Stein. New York: Bergin and Garvey, 1990.

_____. *The Battle for Guatemala: Rebels, Death Squads, and U.S. Power*. Boulder, Colo.: Westview Press, 1992.

Josephus. *Dio Cassius*.

King, Martin Luther, Jr. *The Words of Martin Luther King Jr*. New York: Newmarket Press, 1987.

_____. *Why We Can't Wait*. New York: Harper & Row, 1963.

Kittel, Gerhard, ed. *Theological Dictionary of the New Testament*, vol. 1. Grand Rapids, Mich.: Wm. B. Eerdmans Publishing Company, 1972, p. 781. Quoted in *Foremothers: Women of the Bible*, by Janice Nunnally-Cox. New York: Seabury, 1981.

Kohler, Gernot. "Global Apartheid." In *Toward a Just World Order*. Ed. Richard Falk, Sam Kim, and Saul Mendlovitz. Boulder, Colo.: Westview Press, 1982.

Krueger, Chris, and Kjell Enge. *Security and Development Conditions in the Guatemalan Highlands*. Washington, D.C.: Washington Office on Latin America, 1985.

LaFeber, Walter. *Inevitable Revolutions: The United States and Central America*. New York: W. W. Norton, 1984.

Lebacqz, Karen. *Justice in an Unjust World: Foundations for a Christian Approach to Justice*. Minneapolis: Augsburg, 1987.

_____. *Six Theories of Justice: Perspectives from Philosophical and Theological Ethics*. Minneapolis: Augsburg, 1986.

Lester, Muriel. *It Occurred to Me*. New York: Harper and Brothers, 1937.

Linz, Juan J. *The Breakdown of Democratic Regimes: Crisis, Break-*

down, and Reequilibration. Baltimore: The Johns Hopkins University Press, 1987.

Lovell, W. George. *Conquest and Survival in Colonial Guatemala: A Historical Geography of the Cuchumatán Highlands 1500-1821.* Montreal: Queen's University Press, 1985.

McAdams, Doug. *Political Process and the Development of Black Insurgency, 1930-1970.* Chicago: University of Chicago Press, 1982.

McGinnis, James. *Bread and Justice: Toward a New International Economic Order.* New York: Paulist Press, 1979.

McManus, Philip, and Gerald Schlabach. *Relentless Persistence: Nonviolent Action in Latin America.* Philadelphia: New Society Publishers, 1991.

Menchú, Rigoberta. *I, Rigoberta Menchú.* Ed. Elisabeth Burgos-Debray. New York: Verso, The Alpine Press, 1984.

Miller, Francesca. *Latin American Women and the Search for Social Justice.* Hanover, N.H.: University Press of New England, 1991.

Monteforte Toledo, María. *Guatemala: Monografia sociologica.* Mexico City: N.p., 1959, pp. 47-50. Quoted in *Gift of the Devil: A History of Guatemala.* Toronto, Ont.: Between the Lines, 1984.

Moore, Barrington. *Injustice: The Social Bases of Obedience and Revolt.* New York: Macmillan, 1978

Morris, Aldon, and Cedric Herring. "Theory and Research in Social Movements: A Critical Review." In *Annual Review of Political Science,* vol. 2. Ed. Samuel Long. Norwood, N.J.: Ablex, 1987.

Mott, Stephen Charles. *Biblical Ethics and Social Change.* New York: Oxford University Press, 1982.

Nairn, Allan. "Guatemala." In *With Friends Like These: Americas Watch Report on Human Rights and United States Policy in Latin America.* Ed. Cynthia Brown. New York: Pantheon Books, 1985.

Nash, Helen, Helen Safa, and contributors. *Women and Change in Latin America.* South Hadley, Mass.: Bergin and Garvey Publishers, 1985.

National Conference of Catholic Bishops. *Economic Justice for All: Pastoral Letter on Catholic Social Teaching and the U. S. Economy.*

Washington, D.C.: National Conference of Catholic Bishops, 1986.

Navarro, Marysa. "The Personal Is Political: Las Madres de Plaza de Mayo." In *Power and Popular Protest: Latin American Social Movements*. Ed. Susan Eckstein. Berkeley: University of California Press, 1989.

Nouwen, Henri. *Gracias!* New York: Harper & Row, 1983.

Nunnally-Cox, Janice. *Foremothers: Women of the Bible*. New York: Seabury, 1981.

Nyrop, Richard F. *Guatemala: A Country Study*. Area Handbook Series. Washington, D.C.: The American University, 1983.

Oficina de Derechos Humanos. *Informe anual 1991*. Guatemala City: Arzobispado de Guatemala, 1992.

Oliver, Pamela. "Bringing the Crowd Back In: The Nonorganizational Elements of Social Movements." In *Research in Social Movements, Conflict, and Change*, vol. 11. Greenwich, Conn.: JAI Press, 1989.

Origen. *Against Celsus*, 5.33 and 3.8. Quoted in Wink, Walter. *Engaging the Powers*.

Paláez, Severo Martinez. *La patria del criollo*. San Jose, Costa Rica: Editorial Universitaria Centroamericana, 1979.

Palmer, Parker. *Company of Strangers: Christians and the Renewal of American Public Life*. New York: Crossroad, 1981.

Piven, Frances Fox, and Richard A. Cloward. *Poor People's Movements: Why They Succeed, How They Fail*. New York: Vintage Books, 1979.

Romero, Oscar. *Voice of the Voiceless: Four Pastoral Letters and Other Statements*. Maryknoll, N.Y.: Orbis Books, 1990.

Ruddick, Sara. *Maternal Thinking: Toward a Politics of Peace*. New York: Ballantine Books, 1989.

Salinas, Gloria Ardaya. "The Barzolas and the Housewives Committee." In *Women and Social Change in Latin America*. Ed. June Nash and Helen I. Safa. South Hadley, Mass.: Bergin and Garvey, 1986.

Schaef, Anne Wilson. *Women's Reality: An Emerging Female System in a White Male Society*. New York: Harper & Row, 1985.

Schlesinger, Stephen, and Stephen Kinzer. *Bitter Fruit: The Untold Story of the American Coup in Guatemala*. Garden City, N.J.: Doubleday, 1982.

Schroder, Hannelore. "The Economic Impoverishment of Mothers Is the Enrichment of Fathers." In *Women, Work, and Poverty.* Ed. Elizabeth Schüssler Fiorenza, Anne Carr (English language ed.), and Marcus Lefebure. Edinburgh: T. and T. Clark, LTD, 1987.

Secretaria General del Consejo Nacional de Planificación Económica and UNICEF. *Analisis de situación del nino y la mujer.* Guatemala City: SEGEPLAN and UNICEF, 1991.

Sharp, Gene. *The Politics of Nonviolent Action.* Boston: Porter Sargent, 1973.

Simon, Jean-Marie. *Guatemala: Eternal Spring-Eternal Tyranny.* New York: W. W. Norton, 1987.

Smith, Jackie M., ed. *Women, Faith, and Economic Justice.* Philadelphia: Westminster Press, 1985.

Stackhouse, Max. *Creeds, Societies and Human Rights: A Study in Three Cultures.* Grand Rapids, Mich.: Eerdmans, 1984.

Stanfield, Pedro. "Guatemala: When Spring Turned to Winter." In *Relentless Persistence: Nonviolent Action in Latin America.* Ed. Philip McManus and Gerald Schlabach. Philadelphia: New Society Publishers, 1991.

Stassen, Glen. "Critical Variables in Christian Social Ethics." In *Issues in Christian Ethics.* Ed. Paul Simmons. Nashville: Broadman Press, 1980.

————. *Just Peacemaking: Transforming Initiatives for Justice and Peace.* Louisville, Ky.: Westminster/John Knox, 1992.

————. "The Struggle Against Injustice: Narrative of Our Time." Forthcoming in *Theology without Foundations.* Ed. Nancey Murphy, Mark Nation, and Stanley Hauerwas. Nashville: Abingdon Press.

Stavenhagen Rodolfo. *Derecho indígena y derechos humanos en América Latina.* México: Instituto Interamericano de Derechos Humanos, 1988.

Swomly, John Jr. *Liberation Ethics.* New York: Macmillan, 1972.

Tamez, Elsa. *Against Machismo.* Oak Park, Ill.: Meyer-Stone, 1987.

Tertullian. *On Idolatry,* 19.3. Quoted in *Engaging the Powers,* by Walter Wink.

————. *The Chaplet,* 11.4. Quoted in *Engaging the Powers,* by Walter Wink.

United Nations Children's Fund. *The Invisible Adjustment: Poor*

Women and the Economic Crisis. Santiago, Chile: UNICEF, The Americas and the Caribbean Regional Office, 1989.

_____. *Los niños de Guatemala*. Guatemala City, Guatemala: UNICEF, 1991.

_____. *The State of the World's Children 1991*. New York: Oxford, 1991.

United Nations Development Programme. *Human Development Report 1991*. New York: Oxford University Press, 1991.

Walzer, Michael. *The Company of Critics: Social Criticism and Political Commitment in the Twentieth Century*. New York: Basic Books, 1988.

_____. *Exodus and Revolution*. New York: Basic Books, 1985.

_____. *Obligations: Essays on Disobedience, War, and Citizenship*. Cambridge, Mass.: Harvard University Press, 1970.

_____. "Pluralism in Political Perspective." In *The Politics of Ethnicity*. Ed. Ann Orlov, Stephen Thernstrom, and Oscar Handlin. Cambridge, Mass.: Harvard University Press, 1982.

_____. *Spheres of Justice: A Defense of Pluralism and Equality*. New York: Basic Books, 1983.

Welch, Sharon D. *A Feminist Ethic of Risk*. Minneapolis: Fortress Press, 1990.

Wink, Walter. *Engaging the Powers*. The Powers, vol. 3. Philadelphia: Augsburg Fortress, 1993.

_____. *Naming the Powers: The Language of Power in the New Testament*. The Powers, vol. 1. Philadelphia: Fortress Press, 1986.

_____. *Unmasking the Powers: The Invisible Forces that Determine Human Existence*. The Powers, vol. 2. Philadelphia: Fortress Press, 1986.

_____. *Violence and Nonviolence in South Africa: Jesus' Third Way*. Philadelphia: New Society, 1987.

Worker Rights and the New World Order. El Salvador: National Labor Committee in Support of Democracy and Human Rights, 1991. Quoted in "The Phillips-Van Heusen Campaign: A Struggle for Justice and Basic Rights in the Global Economy," by U.S./Guatemala Labor Education Project. Chicago: U.S./Guatemala Labor Education Project, 1991.

World Bank. *World Development Report 1991.* New York: Oxford University Press, 1991.

Yoder, John Howard. *The Politics of Jesus.* Grand Rapids, Mich.: Eerdmans Publishing Company, 1972.

Zelin, Elizabeth, ed. *Women and Social Change in Latin America.* London: Zed Books, 1990.

Ziegler, Warren. *Mindbook for Imaging a World without Weapons.* Denver: Futures Invention Associates.

Articles

Americas Watch. "Extermination in Guatemala." A condensation from Americas Watch Report, *Creating a Desolation and Calling It Peace. New York Review of Books,* 30 (June 2, 1983), 13-16.

"Arming Dictators." *Defense Monitor,* 21, no. 5 (1992), 5.

Bishop, Katherine. "U.S. Alters Policy for Hearings on Political Asylum." *The New York Times International,* December 20, 1990.

Black, George. "Guatemala—The War Is Not Over." *NACLA Report on the Americas,* 17 (May-April 1983), 7-8.

Brockett, Charles D. "Malnutrition, Public Policy, and Agrarian Change in Guatemala." *Journal of Interamerican Studies and World Affairs,* 26 (November 1984), 477-497.

_____. "The Structure of Political Opportunities and Peasant Mobilization in Central America." *Comparative Politics,* 23 (April 1991), 253-274.

Coats, Stephen. "Made in Guatemala: Union Busting in the Maquiladoras." *Multinational Monitor,* 12 (November 1991), 23-25.

Cooper, Marc. "The Butchers in Bush's Backyard: Death Squads Are on the Loose Again in Guatemala." *New Statesman and Society,* 3 (July 13, 1990), 18-20.

Dowd, Maureen. "Bush Begins His Latin American Tour in Brazil amid Worry over Argentina Strike." *The New York Times International,* Tuesday, December 4, 1990, sec. A, p. 14.

Farah, Douglas. "Indian from Guatemala Wins Nobel Peace

Prize." *The Washington Post,* Saturday, October 17, 1992, sec. A, p. 1.

Farnsworth, Elizabeth. "Guatemala: Who Calls the Shots?" *Mother Jones,* 12 (October 1987), 16, 22, 57.

Girard, René. "Generative Violence and the Extinction of the Social Order." *Salmagundi,* 63-64 (Spring-Summer 1984), 210. Quoted in Wink, Walter. *Unmasking the Powers.*

Golden, Tim. "Exiled Indian from Guatemala Awarded the Nobel Peace Prize." *The New York Times,* Saturday, October 17, 1992, sec. A, p. 1.

Gomez, Fermin. "Violence in Guatemala." *Guatemala Human Rights Commission/USA,* 8, no. 1 (1990), 3.

"Guatemala." *The Defense Monitor.* 21, no. 5 (1992), 5-6.

Gutiérrez, Gustavo. "A Spirituality for Liberation." *The Other Side,* 21 (April-May 1985), 40-43.

Gruson, Lindsey. "Political Violence on the Rise Again in Guatemala, Tarnishing Civilian Rule." *The New York Times International,* June 28, 1990, sec. A, p. 3.

_____. "Resurgent Democracy and the Guatemalan Military." *Journal of Latin American Studies,* 18 (November 1986), 383-408.

Hall, Patricia K. "Military Rule Threatens Guatemala's Highland Mayan Indians." *Cultural Survival Quarterly,* 10, no. 2 (1986), 48-52.

Halpin, Lynne, and John Nelson. "Witness for Peace." *Central America Newsline,* 3, no. 26 (December 16, 1992), 4.

Hollyday, Joyce. "A Shield of Love." *Sojourners,* 12, no. 10 (November 1983), 13.

_____, and Jim Wallis. "Conspiracy of Compassion." *Sojourners,* 14, no. 3 (March 1985), 16.

"Human Rights Fact Sheet." Washington, D.C.: Guatemala Human Rights Commission/USA, 1988.

"Human Rights Review 1991." *Guatemala Human Rights Commission/USA Information Bulletin,* 10, no. 1 (First Quarter, 1992), 1.

Kinzer, Stephen. "Despite Gestures, Guatemala Not Addressing

Rights Abuses." *Austin American-Statesman*, (March 6, 1988), D 6.

Langsley, Stewart, and Ruth Pierce. "Elections that Mean Nothing to the Poor." *New Statesman*, 110 (October 25, 1985), 19-20.

"Many Forms of Rights' Violations." *UN Chronicle*, 22 (1985), 49.

McCamant, John F. "Intervention in Guatemala: Implications for the Study of Third World Politics." *Comparative Political Studies*, 17 (October 1984), 373-407.

McSherry, J. Patrice. "The Evolution of the National Security State: The Case of Guatemala." *Socialism and Democracy*, (Spring-Summer 1990), 121-153.

Millett, Richard L. "Guatemala: Hopes for Peace, Struggles for Survival." *Survival*, 33 (September-October 1991), 425-441.

Menchú, Rigoberta. "A Proud Part of this Moment." *Sojourners*, 20, no. 8 (October, 1991), 26-29.

Morrissey, Monique. "Human Rights: December-February." *Guatemala Human Rights Commission/USA Information Bulletin*, 10, no. 1 (First Quarter, 1992), 10.

Nairn, Allan and Jean-Marie Simon. "Bureaucracy of Death." *New Republic*, (June 30, 1986), 13-16.

Orlando, Catalina Trunk. "Apartheid and Guatemala." *The Little Way: Dorothy Day Catholic Worker*, 3, no. 2 (1991), 1.

Patterson, Franklin. "The Guatemalan Military and the Escuela Politécnica." *Armed Forces and Society*, 14 (Spring 1988), 359-390.

Payeras, Mario. "The Guatemalan Army and U.S. Policy in Central America." *Monthly Review*, 37 (March 1986), 14-20.

Power, Jonathon. "Guatemala: Stirrings of Change." *World Today*, 42 (Fall 1986), 31-35.

Reed, John. "The Dictatorship Has Taught Me the Road." *Latin American Perspectives*, 18 (Fall 1991), 96-103.

"Rigoberta Menchú Tum: Symbol of Peace and Reconciliation Wins Nobel Peace Prize." *Central America Report*, 12, no. 6 (1992), 1.

Salinas, Shannon. "TPS Campaign for Guatemalans." *Guatemala Bulletin*, 2, no. 4 (fourth quarter, 1993), 10.

Schirmer, Jennifer G. "Those Who Die for Life Cannot Be Called Dead: Women and Human Rights Protest in Latin America —Argentina, Guatemala, Chile." *Feminist Review*, 32 (Summer 1989), 3-29.

Sider, Ronald J. Review of *The Evangelical Renaissance*, by Donald G. Bloesch. *Christianity Today*, 18 (1974), 1161.

Simon, Jean-Marie. "In Search of the Disappeared: Guatemalan Women Resurrecting Democracy." *Multinational Monitor*, 7 (October 1986), 4-10.

Smith, Carol A. "The Militarization of Civil Society in Guatemala: Economic Reorganization as a Continuation of War." *Latin American Perspectives*, 17 (Fall 1990), 8-41.

Stassen, Glen. "Michael Walzer's Situated Justice." *The Journal of Religious Ethics*. (Fall, 1994).

_____. "A Social Theory Model for Religious Social Ethics." *Journal of Religious Ethics*, 5, no. 1 (1977), 9-37.

"Supporting Brothers and Sisters in the Struggle." *One World*, no. 112 (1986), 28-29.

Taylor, Richard. "For Penance and Peace." *Sojourners*, 12, no. 8 (September 1983), 14.

"The Testimony of Scripture and of Martin Luther King Jr." *Baptist Peacemaker*, (Fall/Winter, 1992), 16.

Time, June 26, 1944, p. 45. Quoted in *Liberation Ethics*, by John Swomly Jr. New York: Macmillan, 1972.

Tisdale, Jennifer. "Abuse of Women in Today's Guatemala." *Guatemala Bulletin*, 10, no. 4 (First Quarter, 1993), 6.

Tooley, Michelle. "Guatemala—Beyond Struggle, More Struggle." *Forsooth*, 5, no. 1 (December 1993/January 1994), 4.

_____. "Jim Flynn Helps Communities of Population in Resistance." *Forsooth*, 5, no. 1 (December 1993/January 1994), 4.

Torres-Rivas, Edelberto. "Guatemala: Crisis and Political Violence." *NACLA Report on the Americas* (January-February 1980), 24.

United States House Committee on Foreign Affairs Subcommittee on Western Hemisphere Affairs. "Options for United States Policy toward Guatemala: Hearing, July 17, 1990." Washington, D.C.: U.S. House of Representatives, 1990.

Waller, Douglas. "A World Awash in Refugees." *Newsweek*, 114 (October 9, 1989), 44-45.

Wallis, Jim. "Witness for Peace." *Sojourners*, 12, no. 10 (November 1983), 3.

Willis, Michael. "Rigoberta Menchú: Her Story Is the Story of Her People." *Central America Report*, 12, no. 6 (December 1992), 6.

Wilson, Brian. "Bishops Appalled by UN View of Guatemala." *New Statesman*, 108 (November 23, 1984), 4.

Woozley, A. D. "Injustice." *Studies in Ethics*, American Philosophical Quarterly Monograph Series 7. Oxford: Basil Blackwell, 1973.

Unpublished Works

Dissertations

Kendrick-Lites, Jane. "Divine and Human Vulnerability: Re-imaging Power and Relationship in Pastoral Theology." Ph.D. dissertation, The Southern Baptist Theological Seminary, 1994.

Pamphlets and Other Materials

AVANSCO/PACCA. "Growing Dilemmas: Guatemala, the Environment, and the Global Economy." Guatemala City, Guatemala: AVANSCO/PACCA, 1992.

CONAVIGUA. "CONAVIGUA 1988." Guatemala City, Guatemala: CONAVIGUA, 1988.

_____. "Introductory Statement." Guatemala City, Guatemala: CONAVIGUA, 1988.

_____. "La Voz de los niños pobres de Guatemala." Guatemala City, Guatemala: CONAVIGUA, 1991.

_____. "Las Violaciones de los derechos humanos son una

realidad dolorosa en nuestro pais." Guatemala City, Guatemala: CONAVIGUA, 1992.

_____, speech. Instituto Central America, Quetzaltenango, Guatemala, recorded June 29, 1992.

_____. "Tres años de vida, trabajo, sacrificio, y lucha." Guatemala City, Guatemala: CONAVIGUA, 1991.

Cox, Gray. "Imaging a World Without Weapons."

"Declaración de la Conferencia por la Paz y los Derechos Humanos." January 31, 1992.

Escoto, Jorge. Interview with author. March 26, 1993.

Fuentes, Blanca. Jornados por la Vida y la Paz and APGC, Permanent Assembly of Groups of Christians. Guatemala City, Guatemala, recorded July 22, 1992.

GRUFEPROMEFAM. "Analysis de coyuntura económico." Guatemala City, Guatemala: GRUFEPROMEFAM.

_____. "Analysis de coyuntura política." Guatemala City, Guatemala: GRUFEPROMEFAM.

_____. "Conociendo nuestros derechos laborales." Guatemala City, Guatemala: GRUFEPROMEFAM.

_____. "Las Mujeres luchamos para construir un futuro De paz." Guatemala City, Guatemala: GRUFEPROMEFAM, 1992.

_____. "La Vida de la Mujer y la Familia Indígena," speech given by Elba Marina Villatoro. Guatemala City, Guatemala, March, 1992.

Jornados Por La Vida y La Paz. "Situación de los damnificados por la violencia." Guatemala City, Guatemala: Jornados Por La Vida y La Paz.

Liteky, Charles. Letter to Ronald Reagan. July 29, 1986.

Lopez, Fermina. CONAVIGUA. Guatemala City, Guatemala, recorded July 7, 1992.

Mann, Michael. "To Celebrate Columbus or Not to Celebrate: Is That the Question?" Brown Bag Lunch Series, Kroc Institute for International Peace Studies, Notre Dame, Ind., January 23, 1992.

Nelson, John. Letter to author. August, 1992.

"Position of the Permanent Commissions of Representatives of the Guatemalan Refugees in Mexico, Regarding Several Themes Relative to the First Movement of The Return." (Unofficial translation), November, 1992.

Pro Justice and Peace Committee of Guatemala and World Council of Churches. "Human Rights in Guatemala." Guatemala City, Guatemala: World Council of Churches, October, 1988.

Rader, Jenn. Letter. February 12, 1993.

Rivas, Olga. Interview with author. July 27, 1992.

"Second Continental Gathering Conference Statement." Quetzaltenango, Guatemala, October, 1991.

Tarrow, Sidney. "Struggling to Reform: Social Movements and Policy Change during Cycles of Protest." Western Societies Paper no. 15. Ithaca, N.Y.: Cornell University, 1983.

Tuyuc, Rosalina. Interview with author. Quetzaltenango, Guatemala, June 29, 1992.

United Nations. "Report on the Situation of Human Rights in Guatemala." A/38/485 by the Special Rapporteur, Viscount Colville of Culross (November 30, 1983).

"Urgent Action Report." Citizen Urgent Action Network for Emergency Support (CUANES), December 7, 1992.

U.S./Guatemala Labor Education Project. "The Phillips-Van Heusen Campaign: A Struggle for Justice and Basic Rights in the Global Economy." Chicago: U.S./Guatemala Labor Education Project, December, 1991.

Washington Office on Latin America. "Guatemala Human Rights Conference Report." Washington, D.C., October, 1985.

Index

A

Advocacy, 193, 196
Alvarado, Pedro de, 19, 29-31, 161
Apartheid, 61-62, 107, 161, 168
Arana Osorio, Carlos, 41, 199
Arbenz Guzman, Jacobo, 36-41
Arévalo Bermejo, Jose, 36-39, 41
Assimilation, 163-164, 180, 189

B

Basileia, 123. (*See also* Kingdom of God.)
Beans and bullets, 43
Bellah, Robert et al., 169, 206, 209-210, 212

C

CIA, 39-40, 173, 198. (*See also* Operation Success; Allen Dulles.)
CONAVIGUA, 28, 57, 84-95, 151, 165, 174, 178, 184, 189-190, 195, 202, 226-227
CPRs (Communities of Population in Resistance), 97, 111, 179-180, 225
CUC, (Comite Unidad Campesino), 73-79, 90-94, 132, 165, 174, 184, 189-190, 195. (*See also* Repression.)
Cardenal, Ernesto, 138, 206, 213
Castillo Armas, Carlos, 39, 41
Cerezo Arevalo, Marco Vinicio, 42, 46-48, 50, 59-60, 63, 82-83, 91, 190, 200

Church, 152
    Catholic Action, 41, 91, 165, 199
    human rights, advocacy of, 111, 136, 175
    mission of the, 140, 152-154, 172, 191
Civil disobedience, 23, 35, 120, 122, 156
Civil patrols, 59-61, 83-85, 87-88, 181, 189
Conservative, 32-33

D

Death squads, 41-42, 44
Democracy, 34, 36-37, 39, 44-45, 155, 164
Democratization, 155-156. (*See also* Democracy.)
Disappeared, the, 20, 40, 42, 46, 58, 63, 82, 99, 129, 200
Discrimination, 62, 97, 128, 130, 134, 144-145, 194. (*See also* Injustice.)
Dulles, Allen, 40, 199
Dulles, John Foster, 40, 199

E

El Salvador, 14, 23
    Co-Madres, 23, 79
Elections, 34, 36-37, 40, 42, 44, 46, 57, 102
    1985, 46
Esquivel, Julia, 138, 183, 206, 210, 214
Evil, 27

personal, 113
structural, 27, 99, 103, 107, 113, 135, 140, 172

F

Feminism, feminist, 16, 135, 159-160, 192
Feminist values, 120. (*See also* Feminism, feminist.)

G

GAM (Grupo de Apoyo Mutuo), 28, 57, 79-83, 86, 89-95, 151, 165, 174, 178, 184, 186, 190, 195, 200
GRUFEPROMEFAM (Grupo Feminino Promejoramiento Familiar), 134, 170, 175, 209, 227
God's kingdom, 131. (*See also* Kingdom of God.)
Guerrillas, 15, 19, 41-42, 44, 59, 67-68, 74, 79, 102, 148
EGP (Guerrilla Army of the Poor), 44
FAR (Rebel Armed Forces), 44
ORPA (Organization of the People in Arms), 44
PGT (Guatemala Workers Party), 44
URNG (Guatemalan National Revolutionary Unity), 44
Gutiérrez, Gustavo, 25-27, 96, 141-143, 146, 150-154, 158-159, 164-168, 171-172, 175, 207-209, 215, 223

H

Harrison, Beverly, 183
Hollenbach, David, 25-27, 141-143, 149, 151, 157, 174, 184, 207, 216
Human rights, 20, 50, 54-56, 60, 78-79, 85-86, 88, 91, 109, 139-140, 143-144, 148-152, 154-157, 162, 165, 172, 174-177
abuse, 20, 45, 47, 56-58, 65, 75, 89,
129, 156, 183
church's role, 112, 143, 149, 154, 165, 175-176, 185
civil, 44, 55, 90, 150, 152, 156, 188
economic, 151, 155, 161, 188
groups, 20, 26, 41, 45, 54, 66, 71, 78, 92, 99, 148, 179, 183, 189
political, 44, 150, 152, 155-156, 161, 175, 188
social, 44, 58, 149-152, 156, 161, 188

I

Indians, 20, 42, 70, 76, 91
assimilation, 32, 61
ethnic identity of, 60-62, 161
repression of, 20, 29-31, 43, 76
social control of, 30-32
Indigenous people, 19, 25, 29, 31, 44, 61-62, 69, 75, 77, 98, 109, 155, 161-165, 170-171, 180, 182-183, 189
Individualism, 26, 99, 139-141, 155, 177, 191-192
Injustice, 27, 61, 98-100, 107, 114, 139, 141, 143-148, 154, 157, 159, 164-166, 168-169, 171-174, 176, 179, 182-184, 190
definition of, 98, 145
economic, 59, 63-65, 69, 72, 98, 125, 128, 130, 132, 141, 146, 154, 156, 158, 180
ethnic, 60, 72, 98, 146, 169
gender, 63, 72, 95, 126, 128, 141, 146, 157, 160
political, 146
social, 139, 146

J

Justice, 27-28, 69, 98, 100, 104, 115, 131, 137-148, 152-155, 157, 159-160, 162-163, 165-169, 172, 174-179, 184-189
cultural, 161-164
definition of, 138-139, 141, 144,

159, 165-167, 177
distributive, 144
economic, 77, 126, 131, 152, 156
ethnic, 77
gender, 57, 123, 133, 157, 188-189
political, 141, 156
social, 28, 120, 152-154, 160, 191

K

King, Martin Luther, Jr., 88, 96, 117,
139, 163, 185, 194, 202, 210, 216,
225
Kingdom of God, 116

L

Ladino, ladina, 21, 25, 32, 69, 76-78, 85,
90, 94, 108, 140, 162, 164, 170,
179-180, 189, 197
Land distribution, 38, 41, 47, 62. (*See
also* Land reform.)
Land reform, 37-39, 44, 47
Lebacqz, Karen, 25-27, 141-144, 146,
157, 165-168, 172, 174, 197, 206
Lester, Muriel, 139, 192-193, 210, 217
Liberal, 32-33
Liberation theology, 27, 105, 142, 146-
147, 153, 158-159, 165, 167, 171,
207

M

Mack Chang, Myrna, 96-97
Maquín, Mama, 70-72, 170
Massacre, 150, 182, 186
Panzós, 76-77, 79
Spanish Embassy, 74, 77-79
Medellín, CELAM II, 96, 153
Mejia Victores, Oscar Humberto, 44,
83
Menchú, Rigoberta, 28, 72-75, 77-79,
92-95, 97-98, 170, 176, 178, 185,
189, 201-202, 209, 217
Military, 15, 20, 34, 37, 42, 44, 46, 48,
59, 67-68, 71-72, 75, 83, 108-109,
179

impunity, 59, 102
Model villages, 55, 61-62, 67

N

Nonviolence, 22, 61, 115-116, 118,
137, 198, 202, 204
social change, 24, 72, 77-78, 80-81,
86, 174, 202
strategies, 80-81, 86, 111
Nonviolent action, 118. (*See also* Nonviolent social change.)

O

Okin, Susan Moller, 159-160, 208
Operation Success, 39

P

PACs, 59. (*See also* Civil Patrols.)
Political protest, 90
Poverty, 19, 59, 62-63, 66, 74, 77, 102,
124-128, 131-132, 148, 153-155,
164, 177, 179-181, 183, 187, 190,
194. (*See also* Injustice, economic.)
feminization of, 63-64, 124, 127,
157-158
Power, 37, 122, 156, 189
military, 39, 41, 43, 45-46
new image of, 122, 189
oligarchy, 37, 39, 43, 45
people, 118, 174, 205
Powers and authorities, 27, 95, 99-103,
105, 117, 181
Powers and principalities, 27-28, 100,
118, 136
Puebla, CELAM III, 153

R

Reagan, Ronald, 126, 150, 193
Refugee and refugee camps, 14, 19, 55,
66-68, 121-122, 173-174, 180
January, 1993 Return, 68, 86
La Sombra refugee camp, 71
internally displaced, 20, 66, 96
Reign of God, 114-115, 117, 131, 137.

(*See also* Kingdom of God.)
Repression, government, 69, 84, 93, 148
    CONAVIGUA, 72, 87
    CUC, 77, 79
    GAM, 72
Romero, Oscar, 45, 122, 187, 194, 210, 219
Ríos Montt, Efrain, 43-44, 50, 59, 199

S
Santiago Atitlán, 118-119, 182
Sermon on the Mount, 116, 131-132
Serrano Elias, Jorge, 48, 78
Sin, 27, 172
    personal, 99, 172
    social, 27, 69, 99, 172
Social change, 184, 195
    strategies, 184, 186
Social movement, 93-94, 110, 160
Social movement theory, 89, 93
    political process model, 89-91, 203
    relative deprivation, 89
    value of crowds, 93-94
Solidarity, 143, 159, 172, 175, 178-179, 185-186, 196
Stassen, Glen, 100, 139, 162, 168, 205-206, 208-208, 220

T
Torture, 55, 74-75, 77, 109, 121, 156, 179. (*See also* Repression.)

U
Ubico, Jorge, 34-36, 38, 197
United Fruit Company, 35, 38-39, 41
United Nations, 40, 47, 55-56, 58, 62, 64, 67, 70-71, 75, 92, 102, 197, 200, 208, 220, 228

Declaration of Human Rights, 144
United States, role of, 67, 102-103, 112
    refugee policy, 67

V
Violence, 36, 50, 83, 108, 114, 116-118, 130, 137, 140, 145, 158, 172, 182-184, 187, 189
    gender-related, 56-57, 126, 130, 158
    generalized, 56, 84
    military, 42-43, 93
    systematic, 44, 56, 62

W
Walzer, Michael, 25-27, 141-144, 151, 159-160, 162-163, 165, 168, 173, 175, 196, 207-208, 210, 221
Widows, 63, 84-85, 87, 95, 151, 155, 183
Wink, Walter, 26-28, 99-110, 113-118, 120, 122-123, 126, 136, 181, 203-206, 220-221
Witness for Peace, 15, 50, 92, 111-112, 186, 200, 202, 204, 226
Women, 56
    Guatemala, 64, 71, 84, 94-95, 128, 134, 139, 141, 194
    United States, 21, 105, 111, 119-120, 127, 129, 132-133, 135, 139, 141, 171, 175, 190, 195
Women and social change
    Argentina, 23-24
    Bolivia, 22
    Brazil, 21-22
    Chile, 24
    motherist groups, 23-24
Women peace activists, 120. (*See also* Women and social change, United States.)

The Author

A NATIVE of Lufkin, Texas, Michelle Tooley is Assistant Professor of Religion and Women's Studies at Belmont University (Nashville, Tenn.) and previously taught at Hanover College, Bellarmine College, and Southern Baptist Theological Seminary.

Tooley earned a Ph.D. in Christian social ethics at Southern Baptist and has done graduate study at the Kroc Institute for Peace Study at the University of Notre Dame. She also received degrees from Southwestern Baptist Seminary and Northwestern State University.

An activist in anti-hunger campaigns as well as Central America solidarity groups, Tooley blends activism and academics. She serves on the board of directors of Witness for Peace and Bread for the World. Convinced of the importance of standing with those who experience injustice, Tooley has participated in and led groups to Haiti, Costa Rica, Nicaragua, Guatemala, and several major urban areas in the United States. An ordained Baptist minister, she has been part of an inner-city congregation in Louisville, Kentucky—Jefferson Baptist Community.

Tooley has written a book to empower women and other people of faith in their struggle for justice in their churches and communities. She is eager for women in North American churches to make connections with those who suffer injustice in their own country as well as in such countries as Guatemala.